Seventeenth-Century Poetry:
the Social Context

Seventeenth-Century Poetry: the Social Context

Graham Parry

Hutchinson
London Melbourne Sydney Auckland Johannesburg

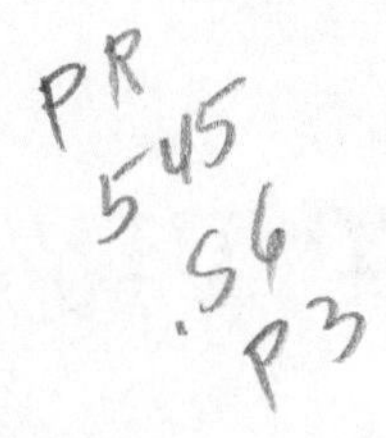

Hutchinson & Co. (Publishers) Ltd

An imprint of the Hutchinson Publishing Group

17–21 Conway Street, London W1P 6JD
and 51 Washington Street, Dover,
New Hampshire 03820, USA

Hutchinson Publishing Group (Australia) Pty Ltd
16–22 Church Street, Hawthorn, Melbourne, Victoria 3122

Hutchinson Group (NZ) Ltd
32–34 View Road, PO Box 40–086, Glenfield, Auckland 10

Hutchinson Group (SA) (Pty) Ltd
PO Box 337, Bergvlei 2012, South Africa

First published 1985

Set in VIP Plantin and Perpetua by
D. P. Media Limited, Hitchin, Hertfordshire

Printed and bound in Great Britain by
Anchor Brendon Ltd,
Tiptree, Essex

British Library in Cataloguing in Publication Data

Parry, Graham
Seventeenth-century poetry: the social context.
1. English poetry—Early modern, 1500–1700—
History and criticism
I. Title
821′.4′09 PR541

Library of Congress Cataloging in Publication Data

Parry, Graham
Seventeenth-century poetry

Bibliography: p.
Includes index
1. English poetry—early modern, 1500–1700—History and criticism. 2. Social problems in literature. 3. Literature and society—Great Britain. 4. Great Britain—Social conditions—17th century. I. Title.
PR545.S6P3 1985 821′.4′09355 84-28888

ISBN 0 09 160731 0 paper

For T & L

Contents

Introduction 9

A note on the texts 15

1 Ben Jonson: Britain's Roman poet 17

2 John Donne: patronage, friendship and love 42

3 George Herbert and the temple of Anglicanism 75

4 Henry Vaughan: social darkness, spiritual light 95

5 Thomas Traherne: the accessible Eden 116

6 The devotional adventures of Richard Crashaw 124

7 Robert Herrick and the ceremonies of innocence 154

8 The Caroline Milton 188

9 Andrew Marvell and providential history 221

Recommended reading 247

Index 251

Introduction

When we read seventeenth-century poetry today, we have to a large extent lost sight of the circumstances of its composition, the manner of its first presentation to an audience, and the designs it had upon that audience. The easy availability of the *Complete Poems* of Donne or Jonson, Vaughan or Milton, allows us to take an overview of a poet's work, and to trace the development of dominant themes and issues through a long career, and by a selective choice to establish a canon of significant poems that satisfies our modern sense of the particular achievement of an individual author. But many of the poems were originally composed for specific occasions, and when published they appeared in fairly small collections; relating as they did to contemporary issues, the first impressions that they made must often have been quite different from what our distant modern appreciation allows. Sometimes when a volume was published it was entirely in accord with the main intellectual movement of the time, as with Jonson's poems of 1616, or Herbert's of 1633; sometimes it appeared at a time quite unfavourable to its contents, because of the rapid change of political circumstances. (This was the fate of Milton's *Poems* of 1645 and of Herrick's *Hesperides* in 1648.) I have tried in various ways to imagine the experience of the seventeenth-century reader on first encountering some of the most important collections. I have been concerned to look at individual volumes of poetry to discover what can be learned from their principle of organization, and from the various signals given by the peripheral matter of a seventeenth-century book. Addresses to the reader often furnish an instructive guide to the character of a work, and dedications provide helpful information about a poet's patronage, enabling us to estimate his probable political and religious affiliations, and alerting us to his conscious poetic intentions. The engraved frontispieces that most volumes carried are a neglected source of information about the way a poet advertised the important themes of his work; and the emblems, images and allegorical figures that crowd the frontispiece often make a visual statement of the author's programme. The epigrams of the title page, usually Latin quotations, help to identify the seventeenth-century poet's sense of affinity with one of the antique poets, such as Horace, Virgil and Martial, who exerted a distant but powerful influence on English literary intentions; the relationship between the Stuart poet and his Roman hero was an unusually creative one. By reviewing all this preliminary material, and by going back and looking at the original structures of the different volumes, I hope to achieve some understanding of the way this poetry communicated its values to its seventeenth-century audience.

Much of the poetry discussed here is social poetry. Stuart England was full of educated men writing to each other in verse, consolidating their friendships in prosperous or adverse times by means of poetry that stressed their shared humanist values or their common religious hopes. Poetry was a serviceable social art that helped to bind the network of Stuart society together: it served to strengthen the ties of kinship, marriage, education and patronage, and to give distinction to the intellectual contact of thoughtful men. The range of subject matter was broad and stimulating, as poets urged their varying conceptions of the good life, discussed their taste in women or art or religion, considered the merits of town, Court or country, argued their political affiliations or personal ambitions, or bestowed an enduring glory on trifles of their fancy; and the 'Country House' genre infuses a small but important group of poems with a notable pleasure in the localness of the English countryside, especially those places that have enjoyed a long association with some distinguished family.

The dominant figure in this scene was Ben Jonson, whose tireless desire was to present his contemporaries in ways that made them fit subjects for the poetry of praise or censure. He enabled educated Englishmen to believe that they belonged to a society whose variety and distinction were worthy of lasting poetic fame. The generous choice of characters and professions that his poetry touched with its idealizing skill helped dignify the age, gave classic depth to its achievements, and made his subjects feel that they were part of a communal advance towards a new spacious order of civilization. The success he achieved was not just a vindication of his personal ambitions but a triumph for the cause of poetry too. Through his example poetry became the fashionable medium for the exchange of courtesies, opinions and judgements of conduct. It was Jonson above all who set the tone of poetic discussion of social affairs, refined the arts of compliment, and carried on a vast poetic correspondence that gave two generations of seventeenth-century writers a common centre of reference. Women as much as men were included in this literary activity, and although in most cases their contributions have vanished, they were addressed on equal terms by their male contemporaries and were expected to participate in the national poetic life.

The other great innovatory figure was John Donne, who created a style and a poetic personality that could project his spirited, witty reactions to the high moments of experience in a way that registered subtleties of thought and feeling with a new brilliance. He renovated the poetry of love, animating it by endowing his lovers with a ceaselessly observant mind and boundless desires. In particular, I try to encourage an awareness of how his poetry is so often an aspect of his relationships with friends and patrons, a means of attracting admiration and respect that might facilitate his movement through the difficult channels of Jacobean society. For Donne, poetry was a skill that might delight his friends, but might also give him access to the circles of power that he wished to be associated with. To recognize the various ways in which Donne's poetry tenaciously clings to the rough surface of his society enlarges one's understanding of its functional value and sometimes helps us to see how a poem can turn a transitory occasion into a permanent addition to our communal experience. By restoring in some measure the local context of these poems, I hope to make the reader more conscious of the immediate claims they made on their first audience, without losing a sense of why they continue to work powerfully on our own imaginations.

Robert Herrick has been chosen for inclusion in this book in order to show how the style of civilized poetic discourse established by Jonson continued on until the disruption of Stuart society in the 1640s. Herrick's understanding of the strength of the ties that bind the country gentleman to the land he owns is matched by an appreciation of the graces and sophistication of the Court culture that developed in his time. These two strains, harmonized by many allusions to the ideal of the good life portrayed in Roman poetry of the Augustan age, express to perfection the ceremonious beauty of the peaceful Caroline world. Again, with Herrick, we are conscious of the ways in which poetry holds together a large number of like-minded people by articulating the values that give order and direction to their lives, while at the same time preserving the finer qualities of their culture in enduring verse – rather in the way that crystal preserves the lily in Herrick's poem on that theme.

My concern with the social dimension of poetry accommodates

religious writing as well as secular. Many of the writers discussed in this book were Anglicans in belief, and the institution of the Church of England and its modes of worship offered them a particular satisfaction and security. As the Church of the State it complemented easily the formal values and the civility of the society it served. In an age so deeply and instinctively religious, it is often difficult to draw the line between sacred and secular, and the religious poetry of the early and mid seventeenth century frequently evokes the social milieu in which it was written, just as social and, later, political verse is often deeply coloured by religious assumptions. George Herbert was the outstanding poet of the Anglican Church in its palmy days of the 1620s and 1630s, and his intense satisfaction in its doctrine and discipline could perhaps only have been expressed in a time of stability and peace. Later events would show how illusory the stability of Herbert's society was, but for him it was real and enduring, and *The Temple* reveals the profound sense of order and benign purpose that informed his world and were reflected in the structure and services of the Church.

We must remember too that religious poetry was a functional art. It was the product of devotional hours, and it served as an aid to meditation; it helped to concentrate the mind on the spiritual drama of the Fall, Incarnation and Judgement, which formed the permanent landscape of the pious man. Here above all the modern reader tends to have an imperfect sympathy with seventeenth-century theological positions, and I have gone to some lengths to try to explain the devotional contexts of certain poets, some of whom (Crashaw, for instance) need to be read in the light of developments within the Anglican Church in the 1630s; others, such as Vaughan and Traherne, who were instinctive Anglicans trying to uphold their faith after the destruction of their Church, show how poetry may become a kind of surrogate Church in a time of adversity. There was much looking back to Old Testament times, as poets sought to establish affinities with the Israelites and affirm that God's spirit was as active in England as it had been in the ancient Holy Land. Religious writers glanced back for reassurance to the early age of the world, but they also peered forward eagerly to the Final Day, which many believed to be close.

One aspect of seventeenth-century religious life that I have tried to emphasize (underestimated in most recent discussions of the poetry) is the deep apprehension of the End that permeated the faith of so many of the writers we encounter here: the conviction that the end of time was near and that Judgement would soon interrupt the sequence of history. It is increasingly recognized that millenarianism, the belief in the imminence of the return of Christ to judge mankind and inaugurate his thousand-year rule amid his saints, was widespread among all classes and sects in the first half of the seventeenth century, and not just the conviction of radical sects or the lunatic fringe. The belief was an integral part of English Protestantism. The success of the Reformation in northern Europe encouraged Protestants to believe that they had entered the long-awaited last age of the world: God was intervening in history, purifying religion, beginning to gather in his saints, fulfilling many of the Old Testament prophecies and initiating the climactic struggle with Antichrist that must precede the return of the Messiah. Contemporary history was insistently interpreted in the light of biblical revelation, and of all the books in the Bible it was the Book of Revelation that was most eagerly read by Englishmen in this period, in order to elucidate the signs of the times and make them conform to the premonitions of the Apocalypse that were so cryptically described in the Bible. There was a wide consensus from high Anglican to radical Puritan that the present generation was living 'in this setting part of time', in Sir Thomas Browne's phrase. The unexpected outbreak of civil war, the collapse of the monarchy, and the trial and execution of the King aroused expectation of some divine event to an intense pitch. For Milton, Christ is our 'eternal and shortly-expected King' and Marvell's poetry is suffused with a latter-day excitement. Both men express the common feeling that English history is under providential control and that these are times when divinity is actively preparing for a revelation. Marvell's judgements on English political leaders – King Charles, Fairfax and Cromwell – are all coloured by these beliefs. Vaughan too in his rural retreat expected the End. He showed no interest in the religious configuration of political events, but was convinced he was living in the night of time and yearned for the dawn of Christ's return.

An important element of English millenarianism was a belief in the restoration of the Earthly Paradise, where Christ would reign with his saints for the thousand years. The garden at the end of time would be a recreation of Eden that stood before time began, but now with the presence of Christ and with no possibility of a Fall. And the site of the restored paradise would be England, God's favoured country in the latter days. The continuing fascination with gardens, paradises and a restored state of innocence in the poetry of the first half of the seventeenth century owes much to the vitality of millenarian ideas, for almost all of the imaginative writers assimilated the belief, even though they might not assent to it, that gardens and garden states had an especial relevance to Englishmen in this time of high religious anticipation.

The most extensive treatment of the matter of paradise is *Paradise Lost*, but the character of that poem as well as its length keep it outside the scope of this book. I have been concerned primarily with the social contexts of poetry and with the devotional contexts of the religious verse: *Paradise Lost*, as an epic, as a grand public poem, has the whole century for its context. Moreover, the personal voice of religious experience is not notably present in *Paradise Lost*, which has much theology and intellectual history, but little inward experience of the sort that would have been recognized by Herbert or Donne or Traherne. With Milton I have rather chosen to concentrate on the *Poems* of 1645, which give access to Milton's ambitions while they are still in the process of formation, and which enable us to assess Milton as an inhabitant of the Caroline poetic world, where he appears as a more courtly figure than is usually observed.

Finally, I should like to express my thanks to Professor Douglas Jefferson of the University of Leeds for the long conversations that have so often brought ideas into a new and revealing relationship, and to my colleague at York, Professor Bernard Harris, for sharing my conviction that the seventeenth century is the most absorbing of all historical periods. Dr Margarita Stocker drew me into the perplexities of the Apocalypse and the premonitions of the End that have found their way into the chapter on Marvell. Above all, I thank my wife Barbara for her many contributions to this book by way of good advice and practical help in preparing the typescript.

Graham Parry
University of York

A note on the texts

I have retained the spelling and punctuation of seventeenth-century texts, both as a guide to pronunciation and also for the sake of greater expressiveness. Since this is a book about the social relations, courtesies and beliefs of seventeenth-century people, I feel that the original spelling helps to evoke the sound of their voices and the style of their manners more successfully than modernized English.

The texts I have used are as follows:

Donne: *The Satires, Epigrams and Verse Letters*, ed. W. Milgate (Oxford 1967).

The Elegies and The Songs and Sonnets, ed. Helen Gardner (Oxford 1967).

The Epithalamions, Anniversaries and Epicedes, ed. W. Milgate (Oxford 1978).

The Divine Poems, ed. Helen Gardner (2nd edn) (Oxford 1978).

Jonson: *The Complete Poetry of Ben Jonson*, ed. William B. Hunter (New York 1963).

Herbert: *The Works of George Herbert*, ed. F. E. Hutchinson (Oxford 1941).

Vaughan: *The Works of Henry Vaughan*, ed. L. C. Martin (2nd edn) (Oxford 1957).

Traherne: *Poems, Centuries and Three Thanksgivings*, ed. Anne Ridler (London 1966).

Herrick: *The Complete Poetry of Robert Herrick*, ed. J. Max Patrick (New York 1963).

Marvell: *Poems and Letters*, ed. H. M. Margoliouth, rev. by P. Legouis and E. E. Duncan-Jones, 2 vols. (Oxford 1971).

Milton: *Poems 1645*, Type-Facsimile (Oxford 1924).

The Poems of John Milton, ed. John Carey and Alastair Fowler (London 1968).

John Milton: Complete Poems and Major Prose, ed. Merritt Y. Hughes (New York 1957).

1 Ben Jonson: Britain's Roman poet

A fair understanding of Jonson's sense of his significance and position as a writer can be gained from the imposing frontispiece of his folio *Works*, published in 1616. Jonson's description of his plays, poems and masques as *Works* was in itself a bold statement, for by using the English translation of the Latin 'opera' he was in effect claiming an exceptional dignity for himself. 'Opera' were serious mature writings that expected the attention of posterity. King James, whose *Works* were also published in folio in 1616, might justly employ that title, writing as a prince of Christendom, but for Jonson to use it of himself as a living poet, in a language whose literary reputation had yet to achieve international recognition, could be regarded as an act of hubris. Nevertheless, Jonson was confident that he had contributed as much as any man to the advancement of literature in England, and deserved fame. The architectural frontispiece of the book (Plate 1) exhibits his many accomplishments, above all his claim to have revived the classical theatre in England: the scheme of the structure depicts the development of the drama from its primitive origins to its modern form of tragicomedy. The vignettes of the plinth show the early stages of drama: we see the chorus dancing in honour of Bacchus in a 'visorium' or amphitheatre, and on the left the 'plaustrum' or theatre wagon containing an actor who must be Thespis, described by Horace as the first master of Tragedy, who had also first developed the individual part or role, and who had carried his art from place to place in a theatrical cart.[1*] The grand figures of Tragedy and Comedy flank the central portal of this scene, Tragedy with her rich robes and her buskins, bearing crown and sceptre against a cloth of state, Comedy in simpler dress with rustic attributes. Their appropriate masks hang by them. In front of the uppermost niche stands Tragicomedy, the latest of the theatre's genres. Framed by the elaborate scrolled and strap-work cartouche over the central entablature is an image of the Roman

* Superior figures refer to the Notes at the end of each chapter.

theatre, probably the theatre of Marcellus, and it is this image of the Roman theatre restored that Jonson wishes the reader to associate most immediately with his achievement. Two other characters complete this group – a satyr and a shepherd playing their pipes in the upper storey of the scene – so that altogether the five figures of the frontispiece express in large terms the scope of Jonson's dramatic, satirical and pastoral art. The pastoral claim was not entirely honest (although Jonson told his friend Drummond that he proposed to write pastorals) but as the genre was central to Renaissance expectations of the complete poet, the shepherd may be held to represent intention rather than fulfilment. Here then was Jonson's triumphal arch, splendidly designed to impress the Jacobean reader. Above the whole edifice rise obelisks wreathed with laurels that symbolize the eternity of poetic fame that he felt to be his due.

Unquestionably the emblems and allusions exhibited here make an assured and uncompromising claim to classical status and enduring value; Jonson was by no means shy about his merits, and throughout his career he expended much energy on advertising himself as a playwright, poet and man of letters, whose very existence in Stuart England added to the lustre of the age. Publishing his works in 1616 as if they already formed a completed body of literature was the central event in his long campaign to gain recognition of the importance of his work and person. Addresses to the King, dedications to members of the aristocracy, appeals to fellow scholars, published letters to the universities and to the Inns of Court, all served to attract attention to his activities and literary intentions; appearances on stage, and the public venting of his quarrels and grievances helped to make his society aware that there were values of style and taste being tenaciously fought for in their midst. Compared to the reticence of Shakespeare and most of the poets and dramatists of the time, Jonson was an excessively noisy one-man band, who kept up a rattle of publicity for nearly forty years. Remarkably, however, he did manage to get himself accepted at his own valuation as Britain's greatest modern man of letters, her most judicious critic, the translator of the classical muses to English soil, and the model exponent of most literary genres. He was the only English poet of the age who could properly claim to have created a school of disciples and friends. The volume of verses of praise, admiration and regret that was published in 1638, the year after his death, offers an enduring testimony to the high place he had attained in the world of English letters. The tribute from Sydney Godolphin, himself one of those accomplished minor poets who grew

Plate 1 The frontispiece of Jonson's *Works*, published in 1616

so vigorously in Jonson's shade, expresses what men of taste and judgement universally felt:

> The Muses fairest light in no darke time,
> The Wonder of a learned Age; the Line
> Which none can passe; the most proportion'd Witt
> To Nature, the best Judge of what was fit;
> The deepest, plainest, highest, clearest Pen;
> The Voice most eccho'd by consenting Men,
> The Soule which answer'd best to all well said
> By others, and which most requitall made;
> Tun'd to the highest Key of ancient Rome,
> Returning all her Musique with his owne,
> In whom with Nature, Studie claim'd a part,
> And yet who to himselfe ow'd all his Art:
> Heere lies Ben : Iohnson. Every Age will looke
> With sorrow heere, with wonder on his Booke.[2]

Jonson's role as 'best Judge of what was fit' was the one which aroused most respect among his admirers. He was pre-eminently a social poet, who drew much of his strength from his creative relationship with the Roman social writers of the age from Augustus to Hadrian.[3] The poets, historians and moralists of that age had exercised a mastery of judgement over the affairs of their society that Jonson envied and wished to emulate. He was a Renaissance moralist, whose stance was ethical and severe, who believed that the judgement of men and manners was the highest responsibility of a poet, and who made it his business to become the arbiter of civil virtue in his time. His aim as a poet was to classicize his society, to cast its leading men into a Roman mould, and to present Stuart England as a new Augustan age that could confidently bear comparison with antiquity. But besides praise, he also wanted to administer censure, in the Roman fashion, on the fads and foibles of his society, on unworthy men and on the degeneracy of morals that even the best times conceal. His own poetic talents were critical rather than lyrical; he prefers to employ a plain style, direct and questioning. There is little concern with surface beauty in his work, but a constant interplay of observation and judgement on the quality of contemporary life. In general, he avoided the standard poetic subjects of his time – matters of love, heroic action, history or romance – and concentrated instead on the appraisal of his immediate social surroundings.

The poets that Jonson most closely identified with were Horace and

Martial, and it was their instruments of social observation, the epistle, ode and epigram, which he adapted to his own ends. In the two collections of poetry that he published in the 1616 folio, the first, the *Epigrams*, echoes Martial, and the second, *The Forest*, is primarily Horatian in tone and content. Martial today is little read, and the epigram regarded as an insignificant genre; in the Renaissance, however, Martial had a considerable reputation as a humanist poet. His books of epigrams are by no means limited to brief satirical sallies, but contain a great variety of material: portraits of all conditions of men from the emperor to beggars and slaves, social scenes, love poems, epitaphs. Jonson's volume deliberately matches the scope of Martial's. Jonson clearly valued his *Epigrams* very highly, for he dedicated them to his chief patron, William, Earl of Pembroke, describing them as 'the ripest fruit of my studies', a mature essay in humanism. Most of the epigrams had been in circulation for years in manuscript, but once they are ordered into a volume they take on a new character as components of a structured whole.

What then do we find here? Jonson opens with an appeal to the reader to take care 'to reade it well: that is, to understand'. Time and again Jonson made this appeal: the prefaces of his plays attempt to explain his intentions, the introduction and commentaries to the masques try 'to make the readers understanders' by pointing out the 'antiquitie and solide learnings' that were concealed behind the brilliant festal display and by alerting the spectators to the 'more removed mysteries' that the masques contained. Jonson's career involved a prolonged effort to educate his audience into an appreciation of the seriousness of his work and the magnitude of his ambitions. Behind the entertaining frontage of his work there is always a profounder purpose: the laughter of the comedies should be accompanied by reflection on character and society, the splendour of the masques by a philosophic understanding of the powers of kingship, the tragedies by a consideration of the nature of political man. The epigram from Horace on the frontispiece of his *Works* translates as 'I do not write to be admired by the crowd. I am content with few readers.' This is similar to Milton's 'fit audience find though few', but it is an unusual sentiment from a man who wrote for the public stage. It suggests that Jonson sought an audience who would understand the larger implications of his work, not just enjoy the immediate effect. He wanted them to recognize the links with the classical world, to catch the allusions, and to observe how he was establishing affinities between ancient Rome and Stuart England, how Roman values were being applied to

English life, and how Roman models were being recreated in an English guise. It is part of the function of a poet to sense the quality of his age, to recognize a consonance between societies in different times and to reveal the secret affinities between them. Jonson's ambition was to raise his own society to classical levels, by presenting the best of that society living up to Roman ideals of virtue and honour, and by using Roman standards of criticism to censure those who failed to live well. Conscious of the genius of Great Britain in his time, Jonson wished to associate that genius with the style and values of Augustan Rome, which for a Renaissance humanist expressed the permanent ideal of civil and moral excellence. He wanted to prove that England for the first time in its history could look back to Rome with an equal eye. A parallel endeavour was being made through architecture by Jonson's collaborator and rival at Court, Inigo Jones, who was designing buildings in the authentic style of first-century Rome for the leading men of Stuart England. Like Jonson's poetry, Jones's designs are also full of allusions to Roman models, as some learned and understanding eyes might perceive, but the elegant unity of his architecture can be enjoyed without a knowledge of his sources. In Jonson's work, however, there are occasions when his frequent classical references intrude as pedantry. Nevertheless, both the architecture and the poetry are monumental exercises in the application of classical learning to modern life, a characteristic feature of the Renaissance mind.

A fine example of the integration of ancient and modern is the epigram 'Inviting a Friend to Dinner', where Jonson's invitation evokes a scene of civilized hospitality which gathers together some of the central strands of the humanist ideal of the good life. The tone has a certain ceremoniousness which is friendly rather than formal:

> Tonight, grave sir, both my poore house, and I
>   Doe equally desire your companie:
> Not that we thinke us worthy such a ghest,
>   But that your worth will dignifie our feast,
> With those that come; whose grace may make that seeme
>   Something, which, else, could hope for no esteeme.
> It is the faire acceptance, Sir, creates
>   The entertaynment perfect: not the cates.

The epigrammatic wit of the last couplet alerts the reader to the fineness of feeling that informs the whole poem. Then Jonson describes the fare, choice but simple:

Yet shall you have, to rectifie your palate,
An olive, capers, or some better sallade
Ushring the mutton; with a short-leg'd hen,
If we can get her, full of egs.

The perfection of the evening will be the wine

Which is the Mermaids, now, but shall be mine:
Of which had Horace, or Anacreon tasted,
Their lives, as doe their lines, till now had lasted.

But nothing to excess: 'we will sup free, but moderately'. At such a meal the intellect is catered for as well as the senses:

my man
Shall reade a piece of Virgil, Tacitus,
Livie, or of some better booke to us,
Of which wee'll speake our minds, amidst our meate.

The poem conveys a delightful sense of shared tastes and moderated pleasures; there is the prospect of free discussion elevated by wine, of mutual trust and understanding, of harmless pleasures convivially enjoyed. An ideal of friendship is being celebrated here, one that has a long history, for Jonson draws on at least three of Martial's epigrams, all of them invitations to a dinner, as well as a satire of Juvenal and an epistle of Horace.[4] From these sources come the detailed descriptions of the rather frugal meal, the promise of good literature with the meal, the promise also that the poet will not recite his own verses, the particular concern for the wine, its character and provenance, and the assurance that no harm can come to guests gathered in the security of friendship. Jonson has Englished all this, and makes the recipient of his poem feel that he too is a naturalized citizen of Rome, sharing the same liberal civilized values as an educated Roman of the first century. Certainly a way of life comparable to that described by Martial or Horace existed in Jonson's time: literary friendships flourished as always, books were read at some men's tables, poets did recite their verses in private company, and the pleasures of good food and wine and talk had not diminished since antiquity. Very probably Jonson's poem had originally a practical function, sent as a dinner invitation to one of his scholarly friends, such as Camden, Cotton or Selden – to someone at any rate who would catch the allusions and recognize the kind of compliment that was being paid.

Many of the *Epigrams* were directly addressed to the circle of his friends and patrons. (It is difficult to draw a line between the two groups because Jonson rarely accepted patronage without friendship.) Today's taste tends to scorn the poetry of compliment: we are still conditioned by Romantic values of sincerity, and feel that admiration and flattery allow too much play to false sentiment and are probably tainted with self-interest. But we should remember that in western society until late in the eighteenth century compliment was always one of the minor arts that aided the cohesiveness and smooth operation of society, allowing artists to project their ideals of social behaviour on to their contemporaries. In Jonson's case, besides desiring the immediate social benefit that compliment might bring, he was anxious to celebrate English men of merit in order to declare to posterity the distinction of his society. William Drummond, the Scots poet whom Jonson visited when he walked to Scotland in 1619, noted as the first item in his 'Conversations' (the record of their literary discussions together) that Jonson

> had an intention to perfect an Epick Poeme intitled Heroologia of the Worthies of his Country, rowsed by fame, and was to dedicate it to his Country, it is all in Couplets, for he detesteth all other Rimes.[5]

We do not know if Jonson made any progress with this poem, or whether the manuscript was one of those burned in his library fire in 1623. It would have been a companion poem to Drayton's *Poly-Olbion* (1612), which celebrates the natural beauties of English counties, their curiosities, customs and great men.

The cult of worthies was an aspect of the national pride fostered by Reformation and Renaissance, and promoted by the Tudor historians. Foxe's *Book of Martyrs* honoured the heroes of Protestantism; the heroes of the Armada were praised in ballads and popular poetry. Shakespeare's history plays introduce many historical worthies among the minor characters. British heroes were a popular theme in the Court masques. There is in fact a long tradition of such writing, culminating in Fuller's *Worthies of England* in 1662. As Jonson wrote in 'Discoveries', men of worth 'are the Stars, the Planets of the Ages wherein they live, and illustrate the Times'.[6] In the poems that he published, however, Jonson chose not to praise historically famous men; he wanted rather to distinguish the men known to him individually, so that he could introduce a gathering of eminent men whose excellence he could personally endorse. It was important that he should make these personal endorsements, for they helped to define his status as a poet; by his knowledge of men and manners, by his acquaintance with the high standards of antiquity, and by his abilities as a judge of morals and achievement he had a right to pronounce authoritatively on his contemporaries.

The portraits of mind and character that he draws in these poems are of many kinds. There are soldiers of the calibre of Sir Horace Vere and Sir John Radcliffe, who uphold England's long military tradition, statesmen such as Salisbury and Suffolk, a brilliant circle of cultivated women, fellow poets, musicians and actors. Prominent among his heroes are scholars, such as 'reverend' Camden, once his schoolmaster, later his friend and the greatest historian of the age; and Sir Henry Savile, Warden of Merton College, afterwards Provost of Eton, who founded chairs of geometry and astronomy at Oxford, translated Tacitus, and possessed an immense knowledge of the classical world and of the theology of the Church fathers. The example of such a scholar as Savile gives distinction to the times and raises the spirit of critical inquiry which is essential to the intellectual health of society:

> We need a man, can speake of the intents,
> The councells, actions, orders, and events
> Of state, and censure them: we need his pen
> Can write the things, the causes, and the men.
> But most we need his faith (and all have you)
> That dares nor write things false, nor hide things true.

Jonson's ideal of the humanist scholar is most fully laid out in the epistle to John Selden, lawyer, jurist, antiquary, a great philologist of ancient languages, and the author of a remarkable book on comparative religion.[7] One of the most learned men in Britain, Selden was a close friend of Jonson. They exchanged books and manuscripts and had a common passion for clearing the half-obscured paths of antiquity. Jonson can credibly begin, 'I know of whom I write', and confidently summon Selden to judgement:

> Stand forth my Object, then you that have beene
> Ever at home: yet, have all Countries seene:
> And like a Compasse keeping one foot still
> Upon your Center, doe your Circle fill
> Of generall knowledge; watch'd men, manners too,
> Heard what times past have said, seene what ours doe:
> . . .
> What fables have you vext! what truth redeem'd!
> Antiquities search'd! Opinions dis-esteem'd!
> . . .

> . . . how rectified,
> Times, manners, customes! Innovations spide!
> Sought out the Fountaines, Sources, Creekes, paths, wayes,
> And noted the beginnings and decayes!

The image of the compass well suggests the ranging intellect of the Renaissance scholar, whose centre remains firmly set on truth established by unprejudiced inquiry. Tireless research, the weighing of evidence, rejection of fables, superstition and erroneous beliefs, the gradual elicitation of truth according to the best available light – such are the slow but admirable achievements of Selden, and it is thanks to such people that culture is raised, learning is advanced, and societies establish their claim to be honourably remembered in the history and progress of the race. Jonson's praise of Selden might equally well have been applied to others of his contemporaries, such as Ralegh and Bacon, whose achievements he appreciated in later poems. England in Jonson's time was alive with intellectual curiosity, and part of Jonson's function as a poet was to encourage this activity and proclaim the growing stature that it gave to this new empire of the north.[8]

He praised too the translators for ferrying in new ideas from abroad or for making the thoughts of antiquity freely available. The business of trans-shipping the literary spoils of antiquity into England was one of the necessary tasks of the age, and Jonson was careful to applaud this intellectual traffic of translation in a number of approving poems. To Chapman on his translation of Homer he wrote:

> What treasure hast thou brought us! and what store
> Still, still, dost thou arrive with, at our shore,
> To make thy honour, and our wealth the more!

These brief addresses to men in the public eye show us the vast range of Jonson's acquaintance with Jacobean society, and enable us to understand why he was so confident about his ability to judge all kinds of men, for his life touched most of the moving powers of the time. We also come to realize the compactness of Jacobean society, centred as it was on the Court, where Jonson had free access. The *Epigrams* push us into that crowded, vainglorious Jacobean world, overdressed and underwashed, where scores of assertive characters were straining to display real or imagined talents in a tense, competitive setting. The fops, the frauds, the charlatans are mingled in with people of known merit in this throng of vigorous poems whose very disorder (following the calculated disarray of Martial) captures the energy of the Jacobean scene, the poet jostling to and fro, and smiling, shrinking, pausing to compliment or scorn, always in the middle, tirelessly judging the mêlée. King James is glimpsed from time to time, not as he is seen at the masques, alone, a demigod on his chair of state, but moving unceremoniously in the press of Court life, sandwiched between Sir Cod and Censorious Courtling (*Epigrams* 50, 51, 52). Some of Jonson's best moments in the *Epigrams* come when he flicks off these nauseating Court flies with a proper disgust, as in number 15:

> All men are wormes: But this no man. In silke
> 'Twas brought to court first wrapt, and white as milke;
> Where, afterwards, it grew a butter-flye:
> Which was a cater-piller. So t'will dye.

The finery cannot conceal the baseness of the man beneath, and the poem which so deftly identifies the type and drops its hopeless verdict is a model of Jonsonian observation and laconic wit. There are many such odious men in the *Epigrams*, but over all, merit predominates.

The impulse to weigh and judge the foremost men of his age never left Jonson; throughout his career he continued to advance men and women into the light of their deserved renown. The poem on Shakespeare is one of his best known later exercises, although it is a poor performance. The occasion was the publication of the folio edition of Shakespeare's works in 1623, an event that tacitly acknowledged the success of Jonson's own venture of 1616. It spends too long beating towards its subject, floundering so much that Jonson has to call himself to attention as late as line 17 in order to force himself to some purposeful writing:

> I, therefore will begin. Soule of the Age!
> The applause! delight! the wonder of our Stage!
> My Shakespeare, rise.

Jonson expends a good deal of poetic energy on predictable comparisons, limp puns and conventional classical furnishings. The poem persists in anthologies because it is by Jonson upon Shakespeare, because it offers a few misleading glimpses of that elusive career ('thou hadst small Latine, and lesse Greeke') and because it occasionally strikes off an undeniably memorable line ('He was not of an age, but for all time'). Yet it does not achieve any remarkable criticism of Shakespeare as a dramatist, nor convey any experience of his power; instead, Jonson largely contents himself with literary comparisons to the advantage of Shakespeare. Jonson's driving conception is that

Shakespeare has surpassed the greatest writers of Greece and Rome in both tragedy and comedy, and his brilliance is evidence that the genius of the drama has now passed to England, in common with so much of the culture of antiquity.[9]

> Triumph, my Britaine, thou hast one to showe,
> To whom all Scenes of Europe homage owe.

When we consider Jonson's own sense of himself as a writer who has rivalled the ancients – a sense which is explicit on the title page of his *Works*, implicit throughout his poetry – we begin to understand that he really wished to acclaim Shakespeare as a fellow neo-classic engaged in recreating the ancient canons of taste in the northern isles, the new home of the Muses.

The Shakespeare poem, like the inferior poems addressed to Donne, shows Jonson quite disconcerted when in the presence of the greatest contemporary writers. He seems unable to take the measure of their achievements, although he was by no means reluctant to praise. Jonson was so self-centred in his preoccupations, so committed to the revival of Roman values, that he had difficulty in appreciating the very different literary development of Shakespeare or Donne.

The great world needed poets, and Jonson in particular, to praise its present actions and mediate with posterity. That was one of Jonson's enduring convictions, and he carried it out to best effect in the brief collection of poems called *The Forest*, which followed the *Epigrams* in the 1616 folio. As he explains, the title is a translation of 'Sylva', a title given to some collections of Roman poems to indicate 'their diverse nature and matter' as many sorts of tree grow promiscuously in one wood. Jonson's *Forest* is rather thinly planted, containing only fifteen poems, but all of the finest growth. Several of them are epistles in the manner of Horace, who provides Jonson with his most congenial mode for social poetry; Jonson developed a versatile couplet form of variable length and stress, which he used as the English equivalent of the Roman elegiac couplet. Here he can achieve that civilized tone of voice, familiar and judicious, that is one of the most serviceable contributions he made to the poetry of his time. He liberated men to talk intelligently in verse about questions of personal relationships, ethics and duty that compose so much of the texture of civilized living, not in the dense, strenuous, intellectual way that Donne had pioneered in his epistles, elegies and satires, but in a more relaxed and engaging manner, which was a mark of the well-educated gentleman of the first Stuart age.

The outstanding social poems of *The Forest* are 'To Penshurst' and 'To Sir Robert Wroth', both probably written about 1611–12, both in praise of the style of life maintained by the Sidney family: Penshurst was the seat of Sir Robert Sidney, brother of Sir Philip, while Wroth was married to Sir Robert's highly cultivated daughter Mary. Jonson had enjoyed the hospitality of both families, and his way of repayment was by poetry, the acceptable currency for such transactions. After all, Jonson was offered patronage and hospitality partly in the expectation that he would celebrate his benefactors. Poems of complimentary address such as these may have been sent first as letters to their dedicatees, but most probably they were read aloud at the table of the patron and a fair copy was presented, before they began their career in manuscript or were declaimed by Jonson at the public gatherings of his 'tribe', finally reaching a wider audience when they were set in print and published. Jonson's tactic in almost all these poems is to cast the individual or the family in an exemplary role, and the cumulative effect of these epistles is to create the impression of a civilized humanistic society, high minded, generous and dignified, balancing the pleasures of society with the refreshments of the natural world, an aristocracy of the mind and spirit whose existence raised Stuart England to the level of Jonson's permanent standard of reference, the society of Augustan Rome as represented by its approving poets.

'To Penshurst' is today widely regarded as the *locus classicus* of this social ideal. It begins with an appreciation of the house, modest, venerable and decent like the family it contains. Penshurst is no ostentatious case of over-building, quite unlike the prodigy houses that certain Elizabethan and Jacobean courtiers had vaingloriously built. All here is for use, not display, and Jonson's concern is to show that Sidney's wealth is expended in the common good, not selfishly applied to private ends. The estate of Penshurst that Jonson so approvingly describes is an ideal enclosed world of right order, harmony, fertility and good will. Nature is responsively at the service of its liberal lord, whose careful husbandry ensures the continuance of this happy state. The community thrives on a mutual exchange of respect and kindness between the family and its tenantry, expressed most fully in the generous hospitality of the house. Hospitality was central to Jonson's image of the good life, yet the forms he most appreciated, the house and table open to all comers – the 'liberal boord' of the poem –, the family mixing freely with the guests with no division of rank or fare, all this was already becoming an obsolete custom in his time, for few noblemen were disposed to tolerate the expense, nor wanted this openness in early Stuart England. The Sidneys maintained a medieval and Tudor style of housekeeping, which was more truly communal than the socially separated modern manner; they were survivors of an older, nobler age. Jonson himself enjoyed this hospitality to the full, but the highest mark of approval is that it could accommodate the King, who had descended on Penshurst without notice, 'as if it had expected such a guest.' Rustics, farmers, poet and King, all find a ready welcome at this admirable house. And what kind of family can create such an hospitable ethos? One that has been raised in the spirit of Christian humanism, where religion is allied to 'the mysteries of manners, armes and arts' – a fine, strong Jonsonian line, with its weighty abstractions and its plain, firm assertion of right values.

The poem abounds with wit of a distinctively Jonsonian kind, characterized by a sense of the fitness, neatness and order of things, often unexpectedly discovered by the poet's eye. The fish and fowl that yield themselves up so readily have a proper sense of their own duty, the 'ripe daughters . . . whose baskets beare / An embleme of themselves, in plum or peare' are modestly asking to be plucked for marriage, the tidy rooms of Penshurst are literally fit for a king, and are rewarded by the unannounced arrival of King James. The language everywhere assures us that rightness and moral order prevail. This is a remarkably discreet poem too, and its discretion is part of its wit: the most important figures of the scene, Sir Robert Sidney and his wife Lady Barbara, are never mentioned by name, nor is the genius of the place, Sir Philip Sidney. Instead they are tactfully alluded to, a device which strengthens the intimacy of the poem and the feeling that the community of Penshurst is one large extended family. A learned reader in the seventeenth century might recognize that significant sections of the poem are derived from Roman sources, Martial especially, but also Virgil and Juvenal, yet so skilfully have the details of the Latin poems been adapted to the English setting that they remain unobtrusive, although they give a cultural depth to the poem and suggest a natural affinity between the idealized life of first-century Rome and the quality of life attained by the Sidneys.[10] Moreover, from well-chosen fragments of Roman poetry Jonson has assembled a poem that itself will become the origin of a minor genre, the country house poem, whose line includes Carew's 'To Saxham', Herrick's 'Panegyrick to Sir Thomas Pemberton', and Marvell's 'Upon Appleton House'.[11]

The verse epistle 'To Sir Robert Wroth', which follows 'To

Penshurst' in *The Forest*, extends this picture of felicity. Closely modelled on Horace's second Epode, in praise of the country life, it mythologizes Sir Robert's life on his Middlesex estate into a timeless ideal of rural contentment. Living securely on his own lands, Wroth exercises his good stewardship to regulate the fertile cycle of the natural year:

> The mowed meddowes, with the fleeced sheepe,
> And feasts, that either shearers keepe;
> The ripened eares, yet humble in their height,
> And furrowes laden with their weight;
> The apple-harvest, that doth longer last;
> The hogs return'd home fat from mast;
> The trees cut out in log; and those boughes made
> A fire now, that lent a shade!

His harmless sports and liberal hospitality contribute to his peace of mind and generosity of spirit. The temperate pleasures of his country life preserve Wroth from the wasteful prodigality of the Court, which Jonson as moralist here condemns (even though, in another role, he was one of the prime movers of Court entertainment). The final meditation on the good life emphasizes the right relationship between man and heaven that Wroth exemplifies, for he has a natural piety that acknowledges the need to respect God as well as nature:

> God wisheth, none should wracke on a strange shelfe:
> To him, man's dearer, then t'himselfe.
> And, howsoever we may thinke things sweet,
> He alwayes gives what he knowes meet;
> Which who can use is happy: Such be thou.
> Thy morning's, and thy evening's vow
> Be thankes to him, and earnest prayer, to finde
> A bodye sound, with sounder minde;
> To doe thy countrey service, thy selfe right;
> That neither want doe thee affright,
> Nor death; but when thy latest sand is spent,
> Thou maist thinke life, a thing but lent.

Wroth is Jonson's best example of the Happy Man, a favourite seventeenth-century topos that derived much of its material from Horace, with accretions from Virgil, and received its modern impetus mainly from Jonson in the poems of *The Forest*. The pleasures of the country life rather than the distractions of the city or Court, modest desires and the free exercise of virtue, civil and domestic concord, an elevated spirit, and a God-fearing cast of mind which recognizes the blessings attainable by man, as well as his natural limitations – all these contribute to the theme.[12] It formed part of the larger concern with the golden age that preoccupied Jonson in many of his masques and entertainments for the nobility. Although Jonson could be one of the most venomous writers of his time, one side of his poetic character was highly idealistic and zealous to promote the fiction of an English golden age under the peace-loving King James, who reigned wisely over the 'Fortunate Isles' of Great Britain, which lay separate from the world and enjoyed God's special blessings and protection. This fable was in part propaganda for the new Stuart dynasty, but it was also a means to allow Jonson to consider the highest conditions of human happiness, and it provided a context of ideas in which he could set his most admired patrons and friends. One of the functions of poetry in this time was the presentation of ideal states that men might aspire to and might on occasion reach, and Jonson could be the most eloquent of prophets declaring a Jacobean age of gold. This is the 'Saturn's reign' in which Wroth lives, and which is proclaimed again in the lines, 'Such, and no other was that age, of old,/Which boasts t'have had the head of gold.'

An age of gold is naturally peopled by heroes – and for Jonson the word 'hero' implied a state between mankind and divinity, a demi-god, a man who by his qualities and achievements had risen above the rest of his race to a condition of sublimity, a secular saint, in fact. (The young noblemen who danced in the masques at Whitehall are frequently described as 'heroes'.) The heroes of Wroth's world are the Sidneys, his wife's kinsmen, who have abandoned their rights of title and rank in this happy state where the hierarchy of society is irrelevant.

> And the great Heroes, of her race,
> Sit mixt with losse of state, or reverence.
> Freedome doth with degree dispense.

It is a measure of Jonson's vast admiration for the Sidneys that he should reserve them for this special status. We get a close-up of one of them, Lady Mary Wroth's brother, in the 'Ode to Sir William Sidney', written in 1611 on his coming of age, which is printed later in *The Forest*. In its rapid, bounding stanzas Jonson urges the young Sidney to pursue honour and renown, adding to his great family's store. So far Sir William had not been a youth of promise, but in the idealizing world of poetry, that failure could be overlooked, for Jonson was so committed to promoting the Sidneys that all must appear in a distinctive light. His position is declared in the opening stanza, which is typical of the whole in the way the clear English sense flows through the complicated form:

> Now that the harth is crown'd with smiling fire,
> And some doe drinke, and some doe dance.
> Some ring,
> Some sing,
> And all doe strive t'advance
> The gladnesse higher:
> Wherefore should I
> Stand silent by.
> Who not the least,
> Both love the cause, and authors of the feast?

We notice that Jonson is often present on the edge of his poems, associating himself with his noble subjects and subtly implying his own stature by his strong, plain language and his informal tone of authority. He likes, too, to remind his patrons of the reciprocal need of great spirits for great poets. In his epistle to Elizabeth, Countess of Rutland, who was Sir Philip Sidney's daughter, he reflects on the classical commonplace that only poets perpetuate the nobleness of life:

> Madame, thinke what store
> The world hath seene, which all these had in trust,
> And now lye lost in their forgotten dust.
> It is the Muse, alone, can raise to heaven,
> And, at her strong armes end, hold up, and even,
> The soules, shee loves.

The Sidneys were the foremost of the souls that Jonson loved, and to round out our sense of his commitment to them, we should remember also the several poems inscribed to Lady Mary Wroth, Sir Robert Sidney's daughter, a woman of considerable intellectual sensitivity, to whom Jonson dedicated *The Alchemist*. Both Lady Mary and her cousin Elizabeth, Countess of Rutland, wrote poetry, mainly conventional love poetry, but their shared interest in the art helps to explain why Jonson was a welcome guest at their tables and the object of their friendship.

Jonson found literary relationships with great ladies easy to sustain, and some of his finest poems are addressed to women from whom he received sympathetic hospitality. Perhaps the most remarkable of these was Lucy, Countess of Bedford, the foremost lady of Jacobean cultural life. She was the close companion of Queen Anne for many years, a noted performer in the masques at Court, and a great encourager of literary men and musicians. Among her entourage of poets could be found at various times Donne, Chapman, Drayton and Daniel. Jonson dedicated several of his epigrams to the Countess, and clearly regarded her friendship with intense satisfaction. Later on, Jonson moved into the orbit of Lady Venetia Digby, another lady of cultural sophistication and one of the great beauties of the age. At her death in 1633 Jonson sent her husband, the alchemist and adventurer Sir Kenelm Digby, an ambitious and florid sequence of poems celebrating her noble ancestry, the beauties of her body and mind, and her death and apotheosis. The poems are in general over-strenuous, and not among his better work, but they testify to the intense attachment he had to Lady Digby, 'whom he dared call his Muse'. On another level, but in a better poem, set in *The Forest*, he praises the quiet retired life of Katherine, Lady Aubigny, who was the wife of his first patron Esmé Stuart, a cousin of King James; her modest bearing in a time of extravagance and licence prompted the poet's highest moral approval.

Jonson's serious appraisal of feminine lives represented a new development in English letters: his poems to the great ladies of his time are contributions to a humanist view of society in which men and women move on equal terms, in which character, although conditioned by ancestry and breeding, is essentially a conscious creation of a liberal spirit. Qualities of mind and morals in women attracted Jonson much more than their physical beauty. Donne also in the early years of the century was addressing verse letters to women he esteemed, but they are not nearly as prominent in his work as are Jonson's poems to the ladies who patronized him. Jonson even intended to write a long poem on the female worthies of the kingdom, but he never delivered it.

Friendship with women and admiration for their qualities form the basis of many of Jonson's poems. Love is an emotion he rarely expresses, as he freely admits in the opening poem of *The Forest* ('Why I write not of love'), where he mythologizes his inadequacy in a neat but unfeeling fiction. He recognizes, however, that most readers expect a poet to treat love, so he wishes to defuse these expectations immediately. His private life seems to have been unruffled by feelings of love, and on the rare occasions when he touches the subject in poetry, he does so best by means of translation, as in the famous 'Come my Celia, let us prove,/While we may, the sports of love', and 'Kisse me, sweet', both of which were transplanted from *Volpone* into *The Forest*, and were translated from Catullus into witty, pointed couplets that tell of the secret delights of furtive love.

Jonson's skills are better shown in the poetry of compliment than in that of love, and the height of his art is reached in the song, 'To Celia'.

> Drinke to me, onely, with thine eyes,
>   And I will pledge with mine;
> Or leave a kisse but in the cup,
>   And Ile not looke for wine.
> The thirst, that from the soule doth rise,
>   Doth aske a drinke divine:
> But might I of Jove's Nectar sup,
>   I would not change for thine.
> I sent thee, late, a rosie wreath,
>   Not so much honoring thee,
> As giving it a hope, that there
>   It could not withered bee.
> But thou thereon did'st onely breath,
>   And sent'st it backe to mee:
> Since when it growes, and smells, I sweare,
>   Not of it selfe, but thee.

Here the elegance of expression, perfectly controlled by the metrical movement, results in a poem of exquisite civility. The exchange of glances, the kiss left within the cup, seem to hover like an assurance of immortality, and the second half of the poem extends this hyperbole: the natural decay of roses is arrested by the divine power of Celia's beauty, and their qualities are transformed by the mysterious perfume of her divinity. Even though the love token of the rosy wreath is returned, the poet can find in the circumstances of its rejection new grounds for exalted compliment, which furnish new proof of his devotion. The neat wit of this beautifully turned poem became the model for the Cavalier lyrics of the 1630s: the gallantry, the lightness of touch, and the deft arguments of Lovelace, Suckling and Waller were all anticipated by Jonson a generation before they began to write.

'Drinke to me, onely' stands as an isolated exercise in high compliment: it has no context and no occasion. But Jonson later wrote a suite of poems which also contributed to the thematic stock of the Cavalier poets and which had a partially realized setting. 'A celebration of Charis' professes to characterize the ageing poet's infatuation with a Court beauty and records the progress of their relationship. Charis is probably a conventional fictional mistress – her name could mean Grace, in the social and aesthetic sense of the word, or it could be an alternative name for Venus. The poet sees her, and knows instinctively that her love can be restorative of nature's decay, as with Celia and the rosy wreath:

> this is she,
> Of whose Beautie it was sung,
> She shall make the old man young.
> Keepe the middle age at stay,
> And let nothing high decay.

Inflamed with love, the poet engages in several transactions with Cupid to ensure her conquest, but nevertheless falls her victim. 'Her Triumph' forms one of the most memorable sections with its masque-like air of high artifice as she enters in her chariot, shedding a spiritual radiance around. The final stanza of this poem, like a song from a masque, achieves both reverence and sensuous delight in its awe-struck, hushed admiration:

> Have you seene but a bright Lillie grow,
> Before rude hands have touch'd it?
> Ha' you mark'd but the fall o' the Snow
> Before the soyle hath smutch'd it?
> Ha' you felt the wooll of Bever?
> Or Swans Downe ever?
> Or have smelt o' the bud o' the Brier?
> Or the Nard in the fire?
> Or have tasted the bag of the Bee?
> O so white! O so soft! O so sweet is she!

The repetition of initial words induces a ritual note of worship, yet the language suggests that the goddess may not be inviolable: the 'rude hands', the soiled snow and the tasted bee-bag (whatever that might be!) suggest the possibilities of enjoyment. The delicacy of anticipation here is outstanding, and one can see the qualities of Jonson's verse that Herrick must have responded to.

The poet does exact a kiss from Charis, and in the poem 'Clayming a second kisse by Desert' we catch a glimpse of the social world in which Charis moves:

You were more the eye, and talke
Of the Court, to day, then all
Else that glister'd in White-hall.

As the masquing interlude of the Triumph indicated, we are at Court, where Charis shines, and dances like one who 'might all the Graces lead'. Here, preoccupied with her beauty and keeping men in suspense, she promises she will give her own opinion of whom she would like to take in love. By now the intimacy of the relationship has ceased, and we have moved into a more public scene where courtiers of all kinds gather expectantly around. Her choice would fall on some well-born, frenchified gentleman, high-spirited and bold, yet a novice in love. So much for stout Jonson's hopes. But the sequence ends unexpectedly when another lady intervenes with a greater frankness:

For his Mind, I doe not care,
That's a Toy, that I could spare:
Let his Title be but great,
His Clothes rich, and band sit neat,
Himselfe young, and face be good,
All I wish is understood.
What you please, you parts may call,
'Tis one good part I'ld lie withall

This brings the whole debate down to the level of simple physical satisfaction, and makes one conscious of the elaborate social superstructure that civilized men and women have set up to conceal their animal natures. The final poem, however, does not necessarily invalidate the preceding rituals of courtship; it is merely put forward as one point of view among many.

The attractions of the Charis sequence and its usefulness to the later Cavalier poets lie in its range and variety of attitudes and moods: its intimate and public phases, the witty, whimsical exploitation of the mythology of love, the elegant coquetry of courtship. When the climate of feeling at Court changed from the grossness of King James's time, with its clouds of homosexual emotion, to the refined amorousness that Charles and Henrietta Maria encouraged in the years following the death of Buckingham in 1628, then the inventiveness of Jonson's love poetry could be variously developed in a thoroughly receptive atmosphere.

Some time in the early 1630s, Jonson gathered together the verse he had written since 1616 under the title *Under-Wood*, explaining they were 'lesser Poems, of a later growth' than *The Forest*. (Jonson liked these woody analogies, for he also called his collection of literary observations *Timber* – the usable stock of experience derived from a lifetime of poetry.) He never in fact published the up-dated version of his writings, and it fell to his literary executor Sir Kenelm Digby to bring out a two-volume folio edition of his *Works* in 1640–1. *Under-Wood* is a thoroughly miscellaneous collection which shows how vigorous and varied his poetry remained until his breakdown through sickness in 1631. The concerns of his later poetry stay fairly consistent with his earlier work: there is a great deal of verse that flatteringly evaluates the lives of his friends or extols them in their death, but these examples of virtuous living are increasingly overshadowed by satire on the degeneracy of the age, a topic earlier confined to short epigrams but now becoming the subject of lengthy epistles. There are a few religious poems, unmemorable because of their low level of conveyed experience, and a number of love poems, of which the most appealing is the Charis sequence. The really new development lies in the direction of poems about Jonson himself, exercises of self-scrutiny and assessment which project the satisfactions and disillusionments of the ageing poet.

This last group includes 'An Ode. To Himselfe', the elegy 'Let me be what I am', the 'Execration upon Vulcan', a long satirical lament for the loss of a great quantity of his literary work by a fire in his chambers, which he half suspects to be a judgement on him, and the engaging letter to 'One that asked to be Sealed of the Tribe of Ben.' Having long freely criticized those who failed to strive for distinction in their public and private life, he doesn't hesitate to round on himself when he feels his own resolution slackening.

> Where do'st thou carelesse lie
> Buried in ease and sloth?
> Knowledge, that sleepes, doth die;
> And this Securitie,
> It is the common Moath,
> That eats on wits, and Arts, and destroyes them both.

The energy and seriousness with which the more religiously minded poets attacked their spiritual falterings, Jonson applied to his failure to uphold the honour of poetry. In his later work there is often a sense of his forcing himself to the task of writing and grinding the poetry out of his dissatisfaction with himself and his age. He frequently suspected that he might have compromised his integrity by too much servility at Court, and by his over-involvement with Court masques, those most extravagant vehicles of royal flattery. He had written these masques virtually every year from 1605 to 1625, and one might say that they were written by the Virgil in Jonson, the celebrator of the Augustan glory of King James's reign. But to the Jonson brought up on Horace, Martial and Seneca, they were extraordinary spectacles of vanity and waste, whole fortunes being consumed in one night of pageantry and feasting. There must always have been some tension between his persona as a Horatian moralist and his role as a masque maker, no matter how honourably he served the King in this capacity. The bitterness of his quarrel with his old colleague Inigo Jones, which occasioned several vindictive poems, registers some of his later unhappiness, in the 1630s, with the business of the masques. Court patronage must however have provided much of his income after he stopped writing plays for the public stage in 1616 until the death of James in 1625. The darker passages of his personal poems sometimes dwell on the corruptions of the Court, and are coloured with feelings of complicity and guilt, yet Jonson was hurt by the neglect shown him by King Charles, a neglect only temporarily amended in 1631, when he was again invited to write the masques, and one has the impression that the last decade of the poet's life – he died in 1637 – was lived in a conflict of distress at the failure of Court patronage and irritation at needing such support.

The satisfactions of his later life lay undoubtedly in the conviviality of the poetic gatherings in various taverns and houses at which he was the central figure and where he enjoyed the admiration of the younger poets and wits who congregated there. The magnetism of Jonson's personality is not readily felt through the depth of time that separates us from him, but the response of his younger contemporaries is incontrovertible proof of his energizing presence and wit. Herrick, Carew, Suckling, Randolph and Brome came together with noblemen like Lucius Cary (Lord Falkland) and William Cavendish (Earl of Newcastle) at these poetic feasts which they remembered for the rest of their lives. From him they learnt the delights of living in a world where poetry flickered over every occasion and illuminated all the relationships of their social lives; they also learnt how to handle the intricacies of verse forms and to find the tone appropriate to the serious or frivolous moments of experience; he could best teach how to manage a masque or compliment a mistress, honour a patron or bury a friend. The fact that his poetry was not densely interwoven with his personality and experience, but was relatively formal and literary, made it all the easier to imitate. On his side, Jonson was reassured that his old faith in friendship would sustain him to the end. As he told the poet who wished to join his fraternity, friendships 'such as are square, well-tadged and permanent' are one of the chief gifts of heaven. Throughout his career he had written poetry that had encouraged an intelligent, ethical, civilized approach to life, and he had thrown himself into the cultural activities of his time more energetically than most of his contemporaries; the admiration and love that he aroused in return showed how humanly rewarding a lifetime spent in the service of poetry could be.

Notes

1 See Horace, 'Of the Art of Poetrie', Jonson's translation, lines 391–5. For an extended discussion of the 1616 frontispiece, see M. Corbett and R. Lightbown, *The Comely Frontispiece* (London 1979), pp. 145–53.
2 *Jonsonus Virbius or The Memorie of B. Jonson Revived by the Friends of the Muses*, 1638. Printed in *Ben Jonson*, ed. C. H. Herford and P. and E. Simpson (Oxford 1947), vol. XI, p. 450. The *Virbius* of this unusual title alludes to 'the name given to Hippolytus the favourite of Diana when Aesculapius restored him to life after his murder, and Diana took him to her shrine at Aricia' (Herford and Simpson, XI, 428, from Virgil, *Aeneid*, VII, 764–77). The name therefore expresses ideas of rebirth and sanctification.
3 In particular Virgil, Horace, Martial, Tacitus, Seneca and the Younger Pliny.
4 The raw material for the poem is derived from Martial, *Epigrams*, V.lxxviii; X.xlviii; XI.lii. Also Juvenal, *Satires,* XI, and Horace, *Epistles*, Book I.v.
5 Herford and Simpson, I, 132.
6 By 'illustrate', Jonson means 'add lustre to'.
7 This poem was not printed with the *Epigrams*, though it belongs in spirit with them. It was prefaced to Selden's *Titles of Honor*, published in 1614.
8 Jonson in his masques was very conscious of the imperial possibilities of the newly united Kingdom of Great Britain.
9 This theme of the migration of the Muses from Greece and Rome into England occurs also in the Stuart masques. It appears, for

example, in Jonson's *Fortunate Isles*, and in Davenant's *Luminalia*.

10 See H. A. Mason, *Humanism and Poetry in the Early Tudor Period* (London 1959), pp. 270–89, for a discussion of Jonson's reworking of Martial.

11 Although Pope elaborated the theme on several occasions, it is surprising that this genre did not flourish in the eighteenth century, which was the great age of the country house.

12 For an extended account of this theme in the seventeenth century, see Maren-Sophie Røstwig, *The Happy Man* (Oslo 1954).

2 John Donne: patronage, friendship and love

Whereas much of Jonson's poetry is devoted to honouring the distinguished men and women of his time, and thereby conferring on his society the dignity of a classical age of virtue and accomplishment, a great deal of Donne's is self-advertisement. He wrote much to parade his wit, to entertain and astonish his friends, to attract patrons and generally to announce his availability for employment and advancement in the competitive circles of the Elizabethan and Jacobean Court. Poetry and wit enjoyed a high esteem in those circles: Elizabeth and James both wrote poetry, and most courtiers professed an interest as a sign of their culture. It was a serviceable accomplishment in Court life: it helped to ingratiate one man with another, it might advance amorous affairs, it applied the flattery that was the balm and solace of great men and women at Court – though it could also vent the malice of the disenchanted. The marriages and deaths that shook the Court community were occasions for expressions of joy or grief in verse that helped to formalize the emotions of that varied society. Such was the usefulness of poetry that skill in composition was a definite asset in that small world where talents were aggressively displayed. For Donne, who in the 1590s was moving on the fringes of Court society, it was a means of signalling his presence: here was a witty, spirited, articulate young man hoping for patronage and remunerative office – and his poetry did attract attention.

Donne came from a fairly prosperous London family in trade; on his mother's side there were strong Catholic and literary traditions, for she was related to Sir Thomas More and was the daughter of John Heywood, a minor Tudor playwright and musician. Her son John, born in 1572, was sent to Oxford at an early age to avoid the University's requirement that students over the age of 16 must subscribe to the Articles of the Church of England. He then went on to Lincoln's Inn for the study of law in 1592. Law was only a partial concern, however; he read widely in theology and theological controversy, with a view to clarifying his own position in religion; he studied languages, medicine and alchemy, displaying what he called 'an immoderate hydroptique thirst for learning' of every kind. This passion for learning is well illustrated in his first Satire, where he describes himself cramped in his tiny study:

> Leave mee, and in this standing woodden chest,
> Consorted with these few bookes, let me lye
> In prison, and here be coffin'd, when I dye;
> Here are Gods conduits, grave Divines; and here
> Natures Secretary, the Philosopher;
> And jolly Statesmen, which teach how to tie
> The sinewes of a cities mistique bodie;
> Here gathering Chroniclers, and by them stand
> Giddie fantastique Poets of each land.

But as the poem goes on to admit, the distractions of London also competed for his time. His ambitions lay in the direction of a secretaryship to some great man, or employment in some state office at home or abroad, but in order to gain some such preferment in Elizabethan England, one needed to attract the notice and then the active support of some figure of authority. Without an immediate sponsor, and handicapped by his Catholic connection, he nevertheless began to make a name for himself as a sharp-minded poet in his own circle of friends at Lincoln's Inn, and sought to make some useful contact with the influential families of those friends, all the while exploring the possibility of a career at Court, to which as a gentleman and member of Lincoln's Inn he had access.

His earliest verses are the letters he wrote to fellow students, almost all of whom, Donne implies, practised poetry as a social art. He questions one about the state of 'that mistique trinitee, . . . thy body, mind and Muse'; he asks others about the progress of their studies, whether one has yet reached the secret parts of knowledge, or if another has now satisfied his 'sacred hunger of science'. Always the language is direct, personal in a bright, challenging, intellectual way, and largely free from the poetic conventions of the time. There is scarcely any classical reference, little mythological fancy, and no interest in melodious lines or surface colour. Much of the characteristic material of Donne's later poetry is already to the fore, and displaying a fascination for saints, martyrs, angels and the interaction of souls. For the most part, these early verse letters are inconsequential, attractive measures to consolidate friendship, but later letters offer serious reflections upon experience and morality. One can see this happening in the letter written about 1597–8, 'To Sir Henry Wotton', one of Donne's high-flying friends who would eventually become Ambassador to Venice, and who was at this point a secretary to the Earl of Essex. The poet assures Wotton of the importance of friendship in his life and the need for close sympathetic friends to stimulate his imaginative powers:

> Sir, more then kisses, letters mingle Soules;
> For, thus friends absent speake. This ease controules
> The tediousnesse of my life: But for these
> I could ideate nothing, which could please.

The coinage 'ideate', meaning to invent imaginative notions, seems to be offered as a shining verbal gift to Wotton, the present of a new word to an appreciative friend. Donne's poetry almost always assumed a small intellectual audience who knew the author personally and who were responsive to his ingenuity and mannerisms of style and expression, as well as to his idiosyncracies of subject matter. In the present poem, Donne moves into a discussion of the competing merits of Court, city and country life, evidently making his own contribution to a debate then in progress among the wits of the Essex circle.[1] Typically, the poem descends to intimacies after the generalizations of the discussion: Wotton is urged to maintain his integrity in striking lines very suitable to a political man:

> And in the worlds sea, do not like corke sleepe
> Upon the waters face; nor in the deepe
> Sinke like a lead without a line: but as
> Fishes glide, leaving no print where they passe,
> Nor making sound, so, closely thy course goe.

Donne himself got caught up in Essex's enterprises in 1596, when he volunteered to join the expedition to Cadiz, an immensely popular excursion to damage Spain, which attracted large numbers of footloose gentlemen. For Donne it was an opportunity for adventure after several years at Lincoln's Inn, a chance to show his patriotism and perhaps also to indicate that he had abandoned his Catholicism. He might distinguish himself, make some profitable contact, or simply get killed. He survived, and signed up for a second raid in 1597, on the Azores, under Essex and Ralegh. In the end these risks paid off in two ways: he did make the contact he wanted, and the events of the second voyage provided the material for two poems that were greatly admired at the time. Friendship with his fellow Innsman and adventurer

Thomas Egerton led to a post as secretary to his friend's father, Sir Thomas Egerton, the Lord Keeper of the Great Seal, head of the Court of Chancery – the officer who presided over the House of Lords. It was an excellent appointment, full of variety and promise. The poems that resulted from the Islands Voyage were 'The Storm' and 'The Calme', descriptive pieces that he sent as verse letters to his chamber companion at Lincoln's Inn, Christopher Brooke. Donne rarely gives himself to descriptive writing, but when he does, the busyness of his thoughts constantly translates the scene into other aspects of human life by simile and analogy, as in this passage from 'The Storm':

> And as sin-burd'ned soules from graves will creepe,
> At the last day, some forth their cabbins peepe:
> And tremblingly aske what newes, and doe heare so,
> Like jealous husbands, what they would not know.
> Some sitting on the hatches, would seeme there,
> With hideous gazing to feare away feare.
> There note they the ships sicknesses, the Mast
> Shak'd with this ague, and the Hold and Wast
> With a salt dropsie clog'd, and all our tacklings
> Snapping, like too-high-stretched treble strings.
> And from our totterd sailes, ragges drop downe so,
> As from one hang'd in chaines, a yeare agoe.

Note this early preoccupation with the Last Day that would worry the poet all his life, and the many forms of death that assail the ship and crew. (The innumerable guises that death could assume always gave a macabre delight to Donne.) Then again, the animation, the vigour that all things possess even in decay is characteristic. The swaying, tumbling treatment of the basic pentameter aids the effects. Notice how the tension of the over-stressed ropes is caught in the over-stressed line: 'Snáppĭng, lĭke tóo-hígh-strétchĕd tréblĕ stríngs.' Virtuoso effects of an opposite kind abound in 'The Calme', that recounts the purgatorial life on board a ship becalmed beneath a tropic sun. The stillness of

> No use of lanthornes; and in one place lay
> Feathers and dust, to day and yesterday.

remained for Ben Jonson one of the lasting beauties of Donne's verse.[2]

What impresses, and sometimes tires, the modern reader of these poems is the profusion of ideas and images that load the verse.

Consider the lines that describe the misery of heat and inertia at sea:

> Onely the Calenture together drawes
> Deare friends, which meet dead in great fishes jawes:
> And on the hatches as on Altars lyes
> Each one, his owne Priest, and owne Sacrifice.
> Who live, that miracle do multiply
> Where walkers in hot Ovens, doe not dye.
> If in despite of these, wee swimme, that hath
> No more refreshing, then our brimstone Bath,
> But from the sea, into the ship we turne,
> Like parboyl'd wretches, on the coales to burne.
> Like Bajazet encag'd, the shepheards scoffe,
> Or like slacke sinew'd Sampson, his haire off,
> Languish our ships. Now, as a Miriade
> Of Ants, durst th'Emperours lov'd snake invade,
> The crawling Gallies, Sea-gaoles, finny chips,
> Might brave our Venices, now bed-ridde ships.

Beginning with sea-fever (the calenture), the poet proceeds to envisage death in the jaws of a fish, sacrificial victims, the biblical miracle of the children in the oven, sulphur baths, martyrdom, then memories of *Tamburlaine* and the Book of Judges ('Sampson'), followed by a recollection of Suetonius's Life of Tiberius, a satirical view of galleys and a final fantasy of the decaying fleet as a Venice which turns into a floating hospital. Each couplet introduces a new notion, with the density increasing towards the close. This restless fertility of images may be the sign of a plentiful wit, but it is a relentlessly strenuous one that produces incongruous aesthetic results, for although the nominal subject here is 'The Calme', the reader is subjected to continual mental turbulence.

Donne's earlier poems are generally characterized by this excess of intellectual activity and invention cramped into couplets. The Satires and most of the Elegies belong to the 1590s, and were the poems that enjoyed the widest circulation in manuscript. The Satires are part of an outbreak of such writing in that decade, when a new naturalism swept through English verse, reacting against the more formal beauty and dignity of the poetic generation of Sidney, Spenser and Marlowe.[3] There was now a premium on direct, frank observation, outspoken opinions and iconoclastic attitudes, the sign of a new generation bidding for poetic power. The fashions and morals of the Court are a favourite target, yet Donne has no hostility against that institution, only against what he would have called its corrupt humours; but even so, there is no disposition to reform, only to record the bizarre fads of the day. Besides, the audience for his writing lay at Court and at the Inns of Court, where people knew and enjoyed the world he caricatured. Although the second Satire announces, 'Sir; though (I thanke God for it) I do hate / Perfectly all this towne', that is no preliminary to escape, but rather to an enthusiastic involvement in the crowd of bad poets and fancy lawyers he professes to despise. When he goes to Court in Satire IV he meets a threadbare fantastico:

> Towards me did runne
> A thing more strange, then on Niles slime, the Sunne
> E'r bred; or all which into Noahs Arke came;
> A thing, which would have pos'd Adam to name;

who buttonholes him, engages him in a pseudo-scholarly conversation, deluges him with 'triviall houshold trash' of gossip, and touches him for five shillings. The poet pushes on and reaches the entrance to the Presence Chamber, where he observes courtiers fussing with their dress and concealing their defects like actors going on stage, and in particular delights to see one fastidious gallant making sure that all his clothes are in perfect mathematical proportions:

> And then by Durers rules survay the state
> Of his each limbe, and with strings the odds tries
> Of his neck to his legge, and wast to thighes.
> So in immaculate clothes, and Symetrie
> Perfect as circles, with such nicetie
> As a young Preacher at his first time goes
> To preach, he enters, and a Lady which owes
> Him not so much as good will, he arrests,
> And unto her protests protests protests
> So much as at Rome would serve to have throwne
> Ten Cardinalls into th'Inquisition.

The poet is glad to get away from these overpowering scenes to a more modest setting. Yet, one might ask, why did he go to Court at all? The poem acknowledges that the Court has an undeniable fascination, for there is such variety of incident and costume, such dealing in perquisites and favours, that it is difficult for a worldly-minded gentleman to stay away. Besides, even learning has a sort of value there: we hear of Rabelais and Aretino, Holinshed and Stow. For all his disclaimers in the poem, Donne himself was a Court suitor, a hanger-on, a wit-proud amorist, who may well have been pilloried in some other poet's satires. Donne's Satires, along with many of the Elegies, survive because of their documentary power for the sights and smells and intrigues of Elizabethan London. Although the themes of the Satires, with one exception, are trifling, the social observations are constantly referred back to religious issues or classical antecedents; there is a background of morality, but Donne at this early stage is not interested in looking at it seriously.

The exception is Satire III, 'Of Religion'. The subject here is the search for true religion, a matter of considerable relevance to Donne in the 1590s as he questioned where his own allegiance should lie. The poem falls among the Satires because much of it is given over to an account of the various fashions that prevail in religion, and to wry reflections that men are willing to risk their lives in all sorts of brave or foolhardy ventures (as Donne himself did in 1596–7) yet are indifferent to the infinitely more important challenge of eternal life or death, which also needs to be met by a bold, adventurous approach. Among the Satires, 'Of Religion' alone has a steady intellectual development, an argument to unfold and a serious conclusion. The poet writes as an uncommitted man, aware that there are many tenable positions between Romanism and Calvinism, but mistrustful alike of received opinion and of easy answers. The presentation of the different European churches as mistresses of varying attractions should not be seen as a cynical view, because the female personification of 'Religio' was a commonplace in prints at the time, but we can feel that Donne does not approve of any of the men who have fallen easily for such or such a mistress, for all have chosen according to tradition, custom or sentiment. Worst of all is 'Carelesse Phrygius', who 'doth abhorre / All, because all cannot be good, as one / Knowing some women whores, dares marry none', and only slightly better is the Elizabethan student of comparative religion:

> Graccus loves all as one, and thinkes that so
> As women do in divers countries goe
> In divers habits, yet are still one kinde,
> So doth, so is Religion.

Donne himself is caught in a dilemma. He accepts the conventional wisdom that there must be one true Church, yet doubts if we have the capacities to identify it. The motto he hangs up for himself is 'Doubt wisely', which may be compared to Montaigne's motto, '*Que sçais-je*?', for both are sceptical of our ability to attain any true knowledge of the great questions of life and death. Donne is temperamentally attracted to scepticism as a philosophic position, to suspend judgement because of the inadequate quality of information available, and the fact that what we know is relative to the senses, that these senses are limited, and we are in consequence restricted to a world of appearances with no means of knowing what kind of reality may be presumed from these impressions. Yet neither Elizabethan nor Jacobean England had the confidence to tolerate scepticism, especially in matters of religion, and pressures to conform to orthodox State views were strong.[4] Donne pauses in his poem to enjoy the luxury of a sceptical reflection:

> To adore, or scorne an image, or protest,
> May all be bad; doubt wisely; in strange way
> To stand inquiring right, is not to stray.

But he feels the pressure to reach conclusions, so the mental landscape clears, and he introduces this marvellously worked image:

> On a huge hill,
> Cragged, and steep, Truth stands, and hee that will
> Reach her, about must, and about must goe;
> And what th'hills suddennes resists, winne so;
> Yet strive so, that before age, deaths twilight,
> Thy Soule rest, for none can worke in that night.

Donne can imagine the endeavour even if he cannot envisage the Truth – but he insists there is a truth to be found. The journey, he explains, has to be in time, and into history, a return to 'the streames calme head', the origins of Christianity in its primitive days. And the journey is severe, with no certainty of success, yet the intelligent man has a double duty to make it, to God and his soul; otherwise what could a man say to his God at the close of time, the one event Donne was sure of, the Last Judgement? Donne's feeling that one should rely on individual inquiry into matters of religion indicates he has already parted from the Catholic position, but where he will end up is at the moment of this poem an open question. The poem corresponds to that phase which Walton in his 'Life of Donne' described, when he wrote that he 'betrothed himself to no Religion that might give him any other denomination than a Christian'.

The search for truth in religion and for an understanding of his own spiritual condition preoccupied Donne for most of his life. He must have presented himself as an Anglican to be accepted as Egerton's secretary in 1597, but full conviction came slowly, for he admitted later to a long 'irresolution' in religion. By 1610 he could put himself forward as a champion of the Anglican position in *Pseudo-Martyr*, dedicated to King James and aimed at the Catholic community in England, claiming that he had 'surveyed and digested the whole body of Divinity, controverted between ours and the Romane Church'. His ordination took place in 1615, delayed for many reasons, not the least of which was a feeling of unworthiness for holy office. Yet the inclination of his mind towards scepticism did not fade away for many years: it is a feature of his *Paradoxes and Problems*, written at intervals during the 1590s and 1600s; it is present in his treatise on suicide, *Biathanatos*, written around 1608 but not published until after his death (perhaps because of its unorthodox, approving views). Outside the religious sphere, scepticism is a persistent note in the love poems.

The Satires come from a poet caught up in the mainstream of contemporary life to a degree unmatched by any non-dramatic writer since Chaucer, and the love poems intensify that impression. By their nature, love poems tend to be concerned with a closed circuit, but with Donne the actualities of society intrude to an exceptional extent. Just as the four-poster beds of the time were often set in the main living areas of a house, with only curtains to provide privacy, so Donne's love poems, in particular the Elegies, often seem intimately set yet subject to the pressures of life around them. The impetus towards this approach derives from Ovid, whose love Elegies provided the inspiration for Donne's, both transmitting the belief that in the midst of life we are in love, and featuring a confident, extrovert lover, worldly and often cynical, whose behaviour is dominated by strategies of love. (Both the Satires and the Elegies are indebted to Roman originals, but Donne has so totally reworked them in a modern character that they seem typical of his own society.)[5] The most atmospheric of Donne's love poems is 'The Perfume', where the poet is carrying on an affair under the noses of the family in a stuffy Elizabethan household cluttered with sick parents, inquisitive children and 'The grim eight-foot-high iron-bound serving-man', who blocks up the entrance like an ogre in a fable. In spite of the care the lover takes – 'I taught my silkes, their whistling to forbeare, / Even my opprest shoes, dumbe and speechlesse were' – he is betrayed by the smell of the perfume he wears. The success of the poem lies not in the diatribe against perfume with which it ends, but in the quality of the genre details, and the poet's presence at the centre as an unusually observant lover with a gift for dramatizing and exaggerating every incident, so that the reader sees this bourgeois encounter as a tense domestic drama which could be a passage from a play like *Arden of Faversham*. Behind the humorous detail there is a murderous desire to suppress 'thy immortall mother which doth lye / Still buried in her bed, yet will not dye', and 'to embalme thy fathers corse; What? will hee die?' Such violence of emotional mood is common in Donne's poetry, sometimes expressing itself in adoration, sometimes in exasperation or in contempt that may be gratuitously insulting. In 'The Comparison' the poet considers a friend's mistress:

> Like rough bark'd elmboughes, or the russet skin
> Of men late scurg'd for madnes, or for sinne,
> Like Sun-parch'd quarters on the citie gate,
> Such is thy tann'd skins lamentable state.
> And like a bunch of ragged carrets stand
> The short swolne fingers of thy gouty hand.

Her 'best lov'd part' is 'like to that AEtna / Where round about the grasse is burnt away.' The finder of his mistress's gold chain in 'The Bracelet' is cursed to hell, and 'May the next thing thou stoop'st to reach containe / Poyson, whose nimble fume rot thy moist braine.' Sometimes the poet's violence is directed against himself, as in 'His Picture', where in giving his portrait in miniature to his mistress upon his departure for the wars, he foresees that he may return unrecognizable:

> my hand,
> Perchance with rude oares torne, or Sun beams tann'd,
> My face and brest of hairecloth, and my head
> With cares rash sodaine hoarinesse o'rspread,
> My body a sack of bones, broken within,
> And powders blew staines scatter'd on my skinne.

'On his Mistris', a tender farewell, closes with a nightmare vision of his own death which has a quite surreal power:

> nor in bed fright thy nurse
> With midnight startings, crying out, oh, oh,
> Nurse, oh my love is slaine; I saw him goe
> Ore the white Alpes, alone; I saw him, I,
> Assayld, fight, taken, stabb'd, bleede, fall, and dye.

These jagged imaginings and the frequence of violence in the poems reflect a world where cruelty was commonplace, and unexpected violence a hazard of a society noted for its habitual irritability. We may recall the 'friend' in the first Satire, who steps aside to see his mistress, but 'Many were there, he could command no more; / He quarrell'd, fought, bled; and [was] turn'd out of dore.' In real life we only have to remember the fatal quarrels in which Marlowe and Jonson became involved, the ambushes around Court, the ease with which people found themselves in prison, the prevalence of shattering illnesses, and the general beggarly and brutal environment, to understand why there is so much abrasiveness in Donne.[6]

When we turn from the Elegies to Donne's lyric poems, the *Songs and Sonnets*, we sense a shift to a greater refinement in love, towards more stylish relationships. These poems were composed over quite a long period, from the later 1590s until 1610 or so, and they were not published until 1633, but circulated in numerous manuscript collections that friends and admirers made. Donne did not publish his poetry for a number of reasons. Gentlemen were reluctant to publish poetry on the grounds that it was private, very often part of a relationship with somebody else. It had greater value in manuscript, for it could be offered as a gift, read to privileged friends, sent in letters to people one wanted to impress, passed around anonymously to create an effect, declaimed at the various little coteries and drinking clubs that existed around London, slipped to a nobleman so that he could astonish his friends and gain some unmerited prestige or reputation for taste. (Donne's relations with the Earl of Somerset and the Earl of Carlisle are relevant in this regard.) Donne, unlike his friend Jonson, was not a professional poet, and did not seek a broad public reputation or the profits that might come from publication. Poetry was part of his intellectual and emotional currency, and should be in circulation, but only among those who recognized its worth: to publish it would cause it to lose a lot of its value in the private circles where it belonged. Donne did try to bring out a collection in 1614, just before he was ordained, marking the end of his secular life, as it were, but he had difficulty in tracking down his poems and getting copies from friends, for they were in circulation, and apparently he did not keep a record of all that he had written.

His poems were eventually published after his death, but *Songs and Sonnets* acquired their general title only in the second edition of 1635, and even that is misleading, for there are few songs and fewer sonnets. It appears, from the evidence of the manuscripts, that Donne was not in the habit of giving his lyrics titles, so that the titles we know come from an anonymous hand.[7] Each individual poem has its own peculiar brilliance: as a collection it is astonishing. Before we try to establish some context for these poems, we shall look at the kinds of wit that make them so distinctive. An abundance, even a redundance, of wit was always Donne's hallmark as a poet and as a preacher, yet he excelled in many different modes. In the Satires as in the Elegies, his wit takes the form of a relentless application of similes and analogies that force the subject into new associations in virtually every couplet, so that the reader is staggered by the number of odd angles and points of view that can be achieved. However, since one perception is discarded in favour of the next, the effect is often of strenuous mental flailing to keep the subject moving and to meet the expectation of constant diversion that this technique sets up. It is a cracking, laugh-a-line pace that Donne opts for on these occasions. In several of the Elegies, however, he exercises a more spacious and coherent kind of wit when he develops a large extended image or analogy, as with the metaphor of the voyage of discovery in 'Loves Progress', or in the clever exploitation in 'The Bracelet' of the gold coins called 'angels' which he will have to supply for melting down to make a replacement article, enabling him to fantasize with angelological anecdotes. In many of the *Songs and Sonnets* the extended metaphor or 'conceit' is given a new refinement, establishing new points of comparison as it is developed so that the reader's mind is beguiled and intrigued by two series of images, one a fairly slow-moving series that provides information about the situation and relationship of the lovers, the other, superimposed, being a series of rapid transformational effects caused by ideas and sensations enlarging and complicating the relationship.

Ingeniousness of argument was widely esteemed as part of the wit of love, and especially so when accompanied by paradox: one might remember the elaborate and long-winded pleas and professions of Sidney's *Arcadia*. Donne enjoyed this aspect of the art, sometimes developing it outlandishly, and by renouncing the formal beauties of the language of love in favour of direct dramatic diction he created a school of lovers who seem to specialize in remarkable learned proposals and justifications (such as those used to praise ageing beauty in 'The Autumnall' or to argue in favour of nakedness in 'To his Mistris Going to Bed'), and who have escaped from the inhibitions of courtly politeness into unimpeded expressionism. In the *Songs and Sonnets* these characteristics achieve a new economy and distinction. The many different stanza forms encourage a variety of mood and pace and the emotional range is unparalleled outside Shakespeare. The experience of love is no longer contained by traditions and conventions, but is integrated with the wonder-dominated arts and pseudo-sciences of the Renaissance, and this prevalent atmosphere of wonder helps to unite learning and love in the poems.

Given the spectacular novelty of the *Songs and Sonnets* and their notable idiosyncracy, what can we assume about their use and context? For we know that Donne did not hoard his poems or consider them as secrets of his private life. It helps to distinguish different classes of poem within the collection, and this has usefully been done by J. B. Leishman in his book *The Monarch of Wit*.[8] There he makes certain groupings, of which the major are these: the 'deliberately outrageous, paradoxical or cynical poems', mainly concerned with the display of wit, which include 'Womans Constancy', 'The Indifferent', 'Loves Usury', 'Communitie', 'Confined Love', 'Loves Alchymie', 'The Curse', 'The Apparition' and 'Loves Diet'. Then he groups together the less cynical but still primarily ingenious poems, 'The Flea', 'A Jet Ring Sent', 'The Triple Foole' and 'Witchcraft by a Picture'. These are followed by the songs, 'Sweetest love, I do not goe', 'The Baite', 'The Message' and 'Breake of Day', to which should be added 'Goe, and Catche a falling starre'. Eight poems have associations with Lucy, Countess of Bedford, and Magdalen Herbert, who were Donne's patrons in his middle years: 'The Undertaking', 'The Will', 'The Funerall', 'The Primrose', 'The Blossom', 'The Relique', 'The Dampe' and 'Twicknam Garden'. There are four poems which stand as 'serious analyses of love, as distinct from merely witty or paradoxical generalisations upon it': 'Farewell to Love', 'Negative Love', 'Loves Growth' and 'The Exstasie'. The largest group, marked by a greater tenderness and passion, Leishman is 'tempted to suppose' were inspired by Donne's marriage to Ann More: 'The Good-Morrow', 'The Sunne Rising', 'The Canonisation', 'Loves Infiniteness', 'A Feaver', 'Aire and Angels', 'The Anniversarie', the four Valedictions, 'The Dreame', 'The Broken Heart', 'The Computation', 'The Lecture upon a Shadow', 'The Dissolution', 'The Prohibition', 'The Expiration' and 'The Nocturnall'. It must be stressed that these groupings and their associations are a matter of conjecture, aided by a few contemporary remarks that link certain poems to certain persons; such classifications, however, loose as they are, do enable us to make some useful distinctions among the *Songs and Sonnets*.

We may begin with the last-mentioned group. Donne's marriage in 1601 was very much an impulsive love match in an age when gentlemen were inclined to make cautious and prudent marriages based on social and financial advantage. Marrying secretly without the consent of Ann's father offended the stern social conventions of the time, and broke canon law; Sir George More reacted by having Donne briefly imprisoned, and harrying him out of his job as Egerton's secretary. Even after relations were patched up on all sides, Egerton still felt that this indiscretion barred Donne from a secretary's post, where confidentiality and tact were essential. Donne was obliged to retreat into an impoverished state that would endure with occasional remission until his ordination in 1615. Donne did lose all for love, which perhaps explains why several of the *Songs and Sonnets* modulate into a religious key, with the lovers becoming love's saints or martyrs because they have renounced the world for the mysteries of love, as in 'The Canonisation', where the poet can argue that he has attained a state vastly superior to worldly success that more than compensates for his 'ruined fortune'. There the canonized lovers may offer 'a patterne of [their] love' to those who will worship them. A similar tactic is adopted in 'A Valediction: of the Booke', for here the poet urges his mistress, when he is gone, to

> Study our manuscripts, those Myriades
> Of letters, which have past twixt thee and mee,
> Thence write our Annals, and in them will bee,
> To all whom loves subliming fire invades,
> Rule and example found;
> . . . .
> This Booke, as long liv'd as the elements,
> Or as the worlds forme, this all-graved tome,
> In cypher write, or new made Idiome;
> Wee for loves clergie only are instruments.
> When this booke is made thus,
> Should againe the ravenous
> Vandals and Goths inundate us,
> Learning were safe; in this our Universe
> Schooles might learne Sciences, Spheares Musick, Angels Verse.

A literary courtship has its advantages. The couple exert power through the perfection of their love, whatever their wordly state might be, and Donne was attracted by the idea of power. As a lover he liked to imagine himself as a monarch ('The Anniversarie': 'Here upon earth, we are Kings'), a universal emperor ('The Sunne Rising': 'She is all States, and all Princes I'), a conqueror of new worlds, an interceding saint; later he would be grimly satisfied to be the servant of his God, whose omnipotence he so often described in his sermons. It must have been painful to him to be close to power and have no share in it, as he was throughout the years of his marriage, yet in poetry he could exercise dreams of power. He also liked to imagine himself dead, and did so in several of the *Songs and Sonnets*, but even then he envisaged himself with power over the living – as a tormenting ghost in 'The Apparition', as the slaughterer of his friends in 'The Dampe', the preserver of his mistress from dissolution in 'The Funerall', the object of adoration in 'The Relique'. The proximity of death to love in the *Songs* may be a strategy for intensifying relationships, but it also reflects the low life expectancy of the age, when death by sudden disease or in childbirth was so common. Marriages did not normally last very long, and old age was a rare prospect: the hope expressed in 'The Anniversarie' that the couple will 'Attaine / To write threescore' years of love is pure fantasy. Every parting in Donne presupposes a death, all the Valedictions relate the metaphoric death of separation to the possibility of an actual death.

The occasion of a valediction was usually a journey, not just a brief separation. Walton, for example, tells us that 'A Valediction: forbidding Mourning' along with the song 'Sweetest love, I do not goe / For wearinesse of thee' was given by Donne to his wife when he left England in 1611 to travel abroad with Sir Robert Drury, and although Walton's memory has been questioned, for he often confused dates and situations, the occasion would be appropriate to these poems. Each of the Valedictions is a kind of meditation, a secular equivalent to the religious practice of dwelling on a text or topic, extending its significance by illustration or analogy, and pressing out of it as much meaning as possible by the application of pious wit and ingenuity. In fact, a good many of the familiar characteristics of the *Songs and Sonnets* derive from the displacement of meditational techniques from a religious into an amorous setting: the vivid evocation of place, the arguments often aided by conceits to enable a fuller understanding of the situation to develop, the moving of the affections to precipitate a new resolution that will terminate the poem. One Valediction is a meditation on what is literally a text – his name scratched on the window pane; another, 'of the Book', is a meditation on the poems and letters of the lovers and how they may be used to perpetuate their love; 'of Weeping' meditates on lovers' tears; and 'forbidding Mourning' contemplates the phenomenon of lovers parting. The famous conceits of the latitude and longitude of love, of the geographical tear, the aery gold and compasses that appear in these poems function as meditative devices for the exploration of the mystery of love: geometry, spheres, gold and circles are all metaphors of perfection, all working towards an intellectual revelation of love.

These poems, then, may have had their origins in Donne's experience of courtship and marriage. It is quite likely that they began as private poems, but they were badly-kept secrets and he probably soon showed them or sent them in letters to close friends such as Sir Henry Wotton, Sir Henry Goodyere or Christopher Brooke. Most of his friends wrote poetry, and would expect to see Donne's latest 'evaporations', as he once called them. But there is no sign of widespread familiarity with the poems of the *Songs and Sonnets* during the first decade of the century. Jonson seemed unaware of them, for example, and presumably they remained the property of Donne's intimate circle. The first lyric to appear in print was a song, 'The Expiration', which appeared in the 1609 *Ayres* of Alphonso Ferrabosco, a composer associated with the Jacobean Court. One would expect the songs to be rapidly in circulation, for most gentlemen played the lute, and singing was one of the great social pleasures. The window seats at Court and in great houses were favourite places for lute-playing, poetry reading and flirting. Most small social gatherings were likely to break into song at some point, and lutes seemed to hang in every chamber. Donne probably contributed his songs freely to any convivial occasion, and several early seventeenth-century manuscript settings exist to show what pleasure they gave. A song like 'The Baite' was most likely composed to an existing tune that went with Marlowe's and Ralegh's related poems; other poems might have an extempore accompaniment, or be part spoken and part played. Donne assumed that his poems would be taken over by musicians, when he observed in 'The Triple Foole' that no man's poem is truly his own once it gets out of his hands, for it becomes the vehicle for another man's art and pride:

> But when I have done so,
> Some man, his art and voice to show,
> Doth set and sing my paine,
> And by delighting many, frees againe
> Griefe, which verse did restraine.
> To Love, and Griefe tribute of Verse belongs,
> But not of such as pleases when 'tis read,
> Both are increased by such songs:
> For both their triumphs so are published.

Just as the songs were easily launched into Jacobean society, so one imagines were the few poems that attempt some definition of love, notably 'The Exstasie'. The nature of love and the manner of its operation were a standing matter for discussion in cultural circles throughout the Renaissance. The great debate on love that closes Castiglione's book *The Courtier* is the most thorough and articulate exploration of the subject, which continued to divert courtly people until the middle of the seventeenth century. It was especially suitable for mixed companies, and a vast quantity of poetry was written for or as a result of these congenial and often learned exchanges. Donne's relations with his eminent patronesses would be enlivened by witty speculations about love, for these ladies encouraged compliments to fly around and they also allowed certain pretended intimacies or even criticisms within the limits of this game-playing. One can well imagine 'Aire and Angels' being read to the Countess of Bedford or to Mrs Herbert to settle a vexed question about the difference in fineness between a man's love and a woman's:

> Just such disparitie
> As is twixt Aire and Angells puritie,
> 'Twixt womens love, and mens will ever bee.

Even if this poem were not written for such an occasion, it had an evident value in a society where theories and subtleties of love were appreciated. Jonson recounts how he was present at a wrangle over some point of love-lore between the Earl and Countess of Pembroke, was asked for his opinion and told to make it up in verse, the result being 'That women are but men's shadows.' Donne's friend Lord Herbert of Cherbury has a poem entitled 'On a question moved, whether Love should continue forever', which was obviously a contribution to some coterie debate, as were his various poems called 'Platonic Love'. At the Court of King Charles the pastoral dramas and annual masques lavishly explicated the mysteries of the platonic love that united the King and Queen with ideas of virtue and goodness, to the immeasurable benefit of Court and nation. Innumerable ideas and instances concerning the physical and spiritual operations of love can be found in the lengthy section on love in Burton's *Anatomy of Melancholy* (1621), which is a great storehouse of contemporary beliefs, very convenient to those whose imagination needed a stir. 'The Exstasie' would seem to belong to some Anatomy of Love lesson that Donne participated in. It represents his most sustained figuration of the process of love, which here for the most part follows a high-minded neo-Platonic scheme, the steady, reasonable, explanatory tone of the poem suggesting that the speaker is one of 'Love's Divines'.

The lovers are first espied on a traditional trial-ground, the flower-covered bank, with violets (cf. Oberon's 'I know a bank where the wild thyme blows, / Where oxlips and the nodding violet grows'). The speaker does not describe in much detail the preconditions for 'exstasie', in which the soul leaves the body and integrates entirely with the companion soul, but intensity of mutual inter-involvement and a parity of love are essential. The bodies lie motionless, 'like sepulchrall statues', as the transcendent state of ecstasy supervenes. Here beyond speech or expression only a soul in affinity might know of this rarefied union, and Donne rather awkwardly introduces such an observer, while continuing to narrate his experience:

> This Extasie doth unperplex
> (We said) and tell us what we love,
> Wee see by this, it was not sexe,

but rather the fair ideas of the mind, aspects of virtue, goodness, beauty, that are imageless, perceived and enjoyed by the delighted mind in those inexpressible regions where language cannot go. Donne may offer us metaphors of chemistry, and analogies from horticulture and astronomy, but the truth is mystical and language is minimally relevant.

> Wee then, who are this new soule, know,
> Of what we are compos'd, and made,
> For, the'Atomies of which we grow,
> Are soules, whom no change can invade.

This is scarcely informative. Their condition seems angelic, but in order for love to sublimate all the human faculties, it must ultimately involve the body, 'That sense may reach and apprehend, / Else a great Prince in prison lies.' That power can only be released by physical love, and so the poem concludes with a renewed passion for the body. Now whether 'The Exstasie' is one of Donne's most solemn poems of love or is really a platonic shaggy dog story whose purpose is an invitation to love or a 'persuasion to enjoy', disguised by all manner of specious intellectual promises, one cannot with certainty say – but this ambiguity is part of its wit. It is a poem designed to be contentious and provoke a response, and was probably intended for some casuistical circle Donne frequented.

One such circle, membership of which Donne valued greatly, centred on Lucy, Countess of Bedford. Few poets failed to praise the aptness of her name, for she outshone all the other ladies at Court, herself a constellation of talents. She danced brilliantly in the masques, dressed spectacularly, wrote poetry, loved plays, collected paintings and curios and artists of all kinds. She was Queen Anne's closest companion, and like the Queen tended to live apart from her husband, who stayed out of public life after his involvement with Essex's revolt, and later fell victim to illness. Donne was probably introduced to the Countess by Sir Henry Goodyere, who was a friend of the family, and apart from the stimulus and distinction that her friendship promised, Donne must have hoped that she might pull strings for him at Court or find him some post among her extensive family connections. Daniel, Drayton, Florio, Chapman, Jonson and Dowland all enjoyed her patronage, and, like Donne, repaid it with that fawning admiration that so often developed within a Jacobean patron–client relationship. She was considered a good judge of modern literature, and she encouraged writing, bringing different writers together, offering accommodation and occasionally money, and criticizing their work. It was she, for example, who suggested that Florio translate Montaigne's *Essays*.

Her friendship with Donne developed strongly from 1607 onwards, with frequent correspondence and requests from the Countess for copies of Donne's poems. She asked Jonson to get hold of Donne's Satires for her, but Donne must also have sent many of his recent compositions directly to her. In return, she showed him some of her own poems, although courtesy would prevent him from offering any honest opinions. Donne also addressed several verse letters to the Countess, from which we can gauge the character of a Jacobean literary affair between a well-educated poet and a leading member of the aristocracy. Donne usually appears very self-conscious in these letters, adopting a strenuous pedagogical manner, full of propositions and demonstrations deployed in pseudo-reasonings to form conclusions of unqualified adulation:

> Reason is our Soules left hand, Faith her right,
>   By these wee reach divinity, that's you.

Those fortunate enough to be permitted within the circle of her intellectual light must be her saints, among whom Donne wishes to be admitted, drawn by his faith in her god-like qualities to worship and to know her especial genius:

Therefore I study you first in your Saints,
Those friends, whom your election glorifies,
Then in your deeds, accesses, and restraints,
And what you reade, and what your selfe devize.

Composed of so many virtues that she restores the world, she is unique among women:

for you are here
The first good Angell, since the worlds frame stood,
That ever did in womans shape appeare

and by revealing her divine qualities to her elect, she draws them into holiness,

Since you are then Gods masterpeece, and so
His Factor for our loves.

Another letter portrays her virtue purifying the Court, emitting a radiance (for she is Lucy, the shining one) that makes all celestial; she is the translucent temple of Virtue. (Donne was fascinated by the legend of the temple built by Nero in some sort of glass or 'specular stone' where all that happened within could be seen from without.) Elsewhere he writes:

So whether my hymnes you admit or chuse,
In me you have hallowed a pagan muse.

There is a lot of displaced religion in Donne's social and amorous verse, some of it no doubt the result of early Catholic habits of devotion, some merely following the traditional vocabulary of female worship, but the wondering adoration offered to the Countess of Bedford matches the highest panegyrical moments of the Court masques in which she was so prominent. In these ritual entertainments, members of the nobility appeared as the most exalted virtues and powers, such as Intellectual Beauty, Harmony, Justice, Serenity, for part of the function of masque was to reveal the secret qualities of the Court, presided over by the divine majesty of the King himself. In his celebratory poems Donne is extending the convention of the deification of great courtiers beyond the confines of masque into the sphere of patron–client relations. In this new context the hyperbole sounds like idolatry, but to Lucy or to the readers accustomed to the conventions of masque it would not seem immoderate. The Jacobean nobility was used to being viewed in a divine light.

One poem in *Songs and Sonnets* that has strong associations with the Countess of Bedford is 'Twicknam Garden'. The poem has the title in several early manuscripts, and must refer to the Countess's estate at Twickenham, which she acquired in 1607, and which she made the centre of her cultural life. In the verse letter that begins 'Madame, / You have refin'd mee', Donne proclaims that

> The Mine, the Magazine, the Commonweale,
> The story of beauty, in Twicknam is, and you.
> Who hath seene one, would both; As, who had bin
> In Paradise, would seeke the Cherubin.

Access to Twickenham was a distinct privilege, so in using the Countess's garden as a setting for his poem of unrequited love, Donne was both glancing favourably at himself as an intimate of the place, and complimenting the Countess by praising her garden as a place of healing and restoration. The actual garden was a notable horticultural conceit, being laid out on the model of the Ptolemaic universe in concentric spheres of planting, thus offering the opportunity to universalize any event or action that took place there, in the way that the name and shape of the Globe Theatre gave universal relevance to the scenes enacted within. It is possible too that Twickenham garden also figured Paradise, in its choice of trees and plants and orderly layout, with a central fountain running into four streams. Here the love-shattered poet comes to be cured of love's poison and restored by the springtime; Donne had elsewhere praised the Countess for her curative powers against the ills of life:

> But you of learning and religion,
> And vertue, and such ingredients, have made
> A methridate, whose operation
> Keepes off, or cures what can be done or said.

(A 'methridate' is an antidote to poison.) His desire never to leave the garden but to become a piece of ornamental statuary – 'a stone fountaine weeping out my yeare' – is a most ingenious proposition, for he would thereby perpetuate his grief without the discomfort of sensation, yet would also figure as a permanent lover-in-residence to the Countess, an emblem of the love and grief that her perfections inspire in one who cannot hope to attain them. The tear-judging sequence that follows is a pretty display of wit for any audience (though faintly blasphemous, because Christ's tears were held to be the true tears of love), and when the aspersions against women turn suddenly into a celebration of the constancy of one, we can almost hear the murmur of approval that must have greeted this neatly executed conclusion. But whether the poet's distress was fictional or not, an important function of the poem is, by implication, compliment to the Countess for the loan of her garden for the poet's exercise, and for her protective role.

A poem which has often been linked with the Countess of Bedford is the great 'Nocturnall upon S. Lucies Day', largely on account of the prominence of the name Lucy. That she should be the subject of this meditation seems most improbable, for the mood of unmitigated loss and the incontrovertible statement of the death of the poet's love suggest a deeply personal loss, and the poem almost certainly memorializes the death of his wife in 1617, making it the last written of the *Songs and Sonnets*. The overwhelming solemnity of this poem has no equal in English; its sombre measures tread in funeral pace as the poet's mind sinks into a philosophic dejection, its grave wit steadily trying to define the nature of his desolation in a world composed of negativities, 'absence, darknesse, death; things which are not'. The poem is a vigil, a night watch, preparing the soul to follow into the darkness. St Lucy's Day as the shortest day could be an appropriate time for such a meditation as the year attains its nadir of darkness, for that is emotionally appropriate to his state, and he insists that he will remain in that state; time will bring a renewal of life and love to the natural world, but not to the sadly transmuted world that the poet now inhabits. For him this pitch of darkness is the black pathway towards death. The choice of St Lucy's Day may, however, be a dejected compliment to his patroness. Donne's wife died in August, but to write this commemoration in December, when his feelings of loss had matured, would be a fit act of retrospection at the end of the solar year wherein his sun fell; the title suggests that the poem might have been offered to the Countess of Bedford as a sympathetic understander, one who had taken a long interest in the poet's affairs. Nor should it be forgotten that she herself had become more solemn and religious-minded since a near-fatal illness in 1612.

Donne became in effect the Countess's resident elegist for a time, devising poetic wreaths for her cousin Lady Markham and for her friend Mrs Bulstrode, who both found 'a grave frost' at Twickenham in 1609. In 1614 her highly talented younger brother Sir John Harington died, only 22. Donne expended much care on his obsequies, without finding an adequate metaphor for the event; he settled for the triumphant entry of Harington into heaven, but the triumph lacks conviction and the memorable phrase. Nevertheless, a funeral was an important moment when one could honour a family as well as the deceased. Donne tactlessly overstepped the invisible line between patron and artist by sending a begging letter along with the elegy, with a consequent cooling of relations.[9]

The other lady who closely affected Donne's imaginative life was Magdalen Herbert, the pious, witty, well-educated mother of the poets George and Edward Herbert, evidently a good judge of verses herself. She was socially a good deal closer to Donne's level than was Lady Bedford, so that Donne's letters and verses to her have a friendly, even sportive tone. There is some dispute over which if any of the *Songs and Sonnets* developed out of their relationship.[10] Traditionally, the group of poems that appear together in many manuscripts – 'The Dampe', 'The Relique', 'The Primrose', 'The Blossom', 'The Funerall' – have been associated with Mrs Herbert, a belief encouraged by the joke in 'The Relique' – 'Thou shalt be a Mary Magdalen, and I / A something else thereby' – and by the indication in manuscripts that 'The Primrose' was set at Montgomery Castle, the Welsh seat of the Herberts. But the poems could equally well have been composed at Montgomery for the appreciation of Sir Edward Herbert, who resided there, and whose poetry shares many similarities with Donne's. With more certainty, we know that Donne composed his elegy 'The Autumnall' for Mrs Herbert. This is an affectionate exercise in praise of an older woman, which achieves some pleasing harmonies and cadences unusual in Donne's verse:

> No Spring, nor Summer Beauty hath such grace,
> As I have seen in one Autumnall face.
> . . .
> Here, where still Evening is; not noone, nor night;
> Where no voluptuousnesse, yet all delight.

These charms are not permitted to dominate the poem; the disfiguring impulse soon asserts itself, and the poet's imagination engages happily with decay:

> Call not these wrinkles, graves; If graves they were,
> They were Loves graves; for else he is no where.
> Yet lies not Love dead here, but here doth sit
> Vow'd to this trench, like an Anachorit.
> And here, till hers, which must be his death, come,
> He doth not digge a Grave, but build a Tombe.[11]

More evidence, if any were needed, of Donne's fascination with the skull beneath the skin. Death, however, is rarely repose in Donne: bodies are always being dug up again or scattered or resurrected, and subjected to inquiry or interrogation or judgement.

In 1611, friendship, patronage and death combined to provide social and poetic employment. In that year Donne was invited to join Sir Robert and Lady Drury on their continental travels as linguist and companion. Drury was a moderately wealthy man, owning property on the site now called Drury Lane, and he had diplomatic aspirations; Donne had met him through the usual network of Court and legal friends. At the end of 1610, Drury's 14-year-old daughter Elizabeth had died, and Donne used the occasion to compose a long set of philosophic verses that he published in 1611 to mark the anniversary of her death, following them with a second poem in 1612. In a letter to Goodyere he asked pardon for his uncharacteristic 'descent in printing anything in verse', admitting, 'I did it against my conscience, that is against my own opinion', adding too that he had never met Elizabeth Drury. One can only assume that Donne acted under pressure from Sir Robert, who wished to see his daughter publicly commemorated, and in turn the poet may have complied because of his need for support from Drury. The *Anniversaries* enabled Donne to appear in public as a philosophical poet, yet the vein of elegiac hyperbole he adopted to praise Miss Drury bewildered many readers.

Funeral poetry in the seventeenth century habitually proclaimed that the deceased was a paragon and non-pareil, that with him or her all virtue had left the world, and the world itself was left desolate. Donne advanced these claims literally to phenomenal lengths: Elizabeth Drury was the world-soul that animated the whole earth, giving it beauty, colour and proportion; she was 'the intrinsique Balme' that preserved the world from decay, and now she is dead nothing can prevent the terminal decline of the creation. The central exercise in *The First Anniversarie* is 'An Anatomy of the World', where Donne studies the symptoms of decay in man and the universe. Uninhibited by the vastness of the operation, he draws out the evidence, most of it familiar from contemporary controversy, for the degeneracy of nature: man's age has been abbreviated to a span from the immense longevity of the sons of Adam,

> When, if a slow-pac'd starre had stolne away
> From the observers marking, he might stay
> Two or three hundred yeares to see't againe,
> And then make up his observation plaine;

whereas now

> Alas, we scarse live long enough to trie
> Whether a new made clocke runne right, or lie.

Likewise, the stature, nourishment and intellect of man have declined since the Fall: new diseases prevail, the earth has grown deformed, and the heavens themselves, long thought immutable, have been invaded by change as 'the new philosophy' so depressingly discovers. ' 'Tis all in pieces, all cohaerence gone.' Donne never elsewhere contemplated so vast a theme; its magnitude excited all his passion for immensities and universals. The Alexandrian library of his learning is tumbled out without restraint. The disproportion between the occasion and the themes it liberated is baffling, for Donne, invited to write an epitaph, has prophesied the doom of the world. What amazes is his relish for this spectacle of decay, as if his universal pessimism were an entirely invigorating emotion. Not even his control in meditating on the darkness and ignorance of this life, the desirability of death, and the ascent into divine light of Miss Drury's soul, can conceal the utter satisfaction that Donne experiences as he surveys the terrible desolations of time in *The Second Anniversarie*.

He is moving very close to a revelation of the world's end in these poems, and in November 1612 an event occurred that gave a new impetus in this direction, the death of Henry, Prince of Wales. Henry, who died at the age of 18, was a most hopeful prince. Cultivated and warlike and immensely popular, he was the focus of many national aspirations, especially in religion, for his zealous Protestantism aroused expectations that he would become the leader of Protestant Europe and head a crusade against the Catholic powers. He was widely regarded as a providential figure, an instrument of God's designs and a sure sign of God's favour towards England. Prophecy and speculation abounded: he would defeat the Roman Anti-Christ, put an end to the 'jars in religion' that had shaken Europe for a century, and bring about a universal peace. Many believed that this peace would be co-extensive with the final days of the world, and that his reign would create the conditions propitious to the return of Christ and the establishment of the Earthly Paradise.[12] His sudden death was the occasion of immense distress and foreboding, so inexplicable and ominously suggestive of a suspension of God's goodwill. Donne's elegy, one of hundreds printed in 1613 (for virtually the whole poetic community responded to the event), grappled with the injustice of a death which had assaulted both his faith and his reason. It is a cold, intellectual poem, nagging at the mystery of the Prince's death and getting nowhere. He rehearses the hopes that Henry aroused as the 'activ'st spirit to convey and tye / This soule of peace through Christianitie':

> Was it not well believ'd, that hee would make
> This general peace th'eternall overtake?
> And that his times might have stretcht out so far
> As to touch those of which they emblems are?

He acknowledges that Prince Henry's career seemed 'to confirm this just belief, that now / The last dayes came', yet these hopes must now be postponed. He can only offer platitudes in explanation: Henry's death is a punishment visited on a sinful generation, the world does not deserve the hopeful times that Henry's life promised, men must suffer for their sins and errors,

> Therefore wee live: though such a life wee have
> As but so manie mandrakes on his grave.

The idea of living on a grave is congenial to Donne. The ceaseless returnings of his imagination to death and dissolution take place in the larger perspective of the Last Judgement and the resurrection of the body to heaven or hell. Donne was disposed to believe that he was living in the last age of the world, a view widely shared by his Protestant contemporaries, encouraged by the torrent of interpretation and prophecy in sermons and discourses that viewed the Reformation as the beginning of the end, an intervention by God in history to prepare the way for the return of Christ, the Last Judgement and the rule of the saints. Donne was further tempted to believe he might be a member of the final generation, who would not die, but (as St Paul promised) be changed in the twinkling of an eye.[13] In his middle years his thoughts turned with increasing anxiety to the last scene of his life and the world's. The Holy Sonnets in particular, which date from a period of religious crisis through the years 1607–10, when he was tormented by doubts about his worthiness in the eyes of God, visit and revisit the scene of judgement. 'What if this present were the worlds last night?' he proposes to himself in the ninth Sonnet, and the famous evocation of the Last Judgement in the fourth raises the prospect of a fearsomely imminent event:

> At the round earths imagin'd corners, blow
> Your trumpets, Angells, and arise, arise

From death, you numberlesse infinities
Of soules, and to your scattred bodies goe.

If Death should claim him, he has already rehearsed an overwhelming argument to discountenance his adversary: 'Death be not proud' casts off all hesitancy and doubt as he presses home his conviction:

One short sleepe past, wee wake eternally,
And death shall be no more, Death thou shalt die.

We assume that Donne wrote these sonnets as brief, highly disciplined meditations on his sinful condition and on his need for grace, employing the traditional techniques of meditation that he had assimilated from Catholic manuals of devotion. The first of these techniques was the 'composition of place' or 'proposition of the subject', which used graphic images to recreate, often with great dramatic power, the critical religious scene or event that would be the locus of the meditation. Then followed an analysis directed towards an understanding of the situation, extending the subject by similitudes and 'curious inventions', so that it might awaken understanding and move the affections to a firm resolution.[14] This pattern forms the underlying structure of most of the Holy Sonnets, just as it is frequently used to secular ends in the love poems.

Although Donne's religious poems served a private function of spiritual discipline, control of personal fears and encouragement of hope, they also had a social function, for he circulated them to friends so that they could serve the needs of others. In this respect they had a utilitarian value, the more so since Donne's religious experience was not extraordinary or unique – it was compatible with the religious condition of many of his friends – but it had the advantage of being supremely well expressed. He sent, for example, the first six Holy Sonnets with a covering poem to the 'E. of D.', usually identified as the Earl of Dorset, for his judgement. Likewise the circular sequence of sonnets on the life of Christ, 'La Corona' ('this crown of prayer and praise, / Weav'd in my low devout melancholie') was apparently sent to Magdalen Herbert for her use in prayer and meditation.

Donne entered into holy orders in 1615, after much hesitation, and immediately received preferment from King James, who for some time had wanted Donne to join the learned clergy he was trying to build up in England. Thereafter Donne was in receipt of an adequate income, he was no longer desperate for patronage, and since most of his experience of life and religion would now be channelled into his sermons, poetry became a less important means of expression to him. The two moving poems of his later years, the 'Hymne to God my God, in my sicknesse' and 'A Hymne to God the Father', were exceptional productions, arising out of his near fatal illness in 1623. The first Hymn flourishes his wit and learning; the second is unusually simple and direct, but still manages a witty appeal for the forgiveness of sins. Both poems illustrate the Art of Dying as it was practised in the early seventeenth century. A self-conscious pose on one's deathbed was considered admirable, because a well-sustained performance edified the spectators who themselves would eventually have to play the part, and also allowed the dying person to compose his soul, extemporize appropriate prayers and make an exemplary Christian end. The composing of the soul in harmony with a celestial mode is the stated purpose of the 'Hymne to God my God' –

> Since I am comming to that Holy roome,
> Where, with thy Quire of Saints for evermore,
> I shall be made thy Musique; As I come
> I tune the Instrument here at the dore,
> And what I must doe then, thinke now before

– and it proves to be a virtuoso performance. For the last time the cabinets of knowledge are opened up, and all the contents in their different ways reveal the divine plan of salvation. Medicine, cosmography, geography, history, folklore and the Bible combine to promise resurrection through death.

Donne's imaginative faculties were unusually stimulated by the approach of death. His Valedictions are all coloured by the apprehension of death incident to travel; the 'Nocturnall' and the *Anniversaries* derive their sombre power from death; his great sickness of 1623 moved him to write the Hymns and also the *Devotions upon Emergent Occasions*, which record the progress of his illness and the religious thoughts it aroused. When he knew he was dying, in 1631, Donne seized the initiative from death and made it serve his own ends: he appeared in the pulpit at Whitehall, before the King, as a dying man to preach his last sermon, *Death's Duell*, using his body as an eloquent illustration of his text: 'And unto God the Lord belong the issues of death.' At his lodgings at St Paul's he set about turning himself into an instructive work of art. Walton recounts how

> Several charcoal fires being first made in his large study, he brought with him into that place his winding-sheet in his hand, and having put off all his

clothes, had this sheet put on him, and so tied with knots at his head and feet, and his hands so placed as dead bodies are usually fitted, to be shrouded and put into their coffin, or grave. Upon this urn he thus stood, with his eyes shut, and with so much of the sheet turned aside as might show his lean, pale, and death-like face, which was purposely turned towards the east, from whence he expected the second coming of his and our Saviour Jesus. In this posture he was drawn at his just height; and when the picture was fully finished, he caused it to be set by his bed-side, where it continued and became his hourly object till his death.[15]

This picture also provided the inspiration for the portrait attached to *Death's Duell*, published in 1632, for the engraver Martin Droeshout (who had been responsible for Shakespeare's portrait in the First Folio of 1623) worked it up into a powerful *memento mori* (Plate 2). No longer does the bright face of the author encourage the reader to pursue his opinions in the book: here Donne's death's-head declares that he has validated the text with his life. Donne also commissioned a marble statue to be carved of his death-bed tableau, to be used for the effigy on his tomb in St Paul's. It is his last conceit, for it shows him rising from his urn, thus proving that 'death doth touch the Resurrection'.

Notes

1 The debate is outlined by Donne's most recent editor W. Milgate in his edition of *The Satires, Epigrams and Verse Letters* (Oxford 1967), pp. 225–6.

2 See Jonson's *Conversations with Drummond*, in *Ben Jonson*, ed. C. H. Herford and P. and E. Simpson (Oxford 1947), vol. 1, p. 135.

3 Marston, Lodge and Hall all published volumes of satire in the 1590s. Shakespeare responded to the trend by giving his plays a greater satirical bite. Hamlet is very much a contemporary young man.

4 See the excellent discussion of Donne's scepticism in John Carey, *John Donne, Life, Mind and Art* (London 1981), pp. 231–41.

5 See J. B. Leishman, *The Monarch of Wit* (London 1951), pp. 52–90, for a discussion of the relationship between Roman poetry and Donne's Satires and Elegies.

6 For an analysis of violence in Elizabethan and Jacobean society, see Lawrence Stone, *The Crisis of the Aristocracy* (Oxford 1967),

Plate 2 The frontispiece of *Death's Duell*, published in 1632

ch. 5. One suggestion that he puts forward to explain the irritability of the times is that most people were nearly always ill in some way. The prominence in Donne's work of palsy, agues, rheums, sweats, dropsies, pox and plague lends strength to this suggestion.

7 See Helen Gardner's discussion of the titling of the *Songs and Sonnets* in her edition (Oxford 1965), p. 151. The portrait frontispiece (Plate 3) that prefaces the 1635 edition of the *Poems* encourages the reader to associate the poems with Donne's youth, for he is shown there as at the age of 18, fashionable, alert and bold, his hand taking a firm grip on a prominently set sword-hilt to show his spirited character. His motto adds to the defiant air of the portrait: '*Antes muerto que mudado*' – 'sooner dead than changed' – though whether the motto refers to his constancy as a lover or as a soldier is unclear. It has been suggested that this small oval engraving was based on a miniature, possibly by Hilliard; the mediocre quality of the engraving, however, does not enable one to offer much judgement on the original. Izaac Walton, who wrote the accompanying verses, is anxious to undervalue the time of Donne's 'youth, strength, mirth and wit', and by implication the love poems, satires and epistles those years produced, in favour of his maturer age of holy earnestness – but Walton always liked to dwell on Donne's reformation and his progress towards a holy state.

8 Leishman, *The Monarch of Wit*, pp. 178–9.

9 The Countess in effect paid off Donne with a sum of £30, which the poet considered quite inadequate.

10 See Gardner, *Songs and Sonnets*, pp. 251–8, and R. C. Bald, *John Donne: A Life* (Oxford 1970), pp. 180–5, for Donne's relations with Magdalen Herbert and the status of these poems.

11 How old was Magdalen Herbert when Donne wrote 'The Autumnall'? Modern commentators estimate it was written about 1601, when Donne was about 29 and Mrs Herbert (a widow) 34; the poem could be used to document the rapid onset of ageing in early modern England, and it also raises the question of the assumed age of more conventional poetic mistresses. Earl Miner makes some entertaining calculations in his book *The Cavalier Mode from Jonson to Cotton* (Princeton, NJ 1971), pp. 206–9, and figures that most would be in their mid-teens.

12 For a discussion of the high hopes vested in Prince Henry, see G. Parry, *The Golden Age Restor'd* (Manchester 1981), pp. 88–91.

Plate 3 The frontispiece of the 1635 edition of the *Poems*

13 'Perchance I shall never die', he wrote in a letter to Goodyere in 1607. He held out the same possibility to his congregation in a sermon of 1627. See Carey, *John Donne*, pp. 226–9, for an account of Donne's personal hopes for the Apocalypse, and pp. 198–230 for a stimulating investigation of Donne and death generally.

14 The most helpful exposition of these meditative techniques is in Louis Martz, *The Poetry of Meditation* (New Haven 1962), pp. 25–56.

15 Izaac Walton, 'The Life of Dr. Donne', in *Walton's Lives*, ed. C. H. Dick (London n.d.), p. 57.

3 George Herbert and the temple of Anglicanism

None of the difficulties that hampered Donne's social progress lay in the way of George Herbert, yet his career developed in a similar direction, with the disappointments of public employment giving way to a deep satisfaction in the service of the Church. Herbert, born in 1593, belonged to one of the most distinguished families in the country, and grew up in the mainstream of Jacobean intellectual life. He was related to the Earls of Pembroke, who were also Herberts, and through them he could claim kinship with Sir Philip Sidney. His eldest brother Edward became Lord Herbert of Cherbury, a diplomat who served as ambassador to France, a religious philosopher who proposed a system of deism or natural religion that was based on reason rather than revelation, and a poet of some ability. Another brother was Sir Henry Herbert, who led a successful life as a courtier, and became Master of the Revels in 1623. The sustaining figure of the family was their mother, Magdalen Herbert, a cultivated, pious, strong-minded woman, and a friend of Donne, who addressed several poems to her, and who would ultimately preach her funeral sermon, in which he would praise the 'holy cheerfulnesse and religious alacrity' of her life, and the bright culture of her household. She had remarried, after a long widowhood, and her second husband was Sir John Danvers, who led an active political career that gradually became more hostile to King and Court, culminating in his inclusion among the regicides in 1649.

Amid these powerful, varied and stimulating figures, George Herbert grew up, with every expectation that he too would enjoy a public career of some distinction. His education prepared him for such a future: Westminster School followed by Trinity College, Cambridge. At Cambridge he flourished as a classicist, and became the University Orator, responsible for expressing the sentiments of the university, usually in Latin, on national events and on occasions of royal or noble visitation. This was a prestigious post, which normally led on to one of the high offices of state. During his long residence at Cambridge, from 1609 to 1623, he established the connections of patronage that were essential to advancement in this age, associations of the highest order. He had hopes from King James himself, from the King's cousin the Duke of Lennox, he was friendly with Lancelot Andrewes, the most widely admired bishop of the age, and with Francis Bacon, the Lord Chancellor.[1] With all these promising activities and relationships to his advantage, why did Herbert not proceed to eminence as a scholar or statesman rather than turn aside to the minor Church offices that he occupied from 1626 until his death in 1633?

Several explanations have been suggested to account for his failure to gain preferment, all of which have some validity: the alienation of Prince Charles and the Duke of Buckingham by means of a Cambridge speech of 1623 that praised peace at a time when they wanted war against Spain; the political ascendancy of Buckingham, who was hostile to the Herbert clan; the dissolution in 1624 of the Virginia Company with which Herbert and his stepfather Danvers were heavily involved; and the death of his major patrons in 1625–6. Cumulatively these events capsized Herbert's hopes and gave him a lasting dislike of public affairs. Ill health, too, which is often mentioned in his poetry, may have encouraged him to retire from the main thoroughfares of life. Yet one should not underestimate the sense of vocation that moved Herbert to seek the painful satisfaction of a devout life. A clue to his behaviour is given in his poem 'The Pearl', which has a marked autobiographical content:

> I Know the wayes of Learning; both the head
> And pipes that feed the presse, and make it runne;
> . . .
> What willing nature speaks, what forc'd by fire;
> Both th'old discoveries, and the new-found seas,
> The stock and surplus, cause and historie:
> All these stand open, or I have the keyes:
> Yet I love thee.
>
> I know the wayes of Honour, what maintains
> The quick returns of courtesie and wit:
> . . .
> I know the wayes of Pleasure, the sweet strains,
> The lullings and the relishes of it:
> . . .
> Yet I love thee.

> I know all these, and have them in my hand:
> Therefore not sealed, but with open eyes
> I flie to thee, and fully understand
> Both the main sale, and the commodities;
> And at what rate and price I have thy love;
> With all the circumstances that may move:
> Yet through these labyrinths, not my groveling wit,
> But thy silk twist let down from heav'n to me,
> Did both conduct and teach me, how by it
> To climbe to thee.

That mysterious silken thread from heaven, communicating a complex experience by means of an appositely simple image, is characteristic of Herbert's best manner; a familiar object set in an unexpected spiritual context surprises the reader's mind and prompts speculative interpretation within a controlled area. The attractions of the world occupy much of the poem, but they are defeated by the love of God 'let down from heav'n', which reaches the poet and draws him steadily towards a life of devotion. The title further explains the movement of feeling within the poem, for it refers to 'the pearl of great price' of Matthew 13:45, which is the Kingdom of Heaven gained by selling all that one has – in Herbert's case, learning, honour and pleasure. The biblical example, which unquestioningly states the priority of the religious vocation, tells us a lot about the silent processes of Herbert's mind that caused him finally to enter the Church. One should also remember that about the same time that Herbert paused to reassess the direction of his life, his close Cambridge friend Nicholas Ferrar withdrew from public affairs to the small devotional community he established at Little Gidding, and his example may well have influenced Herbert's course.[2]

This community at Little Gidding grew to exercise an influence upon Anglicans out of all proportion to its size during the twenty years following its inception. Ferrar retired to this Huntingdonshire village with his mother, brother, sister and their children, and together they restored the manor house and the little church, and embarked on a life of prayer, work and charitable activity. The pattern of the day was shaped by the requirements of religious observance: short services were held every hour; Matins and Evensong were celebrated, and every night a vigil was kept during which the Psalms were recited. Thanksgiving and prayer dominated the life of the community, which attracted to it many visitors who craved a fuller devotional life than was provided by the ordinary services of the Church of England. Herbert must have been a frequent visitor in the early years, for when he became a deacon in 1626 he held at first the sinecure of Leighton Bromswold, a village only a few miles away from Little Gidding, which he must have seen as a model existence of pious and charitable commitment that would help to shape his own sense of Christian duty and service. Others who sought out Ferrar's home for retirement, prayer and meditation included John Cosin, Richard Crashaw, and even King Charles, who came unobtrusively there on three occasions.

Herbert was ordained a minister in 1630, and was then presented to the living of Bemerton, a village close to Wilton, the seat of the Earls of Pembroke, in whose gift the living lay. It would seem that Herbert served also as chaplain to his cousin Philip, fourth Earl of Pembroke, and his wife Lady Anne Clifford, as well as ministering to the small congregation of country folk at Bemerton. Both at Leighton and at Bemerton Herbert set about restoring the churches, which were in a fairly dilapidated condition. Although one tends to think of this as one of the most vigorous periods of the Church of England, the physical state of the churches themselves was often neglected and sometimes near-ruinous until Laud began to enforce his orders for their handsome maintenance after 1633. Herbert liked order, cleanliness and a subdued beauty in his church life, and did his best to impose them where he could. The plain, well-shaped woodwork that he installed at Leighton still strikes one with its simple harmonies and neat proportions, and we notice that Herbert designed the restoration to give equal prominence to pulpit and lectern, so that preaching the Word and reading the Word are seen to be the primary functions of the Church.

The inspiration for Herbert's particular style of worship would seem to have been Lancelot Andrewes, a man whose reputation for learning and saintliness was acknowledged by all parties in the Church. He had been headmaster of Westminster School, where he had instituted a ceremonious form of worship which Herbert would have practised during his time there. Later a close friendship developed between the two men, who shared a similar Christian temper. 'The beauty of holiness' that Andrewes advocated in Church services and music a generation before Laud's official reforms in that direction appealed strongly to Herbert, who derived profound comfort from the liturgy, rituals and symbolism of the Anglican Church. Its doctrine too always satisfied him. He defended the rites of Anglicanism against Puritan censure in his early sequence of Latin poems, *Musae Responsoriae*, and maintained his conviction that 'The British Church' was 'double-moated with God's grace' in the poem of that title in *The Temple*.

Herbert survived only three years as the rector of Bemerton, leading that life of worship and kindness that caused Izaac Walton to consider him as one of the saints of the English Church when he wrote his biography in the years after the Restoration. At his death, he handed to his friend Nicholas Ferrar the manuscripts of his poems now called *The Temple*, with the request that he burn them or publish them as he thought fit. They appeared in print that same year, 1633. Study of the manuscripts indicates that a good half of the poems, especially those of conflict and doubt, were composed before Herbert took up his post at Bemerton, and date in large part from 1626–9, the years of indecision about the nature of his vocation.[3] The poems too were essentially the products of and aids to Herbert's private devotions; their existence seems to have been unknown until the time of his death, and we do not find individual poems recorded in the commonplace books of contemporaries, as is so often the case with other writers whose verse was passed around to friends before it was published. Herbert's poetry therefore had served its primary function well before the world got a view of it, for it was part praise, part self-scrutiny, and extensively a formalization of the intimate history of Herbert's devotional life over a period when he was making an irreversible commitment to a religious vocation, and enjoying the rewards of a newly-settled conviction.

We do not know if *The Temple* was Herbert's choice of title, but it is certainly apt for the collection, and consistent with his own terse, allusive linguistic usage. An architectural image with spiritual associations is obviously required, for Herbert divided his collection into three parts, the Church Porch, the Church, and finally the Church Militant, where the architectural idea develops into the concept of the living Church. The 'Temple' is one of those typically Herbertian key words, whose meaning is almost illimitable because, though simple in itself, it draws upon immense contexts in the Bible and in religious usage generally. So, the title can allude to the Temple of Solomon, where the worship of God was first formally celebrated, and which is the type of all succeeding churches, including the Church of England; it may allude further to the mysteries of the Temple, which have now been revealed to the faithful Christian through the life of Christ and the books of the New Testament. The Temple is also the body of

Christ, the sacred body that contains all the holy mysteries and sacraments. It stands too for the individual Christian, recollecting St Paul's words: 'Know ye not that ye are the Temple of God, and that the spirit of God dwelleth in you?' (I Cor. 3:16). This continuous interplay between Old Testament and New Testament, between Christ and the individual Christian, ensures that the poems have a far-reaching resonance even when the subject is apparently mundane or trifling. Just as all objects within a church acquire a symbolical power from their presence and function in a sacred place, so Herbert's poems take on a particular intensity of meaning from their setting within the imaginative space of *The Temple*.

Initially we enter 'The Church Porch', a lengthy poem offering moral precepts and advice about the conduct of life that prepares the reader to pass into the church proper by putting him into a fit state of mind: the verses are plain, sober, instructive.[4] They impart useful knowledge of a secular kind, without any revelation of sacred wisdom. Once inside the church, we are led directly to 'The Altar' as the ritual centre of the vital mystery of Christianity.

A broken Altar, Lord, thy servant reares,
Made of a heart, and cemented with teares:
Whose parts are as thy hand did frame;
No workmans tool hath touch'd the same.
A Heart alone
Is such a stone,
As nothing but
Thy pow'r doth cut.
Wherefore each part
Of my hard heart
Meets in this frame,
To praise thy Name:
That, if I chance to hold my peace,
These stones to praise thee may not cease.
O let thy blessed Sacrifice be mine,
And sanctifie this Altar to be thine.

In so slight a work, what worlds of meaning are compressed. We notice first that this is an 'emblem' poem, an exercise in pious wit where the shape of the subject is imaged by the shape of the lines on the page. The language uses the devotional vocabulary of hearts and tears that had been made current by Counter-Reformation writers to illustrate the process of repentance and joy as the hardened heart of the sinful man is touched and reformed by the love of God. The altar itself, built with 'no workmans tool', alludes to the altar which Moses commanded that the Israelites should raise to mark that they had become the people of God when they finally crossed over into the Promised Land.

> Therefore it shall be when ye be gone over Jordan, that you shall set up these stones, . . . and thou shalt plaister them with plaister. And there shalt thou build an altar to the Lord thy God, an altar of stones: thou shalt not lift up any iron tool upon them . . . . And thou shalt offer burnt offerings thereon . . . and shalt eat there and rejoice before the Lord thy God.
> (Deut. 27:4–7)

Given this quotation, one can see that the poem functions on many levels: it is the altar of the Church, evoking the memory of Christ's sacrifice; it represents Herbert's dedication to Christ as a result of the experience of grace; the Old Testament reference shows it to be a thanksgiving to God for guidance into the Promised Land of the Chosen People, which has a New Testament response as a thanksgiving to God for the redemption of the faithful. The key word in the poem is 'sacrifice', which becomes the title and subject of the next poem, but the Deuteronomy reference hints at hidden connections between 'The Altar' and other poems in the collection: Jordan will become the subject of two poems, while the theme of eating sacramentally from the altar will link the first poem of 'The Church' with the last, 'Love'.

Herbert acknowledged this notion of scattered coherences as a principle of organization for *The Temple* in his sonnet 'The Holy Scriptures II':

> Oh that I knew how all thy lights combine,
> And the configurations of their glorie!
> Seeing not onely how each verse doth shine,
> But all the constellations of the storie.
> This verse marks that, and both do make a motion
> Unto a third, that ten leaves off doth lie:
> Then as dispersed herbs do watch a potion,
> These three make up some Christians destinie.

Just as in the Bible one text relates to another, Old Testament verses prefigure New Testament verses, and there is a constant cross-referencing of phrases and meanings, among which a Christian may find his own destiny revealed, so in *The Temple* the poems are held together by innumerable key words and repeated themes through which Herbert's own destiny is unfolded. Behind the poems which form short sequences within the whole, there exists this larger organization, modelled on the Bible's pattern of secret connections, verbal allusions and reiterated experience of the spirit.

So, *The Temple* opens with a sequence of poems that form a recognizable progression: 'The Altar' is aptly followed by 'The Sacrifice', a long poem in which Christ speaks from the cross, reproaching the world for its blindness to his divinity.[5] This is a liturgical poem, formal and doctrinal, in which Christ utters the paradoxes of the faith which place before us simultaneously man's sinfulness and the redemption from sin that Christ's sacrifice has bought. Herbert's instinctive reaction produces 'The Thanksgiving' in two poems, after which he returns to the spectacle of the cross in 'The Agonie', a meditation on the origin of the sacraments and the joy he takes in them. It is becoming clear that Herbert is building up an Easter sequence, and so it continues, with the events of the Passion attended by poems that comment on the consequences of those events for mankind: 'Good Friday', 'Redemption', 'Sepulchre', 'Easter', 'Easter Wings'. Ideologically, the poems of *The Temple* never move far from the Passion, and the poems that deal directly with New Testament material rarely move outside the season of Lent and Easter.[6] The events of Easter culminate in the resurrection of Christ and his ascension; the theological consequences are the liberation of man from the bondage of sin and the offer of salvation to mankind. Within this progression is contained the poet's own experience, for Herbert, like many another Christian, tends to read his own personal history in line with Christ's and dependent upon it, so that there is ultimately a private victory and joy, but only after long tribulation. Moreover, Herbert is inclined to see his own spiritual history as a recapitulation in little of the spiritual history of the world, from the creation and fall into sin to the redemption by Christ. The poem 'Easter Wings', which forms the climax to the Easter sequence, shows again what vast spiritual designs may be compacted within a slender frame. This is another emblem poem, where the shape itself contributes to the meaning by suggesting the image of a bird in flight that characterizes Christ's victory over sin and death, the ascension and the poet's own heavenward ambition.

Lord, who createdst man in wealth and store,
  Though foolishly he lost the same,
    Decaying more and more,
      Till he became
        Most poore:
        With thee
      O let me rise
    As larks, harmoniously,
  And sing this day thy victories:
Then shall the fall further the flight in me.

My tender age in sorrow did beginne:
  And still with sicknesses and shame
    Thou didst so punish sinne,
      That I became
        Most thinne.
        With thee
      Let me combine
    And feel this day thy victorie:
  For, if I imp my wing on thine,
Affliction shall advance the flight in me.

Beginning with the fullness of creation, the first verse paraphrases the history of man, with the Fall occurring in the second line, and man dwindling spiritually and verbally until he is 'Most poore', at which low point Christ enters history and the verse regains its fullness as a result. The divine control of history is made clear in the shape of the verse; we are shown too the Providence that brings a greater good out of the human lapse. The second verse treats Herbert's personal experience that mirrors the universal history: he too declines in a condition of sin, until Christ enters his life at its most hopeless point, with a consequent exaltation, for, through Christ, Herbert participates in the victory over sin and rises the higher for his faith. The poem is crowded with meanings on different levels, yet all is so economically ordered and well crafted that an impression of simplicity prevails, coupled with an assurance of salvation that sounds the more convincing for that simplicity.

Like most men of his age, Herbert felt intimately involved in biblical history: the Fall afflicted him personally, as physical pains and the consciousness of sin daily reminded him. The vicissitudes of the Israelites expressed the changefulness of his own spiritual fortunes, yet assured him that God's watchfulness, if not favour, is constant. He was equally involved in Christ's life, death and resurrection through prayer, meditation and communion. Just as the consequences of sin exist in the perpetual present, so the hope of salvation is available throughout time. The Crucifixion is a permanent event in Herbert's imagination, demonstrating the terrifying powers of sin in the world as they combine to destroy Jesus, yet exhibiting in its outcome the victory of divine love over sin and death, and the promise of everlasting life. Herbert constantly reverts to the Passion as the crisis of the world, where all his own doubts and confusions are clarified and resolved. He commonly speaks of the event in the present tense, as in 'The Agonie', where he dismisses the material knowledge of natural scientists in favour of spiritual knowledge, above all of the divine love that is miraculously revealed at the Crucifixion:

> Love is that liquour sweet and most divine,
> Which my God feels as bloud; but I, as wine.

The spectacle of the Crucifixion causes mingled horror and joy, a paradox that is caught most extraordinarily in 'Easter', where Christ stretched on the cross is imaged as a divine musical instrument that resounds in praise of God:

> The crosse taught all wood to resound his name,
> Who bore the same.
> His stretched sinews taught all strings, what key
> Is best to celebrate this most high day.

Herbert learns to imitate Christ's example in 'The Temper', where he understands that the racking of his spirit by hope and despair is a preparative for a higher concord:

> Stretch or contract me, thy poore debter:
> This is but tuning of my breast,
> To make the musick better.

The musical conceits of 'Easter' and 'The Temper' are part of a network of musical metaphors and allusions that helps to give cohesion to *The Temple* as a whole: affliction, fit employment, dutifulness, poetry, prayer, all may be music of a sort, as well as the conventional kind that Herbert writes about in 'Church-Musick' or 'Even-song'. He set many of his poems to be sung to the accompaniment of a lute, always with the intention of praising God through his art, and with the conviction that 'My musick shall find thee, and every string / Shall have his attribute to sing.' From the music of the spheres and 'church bells beyond the starres heard' to the sighs and strains of Herbert's 'poore reed', all things praise God as a thanksgiving for creation and for the divine Providence that works to lead goodness out of evil.

For Herbert his poetry was a principal means of thanksgiving, yet he was always much exercised by the problems that accompany the writing of religious verse. It is evident that he felt from an early age that he had a mission to Christianize the English muse; in 1620 he had sent his mother two sonnets as a New Year's gift, the first beginning

> My God, where is that ancient heat towards thee,
> Wherewith whole showls of Martyrs once did burn,
> Besides their other flames? Doth Poetry
> Wear Venus Livery? only serve her turn?
> Why are not Sonnets made of thee?

and moving to the assurance of 'since thy wayes are deep, and still the same, / Will not a verse run smooth that bears thy name?' The second sonnet, more mannered and strained, protests 'Sure, Lord, there is enough in thee to dry / Oceans of Ink' and proceeds to a weak abuse of love poetry that adores mortal beauty destined to decay. This concern to vindicate his commitment to religious subjects and to discredit the amorous poetry of his day reappears in his first 'Jordan' poem: 'Who sayes that fictions onely and false hair / Become a verse?' He singles out for disapproval the affected pastoral love poetry then in fashion – William Browne's *Britannia's Pastorals* or William Drummond's verse might illustrate what he disliked. Pastoral verse should be simple, direct, and Christian, in memory of the Good Shepherd. Let it not be distorted then by the artifice of poets, but let it praise God in plain, honest terms. Herbert may well have written this poem as a shepherd or pastor himself, so that the last two lines – 'Nor let them punish me with losse of rime, / Who plainly say, My God, My King' – exemplify the simplicity he recommends. The pursuit of simplicity is a self-imposed ideal. He returns to it in the second 'Jordan' poem, and in the later piece, 'The Forerunners', he repeats that if he can still sing in verse the simple phrase 'Thou art still my God', that is the sum of his poetic ambition. To make his point there, he deliberately lapses into naïve diction to prove that the desire to praise is more important than the artistry of praise: 'He will be pleased with that dittie; / And if I please him, I write fine and wittie.'

Yet of course there is no obligation on the religious poet to practise simplicity. David did not ingenuously praise the Lord, and even

Christ spoke in parables. Herbert himself was sympathetic to a tradition of worship that was intellectually and rhetorically complex, for Lancelot Andrewes and Donne were his close friends, and both of them excelled in the practice of pious wit, the quaint words, trim invention and burnished thoughts that Herbert rejected in 'Jordan' II. *The Temple* contains many examples of rich complexity, for example, 'Sunday', 'Artillerie', 'The Size', the first 'Prayer' sonnet, or 'The Starre', where the poet imagines that a spark of divine love has fallen into his heart like a shooting star, to purify his heart and inflame it with a desire for celestial joys. This touch of heaven may etherealize him, transform him into star-fire,

> That so among the rest I may
> Glitter, and curle, and winde as they:
> That winding is their fashion
> Of adoration.

Those last three lines tell us much about the earlier aesthetic of Herbert's verse, before the ideal of simplicity set in, where indirections find directions out, by means of emblems, metaphors, conceits, analogies, puns, all of which reveal new aspects and glimpses of divinity. Some poems, such as 'Church Monuments', 'Church Musick', 'Church Lock and Key', 'The Church Floor', and 'The Windows', a group that would seem by their subject matter to belong to what appears to have been the early phase of the volume's organization on architectural principles, receive a detailed symbolical interpretation. The large reflective poems, such as 'Man', 'Man's Medley', 'Vanitie', 'Providence', 'Artillerie', 'The Discharge', and 'Miserie', abound in curious speculation and learning all drawn into the service of religion in order to make God's purposes towards man more clear. The same is true of the poems on the virtues – 'Hope', 'Humilitie', 'Frailtie', 'Content', 'Constance' and the like – which are fluently imaginative, working image into image in that easy way Herbert has. The poems on the Christian year and the prayers that make up the Christian day are full of winding flames of adoration.

So why should he want to chasten his style so rigorously and deny the full exercise of his art before God? The answer may be that he considered this discipline as another form of wholesome affliction, curbing his natural tendencies in verse, from which he derived pleasure and satisfaction, and forcing him to submit to a severer, plainer style that he conceived to be of greater spiritual benefit to himself and to his readers. In his later years Herbert seemed concerned to purge poetry of the element of private pleasure that accompanies composition: care for craftsmanship too easily becomes pride in the mastery of the art, a selfish emotion, which detracts from the value of the work as a religious offering. This paradox of religious poetry that is vitiated by the instinctive pleasure of the creator in his craft was best expressed in 'The Coronet', by Marvell, where he suggested that any consciously arranged tribute to the Lord is tainted by its own art. Herbert seems to have developed a similar view, but he was not content to state the paradox, striving instead to write poems of praise that were as nearly artless and de-personalized as he could make them. This is a difficult task, requiring as it does the suppression of so many habitual skills, yet there was something in Herbert that impelled him to go against the grain of his natural inclinations, a suspicion perhaps that those inclinations in poetry as in life encouraged self-indulgence and worldliness. Undertaking the tiny cure of Bemerton may have been the equivalent in his professional life to the enforced simplicity of his later poetry. Such an ideal was not wholly unrealizable, as a number of poems placed towards the end of *The Temple* show: 'A True Hymne' ('My Joy, My Life, My Crowne'), 'Discipline', 'The Invitation', 'The Banquet', 'A Parodie' and 'The Elixir' are all marked by an unusual spareness of manner, as is 'The Posie', brief verses that place before the reader Herbert's own personal motto, 'Less than the least of all God's mercies', a phrase he had inscribed on his ring, marked in his books, and 'which he used to conclude all things that might seem to tend any way to his own honour'.[7] The humility of this verse accords well with the simplicity of manner proposed in the Jordan poems and in 'The Forerunners'. These qualities of humility and simplicity come together most movingly in the last poem of *The Temple*, 'Love', which stands as the achievement of the 'Jordan' ideal and as a spiritual climax to the whole experience of the book, when the humble soul is received by Christ with courtesy and love in a scene of communion that is the reward of perseverance and faith.

The use of the title 'Jordan' well illustrates the multiple meanings possible in the fertile biblical context of Herbert's work. As the sacred river of the Bible, it replaces the Grecian waters that characterized the fresh flow of inspiration in classical and Renaissance poetry – Aganippe or Hippocrene, the springs of Helicon – and so reminds us of Herbert's ambition to make poetry serve the ends of religion rather than those of secular pleasure. In the Old Testament the Israelites had to cross Jordan in order to enter the Promised Land; in the New Testament Christ was baptized with Jordan waters preparatory to his mission, which culminated in the Covenant of Grace. Passage through Jordan is thus a journey into the realm of grace promised to the faithful Christian. As the waters of Jordan are pure and regenerative, so the experience of Herbert's poetry is restorative to a Christian spirit. With its Old Testament–New Testament analogies, and its promise of divine favour, the idea of Jordan belongs to that typical Herbertian pattern where ancient religious history becomes spiritual history bearing definitively on the individual.[8] Finally, the fabled clarity of Jordan waters suggests the simplicity of style that Herbert thinks appropriate to his religious verse.[9] All these justifications of the 'Jordan' manner cannot, however, reduce our pleasure in the 'lovely enchanting language, sugar-cane, Hony of roses' that Herbert poignantly regrets in 'The Forerunners', which had delighted him in earlier days, when he practised richer, more fanciful arts of praise.

Within the poetic architecture of *The Temple*, in with the many poems that re-enact the services of praise in the Church or dwell on the life and death of Christ as the source of the sacraments that sustain spiritual life, we find a number of poems that deal with the phases of faith, the span of hopes and doubts, waverings and resolutions, which make up the familiar experience of post-Reformation Christians. Set as they are in *The Temple*, and in the presence of the Cross, these poems invariably record a final reassurance. The frustration of unrewarded piety, as recorded in 'The Collar', is expressed through language that freely uses sacramental images whose spiritual promise the speaker quite fails to recognize:

> Have I no harvest but a thorn
> To let me bloud, and not restore
> What I have lost with cordiall fruit?
> Sure there was wine
> Before my sighs did drie it: there was corn
> Before my tears did drown it.

The poet exhibits a wilful indifference to the Christian evidences around him, until he is shaken into understanding by the inward voice that is both that of conscience and that of God. Given the way that the events of biblical history fill almost every landscape in Herbert's poetry, and that the very air is suffused with theology, spiritual despondency cannot endure very long before it is corrected by the assurance that the world is regulated by Providence and love. This is not to say that the pain of living is diminished or explained away in

Herbert: rather it acquires a meaning within the context of subordination to one's spiritual condition. The problems of pain and suffering obviously trouble Herbert – and here he must have been representative of a society in which so many people seem to have been chronically sick. Five times he returns to the subject of 'Affliction'. The first of these is the most instructive to a modern reader because it provides a brief imaginative chronicle of Herbert's mature life with its encouragements and checks, leading to a present bewilderment at the breakdown of a once so hopeful career. The psychology of Herbert's delight and distress is particularly vivid in this poem, the impetuous pleasures that accompany the first sense of a divinely ordered world, the inexplicable growth of suffering in the midst of happiness, the series of perverse events that deny him even the satisfactions of his faith: 'Thus doth thy power crosse-bias me, not making / Thine own gift good, yet me from my wayes taking.' God seems indifferent to his devoted servant, gratuitously heaps suffering on him, can find no use for him. Herbert's solution emerges from his discontent, as he suddenly feels how impertinent, even impious, his reactions are, and on the instant he breaks out into a direct prayer of repentance to God for questioning his ways:

> Well, I will change the service, and go seek
> Some other master out.
> Ah my deare God! though I am clean forgot,
> Let me not love thee, if I love thee not.

This direct address to God, or colloquy as it is called, breaks the mood of frustration and prepares the way for a change of heart, but that advance takes place in the next poem in *The Temple*. (This should remind us again not to take these poems in isolation, for they are often phases in a process of spiritual change.) In 'Repentance', Herbert confesses his rashness, palliating it by suggesting that the brevity of our life and the shadow of death cause us to react thoughtlessly. When he declares, with a marvellous economy of phrase, that our life without Christ is 'A steadie aiming at a tombe', we can sense that Herbert's energies are gathering to claim that exemption from death that Christ has offered: 'O let thy height of mercie then / Compassionate short-breathed men' and we know that these energies will carry him through to a new resolution, and so they do, for the next poem is 'Faith', a calmer, more settled poem, expressing confidence that 'grace fills up uneven nature'. Death is discomfited now, in the assurance of faith:

> What though my bodie runne to dust?
> Faith cleaves unto it, counting ev'ry grain
> With an exact and most particular trust,
> Reserving all for flesh again.

So 'Faith' gives rise to 'Prayer', a radiant sonnet of the spirit's power to reach God, a condition that was quite doubted in 'Affliction'. 'Prayer' precedes 'The Holy Communion', where Herbert is restored to contact with God through the sacraments. Words in 'The Holy Communion' such as 'rich furniture', 'nourishment', 'my rebel-flesh', and images of siege relate the poem back to 'Affliction' and mark the distance travelled.

All the poems on the theme of 'Affliction' are closely related to the ones on 'Employment'. The distress Herbert felt in his early years about his lack of satisfying occupation in a world where all creatures except man seemed profitably busy, oppressed him as a form of mental affliction:

> All things are busie; onely I
> Neither bring hony with the bees,
> Nor flowres to make that, nor the husbandrie
> To water these.
>
> ('Employment' I)

But fit employment did come with his entry into the Church, and he also came to realize that the composition of religious verse was also a proper activity for him. 'The Flower' is a late poem, which marvels at the regeneration of spirit he experienced in his last years, after he had entered the Church. His joy at finding his true home and right occupation is seen as the culmination of an entirely natural process:

> And now in age I bud again,
> After so many deaths I live and write;
> I once more smell the dew and rain,
> And relish versing: O my onely light,
> It cannot be
> That I am he
> On whom thy tempests fell all night.

Herbert's religious life cannot be separated from the Church that fostered it even before he took orders: he is in all things a man of faith, which contains and defines and protects him. The sense of order, neatness and control that we receive from his work is due in large measure to the complete compatibility between Herbert and the Anglican Church. He always respected it, and in his later years respect turned to love:

> I Joy, deare Mother, when I view
> Thy perfect lineaments and hue
> Both sweet and bright.
> ('The British Church')

He loved too the language of the Church: 'I like our language, as our men and coast: / Who cannot dresse it well, want wit, not words' ('The Sonne'). There is a settled ground of contentedness in Herbert that comes from this pleasure with the Church, its doctrine, language, furnishings, its effectiveness in spiritual matters, its strength as a social institution. He never knew conflict with it, although he sometimes doubted his worthiness to serve it, and the memory of his doubts about entering the Church troubled him occasionally until the end of his life. But for Herbert, the Church settles everything, providing a complete working context for his spiritual, intellectual and social life. The Church contains, explains and justifies all history from the Fall to the present; knowledge and learning find an honoured place within the Church, but they need that Christian centre if they are to be more than an imposing vanity:

> Philosophers have measur'd mountains,
> Fathom'd the depths of seas, of states, and kings,
> Walk'd with a staffe to heav'n, and traced fountains:
> But there are two vast, spacious things,
> The which to measure it doth more behove:
> Yet few there are that sound them; Sinne and Love.
> ('The Agonie')

The Church is in communion with Christ, whose presence fills the physical building from the lower vaults of death to the upper vaults of the angel-covered roof. Signs and tokens everywhere speak of this presence to the understanding eye of faith, while the sacrifice of Christ and its promise to the faithful sustain the corporate Church, the Church that is the nation at prayer. The strains of suffering and the fear of death are all resolved in the Church, and have their place within a comprehensible scheme that refers all issues to Christ. Everything makes sense to Herbert, and he is fortunate to live within a world that is so intricately well constructed – a world of snug boxes, compact cabinets, birds in nests, nests in trees, trees in tidy rows. Images of circling planets, obedient waves, dutiful stones – things that know their place in a universal order – are expressive of a system whose components are well adjusted, where everything is in tune. The easy intimate tone of voice that Herbert habitually uses suggests a man who is at home in this world, with no need to exclaim about its familiar wonders, but with every cause to be grateful for his privileged residence. Nor does he feel that he alone is benevolently accommodated in this system: it works well for the community of men, and for the race as a whole, so that he is able to write a poem conveying complete sympathy and integration between the created world and its chief tenant, 'Man'.

Man is all symmetrie,
Full of proportions, one limbe to another,
And all to all the world besides:
Each part may call the furthest, brother:
For head with foot hath private amitie,
And both with moons and tides.

. . .

For us the windes do blow,
The earth doth rest, heav'n move, and fountains flow.
Nothing we see, but means our good,
As our delight, or as our treasure:
The whole is, either our cupboard of food,
Or cabinet of pleasure.

The starres have us to bed;
Night draws the curtain, which the sunne withdraws;
Musick and light attend our head.
All things unto our flesh are kinde
In their descent and being; to our minde
In their ascent and cause.

. . .

More servants wait on Man,
Then he'l take notice of: in ev'ry path
He treads down that which doth befriend him,
When sicknesse makes him pale and wan.
Oh mightie love! Man is one world, and hath
Another to attend him.

There can be no questioning the assurance of a poem like this; it draws its strength from a security of belief that later generations would never know.

For Herbert, then, the safeguard of all his assurance, the instrument that mediates between God, man and nature, past, present and future, sin and redemption, death and resurrection, is the Church of England, Herbert's special Temple. He died before the eruption of forces that would destroy his Church a decade later, and in his lifetime it must have seemed as if that Church, enjoying divine favour and the patronage of two devout kings, stood then at its meridian. He had the felicity to live in a religious time that was like his own 'Sunday', when

> heavens gate stands ope;
> Blessings are plentifull and rife,
> More plentifull than hope.

Notes

1 Herbert helped Bacon to translate *The Advancement of Learning* into Latin to give it a European currency. For an extensive discussion of the checks and disruptions to Herbert's life at this time, and for a compact summary of his pre-clerical life generally, see Joseph Summers, *George Herbert: His Religion and Art* (London 1954), pp. 28–48.

2 Ferrar too had been hurt in the débâcle of the Virginia Company, an enterprise which had a strong evangelical intention in addition to its mercantile aim in the New World. One suspects that both men were dismayed at the extinction of this Christianizing mission, which Herbert certainly believed was a critical event in the history of religion, as is evident from his long poem, 'The Church Militant'.

3 For the dating of the poems, see F. E. Hutchinson, *The Works of George Herbert* (Oxford 1941), p. xxxviii *et seq*.

4 The fact that church porches were often used for schools in the sixteenth and seventeenth centuries may help to explain why Herbert uses this poem for the purposes of instruction.

5 Iconographically too the sequence is apt, for altars have commonly the mark of the cross cut into them. 'The Sacrifice' has been studied in great detail, with special respect to its tradition and to its complexity of meaning, by Rosemond Tuve in *A Reading of George Herbert* (Chicago 1952).

6 For this reason, partly, Stanley Fish has proposed that *The Temple* is closely associated with the practice and intentions of catechism, which took place during the season of Lent. See *The Living Temple: George Herbert and Catechising* (Berkeley 1978), which attempts to provide an interpretation of Herbert's work in relation to the methods of catechism.

7 From the Introduction to *The Temple*, 1633. The phrase is a combination of Jacob's words in Genesis 32:10 – 'I am not worthy of the least of thy mercies . . . which thou hast showed unto thy servant' – and St Paul's description of himself as 'less than the least of all Saints' (Eph. 3:8).

8 'Aaron' for example provides a fine illustration of this pattern: the Old Testament priest, arrayed in the symbols of his power, is contrasted with Herbert, the modern man who is all discord and weakness, until Herbert, as priest, enters into Christ, who as the one true priest is the perfected Aaron with the super-addition of grace. Christ redresses Herbert's human failings, and enables him to recapitulate Aaron's role with the addition of Christ's gospel. Thus Herbert 'contains' biblical history (Exodus 28) and the living Christ, and he is transfigured by this experience of assimilation.

9 A brief glance at another 'Jordan' poem will help to show how compact and allusive Herbert is in contrast with a more conventional writer. William Drummond's volume of religious poems, *Flowers of Sion*, published in 1623, contains a Jordan poem under the title of 'An Hymn of True Happiness', where the nymph of the sacred river (how difficult it is to demythologize poetry of its classical personages, though Herbert succeeds in doing so) arises to announce that happiness is not to be found in the pursuit of earthly vanities but in the chaste and pure contemplation of God's attributes, above all his love for the created soul. The symbolical and typological possibilities of the Jordan are hardly touched on, the river existing as a sacred medium from which sweetly phrased theological opinions may emerge. In its lack of intensity, complexity and internal tensions, Drummond's poem is typical of the pleasing, competent but fairly undemanding religious verse of the time.

4 Henry Vaughan: social darkness, spiritual light

Henry Vaughan, unlike Herbert, had no Church to turn to. Whatever spiritual experiences lay behind the poetry of *Silex Scintillans* (1650 and 1655) had to be sustained privately, for the Anglican Church had been dismantled by the Parliamentarians, and its offices and sacraments suspended. Vaughan was a natural Anglican, deprived of his spiritual home, so his recourse was to turn to Herbert's *Temple* as a surrogate Church and to use that poet and his works as a pattern of holiness and inspiration. In consequence, we have the sense of a solitary individual whose devotional impulses are unsupported by any sympathetic institution, and therefore remain essentially intuitive. The wistfulness that pervades Vaughan's poetry may well be caused by the loss of that so recently flourishing Church, now desolate. But before we examine the condition of a religious poet deprived of his Church, it would be helpful to look at Vaughan's earlier literary career, often hastily passed over by critics as indifferent versifying in the manner of Jonson, because there is an evident progression of moods in Vaughan, which makes his transformation from social writer to religious poet more comprehensible.

Vaughan's poems provide some interesting insights into how a man inheriting the tradition of Caroline verse adjusted to the radically changed social conditions of the 1640s. He began with ambition to be numbered among the witty sons of Ben who elegantly rhymed away the years of the Caroline peace with their gallant and amorous verse, but he had the misfortune to be born an age too late, so that when his *Poems* came out in 1646, when he was 24, they fell into a world still racked by Civil War, where their irrelevance must have been obvious. Although he had been at Oxford, and then briefly in London, Vaughan had had no contact with the Court milieu that sustained and validated Cavalier verse, so his lyrics have an unconvincing air of striving to imitate gestures no longer fashionable. He shows in the Preface that he is conscious of his untimeliness, deprecating 'that courage that durst send me abroad so late, and revell it thus in the Dregs of an Age'. He justifies his inadequacies with a quotation from Persius: '*Languescente seculo, liceat aegrotari*' ('When the age grows enfeebled, it is permissible to be sick'). Whether the age has been enfeebled by cultural decadence or by political disruption is unclear, but the weakness of the verse is self-confessed.

Vaughan opens gamely enough, with a poem of friendship to R.W. in the Cavalier mode, but one that already looks forward to death and the uncomplicated freedom of a poetic afterlife, where they will see the ghost of Ben Jonson 'in the shade of his own bayes', accompanied by his 'son' Thomas Randolph. The poem is a diminished version of Herrick's 'Elizium', and allows Vaughan to pay tribute to his poetic mentors. He moves immediately to the main business of the volume, a sequence of Platonic poems, 'To Amoret', indebted particularly to Randolph and to William Habington, whose 'Castara' forms a comparable sequence, and generally to the Court ethos of the 1630s where the cult of Platonic love fostered by Queen Henrietta Maria had been intensely fashionable and poetically debilitating. One can only regret that Vaughan became entangled in this pernicious cult, yet his involvement shows how enticing this exercise of delicate, high-minded wit remained even after its social setting had been swept away. The first half of the *Poems* ends with 'Upon the Priorie Grove', a retirement poem of a kind very common during the period of the Civil Wars and the Commonwealth when sensitive or unfortunate men sought refuge from the brutality of the time in country retreats. Here Vaughan mildly expresses his desire for seclusion and love in his native Breconshire. Nothing very remarkable in this volume, then, one might think, until one turns to the second half, a translation of Juvenal's Tenth Satire. The translation in itself is not especially powerful, but the choice is surprising, for this is the Vanity of Human Wishes satire, full of lofty disillusion with the affairs of the great world. So many of the Roman poems translated in the seventeenth century offered an implicit commentary on contemporary affairs that one suspects that any reading of this poem in the 1640s would be coloured by recent events. Whether Strafford's fall is shadowed in Sejanus' fate and whether the bloody chronicle of Roman history is seen to be extended into the calamities of England are analogies freely available. But the sombre seriousness of the poem, when set against the airiness and preciosity of the Caroline poems in the same volume, overshadows the futile gaiety of those lighter verses and exposes their insubstantiality. That Caroline ethos, declared sickly in the Preface to the *Poems*, is doomed by Juvenal's ponderous exempla of ruined men and fallen states.

What course to take next? Vaughan had another volume ready for the press at the end of 1647, but it did not appear until 1651, showing signs of excisions and suppressions that were presumably made to get rid of impolitic references, and published by a friend who seems to have rescued it after the author had turned exclusively to religious verse. The title is *Olor Iscanus*, or the Swan of Usk, Vaughan's native river. The engraved title page (Plate 4) provides as usual some clues to the character of the book. A swan floats on a river between two trees, one of which is definitely an oak, the British tree; the other would baffle any botanist, but I would hazard that it is a palm tree drawn by an English artist who had never seen one.[1] Bees are abundant, flowers thrive, the motto is '*Flumina amo silvasque, Inglorius*'. If the second tree is a palm then it would be in seventeenth-century sign language a tree of the ancient world, and Vaughan as the Swan of Usk would be relating ancient matters to modern Britain.[2] The bees and flowers announce the pastoral world, as does the motto, a favourite epigram for pastoral poets, adapted from Virgil's Second Georgic, where it forms part of the proposition that those who cannot aspire to epic themes or sing the high mysteries of nature should content themselves with the humble pastoral: 'I love the waters and the woods, though I gain no fame thereby.' Henry Vaughan, Gent., of the *Poems* 1646 has now become Henry Vaughan, Silurist. The term derives from the Roman name Silures for the British tribe that once inhabited Vaughan's part of Wales. Its adoption by Vaughan indicates his desire to associate himself with his native patch, abandoning the courtier-like pretensions he had tried out in his first volume, but it also marks his involvement with a nationalistic view of history, in which the British people (as distinct from the later English) have as ancient and honourable a past as any race – and the authentic surviving Britons are the Welsh. With this antiquity went the presumption of authority and wisdom.

The opening poem 'To the River Isca' attempts to order the miscellany of information displayed on the title page. Vaughan invents a fiction to describe the westward movement of culture from Greece to England (a commonplace English Renaissance notion), by means of a sequence of poet–river associations, from Apollo by the Eurotas to Vaughan by his Usk. He reminds us too of the peculiar sanctity that poets bestow on the places they have celebrated:

Poets (like Angels) where they once appear
Hallow the place, and each succeeding year
Adds rev'rence to't, such as at length doth give
This aged faith, That there their Genii live.

So we see here Vaughan settling in as the genius of the place, creating an idyllic pastoral world around the Usk, whose stream bears along a freight of virtues, Honour, Beauty, Faith, etc. through a 'Land redeemed from all disorders'. The poet's manner of proceeding has become masque-like, reminiscent of such Caroline masques as Townshend's *Tempe Restor'd* that blithely envisaged England as a pastoral island free from strife and purified by the presence of love and the arts; but although Vaughan has fallen again into the Court mode of writing, he has backed off from the Court-centred vision it was associated with to a remote (Welsh-British) paradise of his own making, his private retreat in a time of trouble.

The precarious safety of that retreat is, however, undermined by the following poem, the sinister and powerful 'Charnel-House'. This is the tomb in Arcadia, the inescapable presence of death in the happy land. The charnel-house, which was the shed where old bones from the churchyard were thrown to make room for fresh burials, intrudes shockingly into the pastoral world of Usk that the poet in his fiction had thought free from 'dead and dying things'. His shock is registered in the sudden exclamation of the opening verse, 'Blesse me! what damps are here? how stiffe an aire?' The jumble of bones, this 'display of ruin'd man', disgusts and chastens the poet, and the poem founders in darkness both physical and spiritual:

the grudging Sun
Calls home his beams, and warns me to be gone,
Day leaves me in a double night.

The disharmony set off by the two leading poems continues throughout the volume. Poems proper to the pastoral world, poems of friendship, of the country life, of nymphs 'exempt from common frailtie', of happy marriage, have their pleasures broken into by the elegies to the untimely dead that are interspersed among them: to Mr R. W. slain at Rowton Heath 1645, to Mr R. Hall slain at Pontefract 1648, and the epitaph to King Charles's daughter, Elizabeth, whose ill-fated life and premature end seem to sum up the violated innocence of the times:

Plate 4 The frontispiece of *Olor Iscanus*, published in 1651

> Thou seem'st a Rose-bud born in Snow,
> A flowre of purpose sprung to bow
> To headless tempests, and the rage
> Of an Incensed, stormie Age.

The spirit of the charnel-house cannot be exorcised, and it returns time and again to strike at the scenes in which the poet shelters. The alternations of concord and grief extend even into the translations that fill the later pages, for the bitter words of Ovid in exile jar with the pleasures of rural retreat as expressed by the neo-Latin Polish poet Casimire.

Olor Iscanus then is a curious work, showing the difficulties of a poet with a vocation but no certainty of direction. Many verbal borrowings have been noticed, mainly from Jonson and the Cavalier poets – Vaughan had either a very good memory or an imagination that was illuminated by his reading – and many of the poems have that derivative air that was almost inescapable in the Jonson circle. Yet the verse has quality and variety, and there is an obvious if self-conscious recognition that both the pastoral and the Cavalier worlds he is attracted to are inadequate for his needs, do not satisfy him imaginatively, and cannot control the invasion of death or the malignity of the age.

Even with these thoughts in mind, *Silex Scintillans* comes as a surprise, published in 1650, just over two years after the date of the dedication of *Olor*. Vaughan had shown no sign of religious susceptibility in his writing to date, and here, suddenly, is one of the finest collections of religious verse of the century. One might here glance aside at Herrick for a comparison: he had achieved fame for his social verse, but published a religious collection, *Noble Numbers*, with his *Hesperides* in 1648. Many of these were ceremonial poems, and there seems to be no profound enlarging experience behind individual poems. Herrick was after all a clergyman who might be expected to versify his piety, and the results were pleasant but unremarkable. But the divine wind bloweth where it listeth, and it blew with unexpected power through Henry Vaughan, who suddenly spake in tongues in 1650. The causes of this change remain obscure, although the literary agents of the change are fairly clear. The death of Vaughan's younger brother William, who seems to be the subject of the elegies in *Silex*, has often been proposed as the catalytic shock that thrust the poet into a spiritual crisis, and this is probably so, for much of the intenser feeling circulates around a sense of loss. But some more positive event also occurred, recorded in the opening poem 'Regeneration', which establishes the key to the collection. The literary 'friend' who assisted Vaughan's conversion was patently George Herbert, whose poetic mannerisms gave shape and language to Vaughan's inward sensations, and whose own testimony of the Christian life fitfully irradiated by grace was an acknowledged inspiration.[3] The Preface to the reissue of *Silex* in 1655 speaks gratefully of 'the blessed man, Mr. George Herbert, whose holy life and verse gained many pious Converts, (of whom I am the least)'. This Preface also contains Vaughan's palinode, the rejection of his poetry of wit and his translations, which he now considers as 'my greatest follies'. He is 'conscious of so much guilt in both, as can never be expiated without special sorrows, and that cleansing and pretious effusion of my Almighty Redeemer: . . . I do here most humbly and earnestly beg that none would read them'. On the whole, posterity has obeyed his advice.

The title page of *Silex* immediately announces the change: it presents an emblem of the flaming heart school, showing a flinty heart struck by a thunderbolt from the hand of God, and breaking into flames of divine love and melting into tears of repentance (Plate 5). The title *Silex Scintillans* translates as 'the flashing flint', which in conjunction with the emblem suggests the familiar condition of the hardened heart buffeted by affliction until it yields a holy fire. The affliction is heaven-sent, one of God's severer means to compel a soul to a religious awakening. Herbert's experience has already discovered this course, and Vaughan's emblem has obvious affinities with Herbert's stony heart in 'The Altar' at the beginning of *The Temple*, the heart that has been broken in pieces and dedicated to the service of God. The theme of affliction threads through the volume in various forms: sickness, the operation of sin, the loss of friends, the extinction of the Church. The motif of the responsive stone shown on the title page also recurs.

What one encounters in *Silex Scintillans* is an experience of conversion, a distinctive series of intuitions about the spiritual world around which certain theological and hermetic ideas have gathered, and a broad presentation of the life of praise and worship strongly conditioned by Herbert's example and language. 'Regeneration' is a spiritual history recorded through a mixture of allegory and emblem, a miniature *Pilgrim's Progress* (and in fact the poem owes much to Herbert's 'The Pilgrimage') which culminates in a high moment of illumination and delight. Vaughan images his youth as a world of pleasure, yet one inwardly blighted by the consciousness of sin:

It was high-spring, and all the way
Primros'd, and hung with shade;
Yet, was it frost within,
And surly winds
Blasted my infant buds, and sinne
Like Clouds ecclips'd my mind.

That distressing sense of sin begins to make a mockery of his pleasured youth, turning his path into 'a monstrous, mountain'd thing / Rough-cast with Rocks, and snow'. At this point an emblem is interjected: at the height of his youth he encounters a pair of scales on which the vain pleasures of his life are weighed against his understanding of his sinful state. Pleasures predominate, even though they are worthless to his spiritual growth; but a voice cries 'Away!' which is both the 'word' of the emblem (i.e. an appropriate word or phrase to be understood in conjunction with the image) and also a voice from the Bible, the voice of conscience and the warning of God to the spirit. He has the good sense to obey, and flees into biblical territory. Vaughan is fond of relocating his life imaginatively in the pastoral times of the Old Testament, when the presence of God was immanent and intermittently visible, and when the land contained true 'prophets and friends of God'. This time of security and closeness to God had an enduring appeal to Vaughan, who in his poetry tried often to turn his Welsh countryside into the Israel of the Patriarchs.[4] One might suggest that in the absence of a formal Church during the Commonwealth years, Vaughan fell back instead on to the numinous pastoral world that the Bible describes before the erection of the Temple, when divinity blazed in the bushes, glimmered in dreams or revealed itself in pillars of fire or cloud. In his Bible-charged imagination, Vaughan could still sense the warm presence of the Creator in the fields of Wales. So it is that the experience at the centre of 'Regeneration' takes place within a grove of trees, a sacred grove, a pastoral antetype of a church, where God is present as in ancient days. What happens in the grove is extraordinary: Vaughan can only describe, cannot explain:

The unthrift Sunne shot vitall gold
A thousand peeces,
And heaven its azure did unfold
Checqur'd wth snowie fleeces,
The aire was all in spice
And every bush

Silex Scintillans:
or
SACRED POEMS
and
Priuate Eiaculations
By
Henry Vaughan Silurist

LONDON Printed by T: W. for H: Blunden
at ye Castle in Cornehill. 1650

Plate 5 The frontispiece of *Silex Scintillans*, published in 1650

A garland wore; Thus fed my Eyes
But all the Eare lay hush.

Radiance, vitality, colour and spice, all in a profound silence. Like Jacob or Esau, Vaughan has known his God. No theology attaches to the experience, which fills the senses with perfections. Awe-struck, the poet withdraws into a more ordinary light. He shows us emblematic scenes, open to conventional interpretations: a cistern full of stones, some sparkling and buoyant, others heavy, dark and immobile – the elect and the damned – whom we meet again on a bank of flowers, where some are asleep at midday while others are awake and responsive to the light. Only the rushing wind that mysteriously blows through the closing section of the poem, whispering 'where I please', renews the sense of the numinous, for we recognize it as the divine spirit that 'bloweth where it listeth' (John 3:8). The closing prayer that Vaughan makes, desiring to be inspired by that spirit, is one we know to have been granted even as it is phrased. Regeneration carries with it the promise of salvation.

The poet here is so intent on dressing up his experience in communicable narrative that its true nature has been disguised by attempts at theological interpretation and by the emblematic accessories. Vaughan was evidently subject to sudden and occasional moments of transcendence, a sense of the spirit in glory, and inevitably in an age of doctrine he was impelled to give these moments a doctrinal gloss and integrate them into the prevailing patterns of expectation. He was fortunate to be able to provide language for these moments at all; they are best described in the famous (but borrowed)[5] phrase, 'bright shoots of everlastingness' in 'The Retreate', or in the lines, 'So some strange thoughts transcend our wonted theames / And into glory peep.'[6] The need to spell out a significance for these moments often diminishes them, as most notably in 'The World', where the breathtaking vision of the opening –

I saw Eternity the other night
Like a great Ring of pure and endless light,
All calm, as it was bright,
And round beneath it, Time in hours, days, years
Driv'n by the spheres
Like a vast shadow mov'd

– a vision which seems to have been the genesis of the poem, is then followed by a series of emblematic tableaux which give the impression of having been meticulously transcribed from some picture or engraving, all illustrative of those classes of men who ignore the light of heaven and are wholly consumed with the dark concerns of the world. Vaughan seems to feel that he must make the moment of transcendence meaningful or profitable by putting it into a morality scene, but in so doing, he causes the sublimity of his vision to dwindle to a homiletic essay on spiritual blindness.

Vaughan is one of the most photo-sensitive poets in the language: glimmering light is one of the recurrent aesthetic effects of his poetry, but it is more essentially an assurance of the divinity that suffuses the created world, a divinity whose presence Vaughan constantly senses but which he never sees specifically revealed – except for the experience of golden light in 'Regeneration', when he knows he has encountered the God in nature. Images of the sun occluded by clouds, of stars faintly perceived through a mist, correspond to his sense of the divine spark of the soul entombed in the darkness of the body; everywhere there is suppressed light, and Vaughan yearns for the day when the radiance of divinity will be unconfined, either at death, which he envisages as a return to 'the world of light', or at the Second Coming, when Christ shall again illuminate the world. The elegy 'They are all gone into the world of light' is one of Vaughan's most poignant expressions of his feelings of exile from the higher world; he thinks of his dead friends with envy:

> I see them walking in an Air of glory,
> Whose light doth trample on my days:
> My days, which are at best but dull and hoary,
> Meer glimering and decays.

In the poem 'The Retreate' Vaughan writes as if he retained memories of a celestial pre-existence, unorthodox perhaps in prevailing Christian thought, but a commonplace of neo-Platonism, where the idea of life as a banishment of the spirit from heaven into the material world to undergo the experience of time and sin at the mysterious command of a god was central.

> Happy those early dayes! when I
> Shin'd in my Angell-infancy.
> Before I understood this place
> Appointed for my second race,
> Or taught my soul to fancy ought
> But a white, Celestiall thought,

When yet I had not walkt above
A mile, or two, from my first love,
And looking back (at that short space,)
Could see a glimpse of his bright-face;
When on some gilded Cloud, or flowre
My gazing soul would dwell an houre,
And in those weaker glories spy
Some shadows of eternity.

Given a conviction of this nature, Vaughan's untiring responsiveness to light in all its manifestations (dawn, sunrise, star-fire, light in water or in jewels) is quite comprehensible. He is dismayed at the indifference of so many of his fellow men to the light of that other world, an indifference that he considers to be the consequence of sin, and time and again he contrasts men's failings in this regard with the dutifulness of the lesser creatures, which are constant in their observance of the heavens. This last is a theme frequent in Herbert, who liked to remark on the purposeful order of birds, bees, trees and flowers, all following their ordained courses, being active and fruitful and beautiful after their fashion, which Herbert interpreted as natural and constant acts of praise on the part of the creation, so different from man's neglect and forgetfulness of his divine origins. Vaughan tends to narrow down Herbert's loved theme to the unorthodox idea that the natural creation remains unfallen and still instinctively performs the rites of praise and thanksgiving due to the Creator.

Vaughan's profound feelings about the natural piety of the creatures permeate his poetry and act as a spur to his own devotions.

Yet, seeing all things that subsist and be,
Have their Commissions from Divinitie,
And teach us duty, I will see
What man may learn from thee.
('The Starre')

All things here shew him heaven; Waters that fall
Chide, and fly up; Mists of corruptest fome
Quit their first beds & mount; trees, herbs, flowres, all
Strive upwards stil, and point him the way home.
('The Tempest')

His poem 'Cock-crowing' expresses most finely and unusually the instructive tie between the creatures and the celestial world; it highlights the doctrine of correspondences that Vaughan entertained, a doctrine that formed a central part of the system of hermetic philosophy professed by Vaughan's twin brother Thomas. This system has been competently explicated by some modern critics;[7] at the centre lies the conviction that all classes of earthly things possess a secret affinity with some star above, and all with the sun. The Creator has instilled a grain of star-fire into all created forms, so that there is a constant interchange of sympathy between heaven and earth, which Vaughan commonly describes as a 'ray' or 'influence', 'magnetism' or 'commerce'. Man himself has a soul which is a portion of God's nature, which should enable him to feel the heavenward stress that runs through all things, but this awareness has been deadened by sin. The star-fire burns brightly among the lesser creatures, however, which is why Vaughan is so attentive to them in his verse. The cock, as the earliest herald of day, seems pre-eminent in responsiveness:

> Father of lights! what Sunnie seed,
> What glance of day hast thou confin'd
> Into this bird? To all the breed
> This busie Ray thou hast assign'd;
>   Their magnetisme works all night,
>   And dreams of Paradise and light.
>
> Their eyes watch for the morning hue,
> Their little grain expelling night
> So shines and sings, as if it knew
> The path unto the house of light.
>   It seems their candle, howe'r done,
>   Was tinn'd and lighted at the sunne.

Even the humblest forms of creation acknowledge their kinship with the heavens:

> Some kinde herbs here, though low & far,
> Watch for, and know their loving star.
>   ('The Favour')

And stones stand fixed in mute adoration:

> So hills and valleys into singing break,
> And though poor stones have neither speech nor tongue,
> While active winds and streams both run and speak,
> Yet stones are deep in admiration.
>   ('The Bird')

Much of Vaughan's verse sounds this note of loving fellowship with the natural world, to which he is united by an aspiration towards the divine source of light. He shares that watchfulness in the poems that are the record of his devotions, as in the memorable lines of 'Midnight', or in 'The Morning-watch':

> O joyes! Infinite sweetnes! with what flowres,
> And shoots of glory, my soul breakes, and buds!
> All the long houres
> Of night, and Rest
> Through the still shrouds
> Of sleep, and Clouds,
> This Dew fell on my Breast;
> O how it Blouds,
> And Spirits all my Earth! heark! In what Rings,
> And Hymning Circulations the quick world
> Awakes, and sings;
> The rising winds,
> And falling springs,
> Birds, beasts, all things
> Adore him in their kinds.
> Thus all is hurl'd
> In sacred Hymnes, and Order, The great Chime
> And Symphony of nature.
> ('The Morning-watch')

Yet for all the freshness of that praise, there remains a ground-note of homesickness in Vaughan, the voice of the exile who yearns for the remote land of his dreams. The elegies, such as 'Silence, and stealth of dayes' or 'They are all gone into the world of light', 'Thou that know'st for whom I mourne', or 'I walkt the other day' are understandably suffused with this mood – Vaughan has no determination to persevere along the ways of life – but it is also present persistently throughout *Silex Scintillans*, because the locus of all contentment lies elsewhere: 'My Soul, there is a Countrie / Far beyond the stars . . .' ('Peace'). Unlike Herbert, Vaughan cannot settle to the tasks and trials of this world, sustained by the Church and the example of Christ. As I suggested at the beginning of this chapter, Vaughan's sense of homesickness, of wistfulness, may have been compounded by the dissolution of the Anglican Church in his time: his natural shelter had been removed. While Herbert composed many poems in *The Temple* that were complementary to the ceremonies of the Anglican

Church, emphasizing the beauty and value of those ceremonies, and affirming his active membership of the Church, Vaughan's Church poems that are scattered throughout *Silex* tend to be written in lieu of the ceremonies they allude to. Poems such as 'White Sunday', 'The Holy Communion', 'Palm Sunday' and the numerous Easter poems are now private recreations of once public services, memories of religious events preserved in verse, no longer confident assertions of the power of the living Church. Muted protest at the Puritan regime's indifference to the high-days of the Christian year can be heard in 'Christs Nativity' (for Christmas was one of the suppressed festivals):

> Shal he that did come down from thence,
> And here for us was slain,
> Shal he be now cast off? no sense
> Of all his woes remain?
> Can neither Love, nor suff'rings bind?
> Are we all stone, and Earth?
> Neither his bloudy passions mind,
> Nor one day blesse his birth?

'The Brittish Church' is a lament for the dismemberment of the Church of England. Vaughan's title repeats Herbert's in *The Temple*, but what was then 'double-moated' with God's grace has now suffered the fate of Christ to be persecuted and condemned. There is little eloquence but strong feeling at the sight of the Church crucified by the Puritans:

> The Souldiers here
> Cast in their lots again,
> That seamlesse coat
> The Jews touch'd not,
> These dare divide, and stain.
>
> . . .
>
> Write in thy bookes
> My ravish'd looks
> Slain flock and pillag'd fleeces.

Although the Church of England has gone, *The Temple* remains, and Vaughan uses Herbert's collection of poems in the way an Anglican would use the Bible or the Prayer Book, quoting and paraphrasing from them constantly. There are few examples of a closer dependence of one poet on another in English: verbal reminiscences, borrowed phrases, common themes abound, yet Vaughan preserves his own character and individuality in the shade of Herbert because his sensibility and orientation are so different. Herbert becomes a spiritual lifeline to an age of greater faith. Vaughan's tribute to him comes specifically in 'The Match', a two-part poem, the first section of which is addressed to Herbert, the second to Christ. Herbert is not mentioned by name, for only biblical figures are named in *Silex*, but his identity is unmistakable:

> Dear friend! whose holy, ever-living lines
> Have done much good
> To many, and have checkt my blood,
> My fierce, wild blood that still heaves, and inclines,
> But is still tam'd
> By those bright fires which thee inflamed;
> Here I joyn hands, and thrust my stubborn heart
> Into thy Deed.

The reference is to Herbert's poem 'Obedience', in which he commits his heart to God and invites any similar-minded man to 'set his hand / And heart unto this Deed, when he hath read' and 'thrust his heart / Into these lines'. Vaughan accepts the invitation, makes a match of it, and offers himself entirely to God in the second part of the poem. So here Vaughan records himself as coming to Christ through Herbert who, as it were, confirms the younger poet in his vocation.[8] Herbert becomes established Church, minister and poetic master all in one, and 'a most glorious true saint' of 'the Brittish Church . . . now trodden under-foot'.[9]

Vaughan's strategy for dealing with the absence of a Church is, as we saw in 'Regeneration', to recreate imaginatively the conditions of primitive religion that the Israelites knew in their earliest age. 'I by backward steps would move' in order to 'tread again that ancient track', he writes in 'The Retreate'. He likes to imagine himself the contemporary of Jacob, watching the angels passing between heaven and earth, inhabiting a world that is charged with the presence of God. He projects himself into the 'white dayes' of Isaac, when 'Religion was / Ray'd into thee, like beams into a glasse', and 'Angels did wind / And rove about thee, guardians of thy minde' ('Isaacs Marriage').

> Sure, It was so. Man in those early days
> Was not all stone, and Earth,
> He shin'd a little, and by those weak Rays

Had some glimpse of his birth.
He saw Heaven o'r his head, and knew from whence
He came. . . .
. . .

Nor was Heav'n cold unto him; for each day
The vally, or the Mountain
Afforded visits, and still Paradise lay
In some green shade, or fountain.
Angels lay Leiger here; Each Bush, and Cel,
Each Oke, and high-way knew them,
Walk but the fields, or sit down at some wel,
And he was sure to view them.
('Corruption')

So in the pastoral world of *Silex Scintillans*

There's not a Spring,
Or Leafe but hath his Morning-hymn; Each Bush
And Oak doth know I AM.
('Rules and Lessons')

Signs and tokens lie everywhere in nature. The mysterious healing waters still run on as of old in 'The Water-fall'; 'Stones are deep in admiration' ('The Bird'); 'Fresh Groves grow up, and their green branches shoot / Towards the old and still enduring skies' ('The Timber'); and

My God, when I walke in those groves,
And leaves thy spirit doth still fan,
I see in each shade that there growes
An Angell talking with a man.
('Religion')

Here is the pastoral world that Vaughan had tried unsuccessfully to create in *Olor Iscanus*, where the literary fictions he had employed were soon proved inadequate by the pressures of experience. The temple of nature that we find in *Silex* is a durable place of the spirit, and in choosing to recreate the conditions of primitive religion, Vaughan gives new force to his eponym, The Silurist, for that too suggests an inhabitant of a primitive British world, the druidical time when nature was still instinct with divinity.

Amid the religious confusions of the Puritan revolution, Vaughan glanced backwards to the earliest times when man was nearest God; but his hopes looked forward to an even closer union, the Second Coming. Nothing marks the generation gap between Herbert and Vaughan more strikingly than the expectation of that event. For Herbert, in 'The Church Militant', Christ will appear in the fullness of time; for Vaughan, 'So by all signs / Our fulness too is now come in' ('The Jews'), and Christ is shortly expected. The political upheavals of the 1640s had brought to a head the millenarian beliefs that had been growing through the century. The conviction that history was entering the latter days was common across the spectrum of belief from Anglicans like Sir Thomas Browne to radical Puritans like the Levellers and the Fifth Monarchy men. The coming of the last days was preached the length and breadth of the land, signs and prophecies abounded, and the shipwreck of the State in the 1640s, the overthrow of the Church, aristocracy and King, fired hopes and fears that history had reached a climax and the Second Coming was at hand. Vaughan is assured that the appearance of his Saviour is imminent: he looks forward to release from the 'sad land' and to Paradise regained. In the Preface to his *Life of Paulinus* (1654), he writes, 'I commend unto thee the memorie of that restorer, and the reward he shall bring with him in the end of this world, which truly draws near, if it be not at the door.'[10] Now is 'this last and lewdest age' ('White Sunday'), when history has degenerated to its end, and a good deal of the watching of the skies that goes on in *Silex Scintillans* is done with an eye that waits for Christ's return, following the injunction of Matthew 25:13: 'Watch therefore, for ye know neither the day nor the hour wherein the son of man cometh.' 'The Evening-watch', 'Midnight' and 'The Morning-watch' are all poems of this kind, full of alertness and expectation. 'The Dawning' is a notable Second Coming poem:

> Ah! what time wilt thou come? when shall that crie
> The Bridegroome's Comming! fil the sky?
> Shall it in the Evening run
> When our words and works are done?
> Or wil thy all-surprizing light
> Break at midnight?
> When either sleep, or some dark pleasure
> Possesseth mad man without measure;
> Or shal these early, fragrant hours
> Unlock thy bowres?
> And with their blush of light descry
> Thy locks crown'd with eternitie;

Indeed, it is the only time
That with thy glory doth best chime,
All now are stirring, ev'ry field
    Ful hymns doth yield,
The whole Creation shakes off night,
And for thy shadow looks the light.
. . .

Yet let my Course, my aym, my Love,
And chief acquaintance be above;
So when that day, and hour shal come
In which thy self wil be the Sun,
Thou'lt find me drest and on my way,
Watching the Break of thy great day.

Dawn is indeed Vaughan's favourite hour, always full of divine possibility. The excitement that accompanies rising light in all his poetry is caused by the hope of a new epiphany. 'Mornings are Mysteries; the first worlds Youth, / Mans Resurrection, and the futures Bud' ('Rules and Lessons'). 'Cock-crowing' too is an apocalyptic poem, with its anticipation of 'thy appearing hour' for, according to Mark 13:35, 'Ye know not when the master of the house cometh, at even, or at midnight, or at the cockcrowing, or in the morning.' One of the indications of the last days was the conversion of the Jews, and the poem 'The Jews' looks forward to that event, when

  that long frost which now benums
Your hearts shall thaw; when Angels here
    Shall yet to man appear,
And familiarly confer
Beneath the Oke and Juniper:
      When the bright Dove
Which now these many, many Springs
      Hath kept above,
      Shall with spread wings
Descend, and living waters flow
To make drie dust, and dead trees grow.

There are two 'Day of Judgement' poems, the first a meditation on the End, the second an urgent plea for the arrival of that End:

O come, arise, shine, do not stay
    Dearly lov'd day!
The fields are long since white, and I

With earnest groans for freedom cry,
My fellow-creatures too say, Come!

But the East never burst into light, and Vaughan's own poetic lights faded. Long afterwards, in 1678, he put forward another collection of verse, *Thalia Rediviva*, a dry miscellany of poems mostly in couplet form to suit the new taste, unremarkable, showing no trace of the author of *Silex Scintillans*. That volume, however, will survive as the record of a rare sensibility and as a surprising history of an unaccommodated Christian in a dark time.

Notes

1 The oak seems to be copied from the one illustrated in James Howell's *Dendrologia* (1640), even the acorns recurring in the same place. I guess the other tree to be a palm by its scaly bark and its odd fruit, which I take to be seventeenth-century dates. (In 'The Palm-tree' in *Silex*, the tree is associated with paradise and heaven.) The whole frontispiece seems inspired by the mention of the river Isca (Usk) in William Browne's *Britannia's Pastorals*, Book 2, Song 3, lines 772–9, where the combination of swans, Isca, flowers, trees and bees occurs.

2 The poet-as-swan motif derives from the Greek legend that Apollo, the god of poetry, was once transformed into a swan. In addition, Plato in the *Phaedo* has Socrates say that Apollo inspires the swan with an unearthly music. Hence also the Pythagorean notion that the souls of poets transmigrate into swans.

3 The sub-title of *Silex Scintillans*, 'Sacred Poems and Private Ejaculations', is the same as that of *The Temple*. The image of the title page is probably derived from Jeremiah 23:29: 'Is not my word like a fire? saith the Lord, and like a hammer that breaketh the rock in pieces?' A related usage occurs in Vaughan's devotional work *The Mount of Olives*, where he prays that God might 'Take away . . . this heart of stone, and give me a heart of flesh, renew a right spirit within me' (*The Works of Henry Vaughan*, ed. L. C. Martin (Oxford 1957), p. 159).

4 The number of nonconformist chapels in Wales today that still carry the names of Bethel, Sion, Shiloah and the like testify to the enduring character of this aspect of religion in Wales.

5 The phrase is taken from Owen Felltham's *Resolves*.
6 From 'They are all gone into the world of light.'
7 Notably by M. M. Mahood in her chapter on Vaughan in *Poetry and Humanism* (London 1950), esp. pp. 271–89.
8 The title 'The Match' presumably has other meanings: Herbert is the match who has inflamed Vaughan's zeal, and also a compatible soul, a match for Vaughan's.
9 *The Mount of Olives*, in Martin, *The Works of Henry Vaughan*, p. 186.
10 Martin, ibid., p. 338.

5 Thomas Traherne: the accessible Eden

Vaughan's name is commonly linked with that of Thomas Traherne, for understandable reasons. Their most intense years were spent in the rural south-west of the country, and both developed their religious life at a critical time in the absence of an organized Church. Both wrote religious poetry and devotional prose, both had experience of transcendence, Vaughan occasionally, Traherne habitually. Traherne, whose poetry and finest prose have come to light only in this century, was a man whose singular apprehensions of innocence and felicity caused him to evolve a complicated system to account for his experiences. His major surviving work, *Centuries of Meditation*, is the superlative revelation in prose of his spiritual life, and is quite unlike any other devotional work of the century. Some recent critics question how much it owes to personal inspiration, and how much to ancient meditative traditions derived from St Augustine or St Buonaventura. Others represent it as primarily a case of Christian Platonism in an English setting.[1] Two manuscript collections of his poems have also survived and have been printed, one in his own hand, the other in the hand of his brother Philip.[2] Between them they record the essentials of a life of praise and delight within a recovered Eden.

The mundane career of Traherne is neither well-documented nor very remarkable: born about 1637 into an artisan family in Hereford, he was sent by a more prosperous relative to Oxford, where he engaged in religious controversy. He was ordained a minister under the Puritan dispensation in 1657, and was sponsored to a rural living at Credenhill in his native county of Herefordshire. At the Restoration he soon confessed his allegiance to the restored Church of England and was re-ordained according to the traditional rites, remaining in his parish until about 1667. During this time his most profitable relationships appear to have been with the devotional circle that gathered round a Mrs Susanna Hopton at Kington. She was a woman of inordinate piety, who attracted the more ardent spirits of the locality into a demanding round of formal prayer and fasting, meditation and celebration, a pattern of behaviour that looked back to the community at Little Gidding, yet was not as organized as that. Circles such as Mrs Hopton's were not uncommon throughout the seventeenth century, as people were attracted into the company of exceptionally devout figures, often women, whose spiritual authority had no official recognition.[3] Traherne's *Centuries* are thought to have been written for Susanna Hopton, with whom he left several other manuscripts when he left Herefordshire for London to serve as Chaplain to Sir Orlando Bridgeman, Lord Keeper of the Seal (probably as a result of a recommendation from the influential Hopton family). Traherne died in 1674, having published only one work, the polemical anti-Catholic *Roman Forgeries* (1673). He lay unremembered until the present century, when his rediscovery added strikingly to our appreciation of the varieties of religious experience attained in seventeenth-century England.

Our interest here is with the poems, which offer a brief spiritual autobiography, and also record an unusual passage of imaginative adventure, for it was Traherne's immense good fortune to be born in Paradise, to lose it once and yet regain it in his maturity. The wonder of these events renders the details of his ordinary life insignificant. In infancy and childhood he enjoyed the god-like gift of seeing the world as if it had been newly created expressly for his delight; no sense of sin or suffering discoloured the perfections of nature or his infinite capacity for joy. At some point in youth a heaviness settled over him ('Solitude' and *Centuries* III:23), the imaginative light faded, and ordinariness filtered into his being. Yet it did not persist: miraculously the faculty of vision was rekindled. The chronology is not important. What matters is that Traherne writes as the inhabitant of an English Eden, gifted with a pre-lapsarian sense of the ineffable beauty and pleasure of all created nature. The uniqueness of his angelic condition is conveyed by the wondering rhythmic progressions of his prose in the *Centuries*, where exclamation and acclamation combine in tireless thanksgivings, and it is reiterated by the lucid rhapsodies of his verse. One may fairly question if his extraordinary condition is, like Vaughan's, another case of the development of unconventional religious states at a time when the formalizing influences of the Church of England were in abeyance, and when some men found their religious instincts most deeply moved by the operations of nature, and looked with sympathy to the numinous times of primitive worship. Vaughan and Traherne seem examples of such behaviour, as arguably do Marvell and Thomas Browne, and even

John Evelyn, as his fascination with sacred groves might testify. Although Traherne grew up during the Commonwealth years under the Puritan dispensation, the region of his religious life is so private and apart that it seems scarcely to touch the boundaries of his age. Some aspects of his theology, such as his assumption that sin is an acquired characteristic, a 'habit' contracted from living in society, are unusual in this period, to say the least, as is his tendency to emphasize his personal experience of paradisal delights rather than the awareness of sin. Instead of the Fall and the Redemption forming the axis of his religious life, the possession of paradise now, the reward of right perception, is his theme.

Paradise was much frequented by Englishmen in the mid seventeenth century. Marvell constantly found himself on its threshold, imaginatively penetrating its secrets; Milton set his epic there; Traherne knew he lived in Eden and could not be dispossessed. Vaughan, Browne, Evelyn and Cowley all had more than a passing interest in paradise and the state of innocence. This interest, shown by writers of a widely differing character, reflects an excitement which was apparent throughout all levels of society and which was caused by the millenarian speculation that reached its height in the 1640s and 1650s. That Christ would soon return to restore the Earthly Paradise and establish his thousand-year rule of the saints in that new Eden at the end of time was for some a profoundly-held belief and for others a faint hope, but it was undeniably an expectation that had very wide currency in the fervent climate of the English Revolution. Paradise was in the air, its restoration a possibility, and people who felt themselves to be living in the latter days had an understandable fascination with the unfallen state of man which the elect of God might taste again.[4] Traherne more than any other writer of this period expresses not merely the hope but the experience of this exhilarating mood, because for him the quality of paradisal life is already known, not just savoured in prospect. He called this quality, in his private language, Felicity.

The element in which Traherne lived was wonder. In the poem of that title, which begins 'How like an Angel came I down', he describes his sense of constant marvelling delight with which he viewed the world as a child:

> I within did flow
> With Seas of Life, like Wine;
> I nothing in the World did know,
> But 'twas Divine.

He knows the world has been created for his pleasure, and that his birthright is an unlimited joy at the beauty of creation. His only duty, like that of Adam, is to give thanks to the God whose provision is infinite. In Traherne's childhood, as in Eden, there was no sense of property, division or limit; nature, towns, people, all appeared radiant and angelic, spectacles of delight in a commonwealth of benevolence. The adult Traherne, the poet, has regained his childhood faculty of wonder through some miracle of spiritual renewal, but it is now deeper because of his knowledge of sin and grief, and his understanding that Christ's sacrifice has enabled him to escape from their oppression. In his poetry he distances his renewed self from his infant self yet unaware of sin, but he constantly revisits the sensations of his childhood as the truest memory of the state of innocence and paradisal happiness. He has been Adam, he was awakened into sin, he has later come to understand and receive Christ's gift, and the consequence is that he enjoys access once more to that pristine bliss.

The *Centuries*, which cover the same area as the poems but extend far further, convey at length Traherne's delight and gratitude at Christ's work – he is incapable of dejection or grief in Christ's presence – but the poems direct their energies to the recovery of that first felicity made possible by Christ without much reference to Christ, as if Traherne deliberately reserved his poetry for the exploration of the new-found-land of his childhood. He alone has been granted a passage back, and most of his poetry is 'news from another country'; he recognizes the uniqueness of his position, yet imagines that the record of his adventures in his verse may enable others to make the journey if they can learn rightmindedness and regain the lost faculty of wonder that will reveal the divinity of creation and the goodness of God. Traherne ordered two sequences of poetry that move along similar lines, and one assumes that, like the *Centuries of Meditation*, they were intended for publication and for the enlightenment of others, but that his intentions were frustrated by early death.[5]

When one tries to characterize the two sequences, one finds that the poems in Thomas Traherne's own hand incline towards description of the state of felicity coupled with theological analysis, while the poems copied by Philip Traherne tend to be more freely imaginative and speculative. In the Thomas Traherne poems, 'Wonder', 'Eden' and 'Innocence' retrieve the memory of awakening in Paradise:

that Day
The anchient Light of Eden did convey
Into my Soul: I was an Adam there,
A little Adam in a Sphere

Of Joys! O there my Ravisht Sence
Was entertaind in Paradice,
And had a Sight of Innocence.
('Innocence')

The Skies in their Magnificence,
The Lively, Lovely Air;
Oh how Divine, how soft, how Sweet, how fair!
The Stars did entertain my Sence,
And all the Works of God so Bright and pure,
So Rich and Great did seem,
As if they ever must endure,
In my Esteem.
('Wonder')

'The Preparative' begins the process of examination:

Divine Impressions when they came,
Did quickly enter and my Soul inflame.
Tis not the Object, but the Light
That maketh Heaven; Tis a Purer Sight.
Felicitie
Appears to none but them that purely see.

'The Vision', 'The Improvement' and 'The Approach' continue the process, and among the ecstatic poems with their characteristic ode-like shape appear more sober reflective poems in couplet form – 'Dumnesse', 'Silence', 'Nature' – that deliver a cooler judgement on his experience. Traherne proposes a Christian Platonist explanation, assuming the pre-existence of the soul, whose essence partakes of the divine nature.

Then was my Soul my only All to me,
A Living Endless Ey,
Far wider then the Skie
Whose Power, whose Act, whose Essence was to see.
I was an Inward Sphere of Light,
Or an Interminable Orb of Sight,

An Endless and a Living Day,
A vital Sun that round about did ray
All Life and Sence,
A Naked Simple Pure Intelligence.
('The Preparative')

The soul contains 'The fair Idea of All Things', so upon entry into life the images of things seen still correspond to their archetype in the divine mind. As a particle of divinity, the soul views the created world with the same intellectual delight as that with which God reviews the forms of things within his own mind. The soul has a power identical with Adam's when, as the image of God, he contemplated the images of creation. In giving delight, these images evoke the memory of the primal Ideas and arouse a desire to become pure spirit, to be reintegrated with the intellectual energy that is God. This theory of 'desire' or 'want' of Platonic perfection is central to Traherne's system, and explains the soul's yearning to be reunited with God. 'Felicity' is the condition of viewing the creation with an Adamitic eye, but the desire to contemplate the ideal Platonic forms in the divine mind may only be satisfied in death, whereupon 'Felicity' will be elevated to a state of 'Glory'. The fullest evolution of these philosophic strains occurs in the poem 'My Spirit', which should be read in complement with 'The Circulation' and 'The Demonstration'. These poems should dispel any lingering notions that Traherne was some naïve mystic, and indicate his affinity with that loose group of thinkers known as the Cambridge Platonists, who tried during the 1640s and 1650s to elaborate a system of belief that transcended the acrimonious doctrinal squabbles that divided English Christians so profitlessly.[6]

So much of the poetry in Traherne's own manuscript deals with abstractions, that it requires great resolution of mind to follow the convolutions of his thought. Meaning is clarified to some extent by repetition and by the slightly shifting approaches to the central subject area in different poems. Traherne is reluctant to use metaphor or imagery, wanting to use 'transparent words' to bring down 'the highest mysteries to sense'. He avoids allegory, emblems or other pictorialisms, preferring to communicate his intellectual experience directly. The curious rhythmic buoyancy does much to induce a mood in which his thoughts strike home. However, the collection of poems transcribed by Philip Traherne introduces us to a more colourful, engaging aspect of the poet, which shows us something of his humanity. Here are the poems that recount how growing involvement with wordly trifles caused him to become 'a stranger to the shining skies' ('The Apostacy'), leading to the desolation of 'Solitude', which mourns the loss of visionary power, a theme continued in 'Dissatisfaction'. He offers two accounts of his regeneration: in 'Poverty' he suddenly grasps that his material dearth is irrelevant, for his true inheritance is the whole of God's creation, all disposed for his delight. This realization is accompanied by his discovery of 'The Bible' and 'Christendom'. The biblical message works on his imagination, reviving memories of perfection, as Eden, Jerusalem and the New Jerusalem combine to arouse him to the search for felicity once more, a search which develops ever more confidence, culminating in 'Insatiableness' and 'Hosanna', a final thanksgiving. The most imaginative of these poems is 'Shadows in the Water', which uses the device of the child's wonderment at the discovery of the upside-down silent world of reflections in a puddle to speculate on the existence of a spirit world that touches our own, divided from us only by a film. It is a poem that provides an analogy with Traherne's own work, which enables the reader, by means of a shift in perception, to cross into a tract of paradise that has lain unnoticed around him.

Traherne seems to have had no poetic model (in spite of the Herbertian ring of many of his titles), and no successor, although something of his temperament reappeared in Christopher Smart, and his visionary consciousness shares something with Blake's. He belongs properly to the new frontier of religious experience during the Commonwealth, when the breakdown of formal patterns of worship liberated some powerful religious minds to make remarkable private advances that would have been unlikely in a more orthodox time.

Notes

1 See in particular Louis Martz, *The Paradise Within* (New Haven 1964); A. L. Clements, *The Mystical Poems of Thomas Traherne* (Harvard 1969); and Patrick Grant, *Transformations of Sin* (Toronto 1974).

2 For an account of the two manuscript collections, see the Introduction to H. M. Margoliouth's edition of the *Centuries, Poems and Thanksgivings* (Oxford 1958).

3 One might instance the devotional groups around Magdalen Herbert or Lady Anne Clifford, at a socially elevated level. The Countess of Denbigh seems to have stimulated religious purposes

among her friends, e.g. John Cosin and Richard Crashaw. Crashaw seems also to have frequented a group around the anonymous lady to whom he wrote the 'Prayer Book' verses. Margaret Godolphin was the cause of a great deal of devotional ardour on the part of John Evelyn.

4 Revelation 20 and 22 were commonly conflated with the first chapters of Genesis and the Song of Solomon to produce the images of paradise that were current in the seventeenth century. See Charles Webster, *The Great Instauration* (London 1975), pp. 1–32; and Stanley Stewart, *The Enclosed Garden* (London 1966), chs. 2, 3 and 4. For recent studies of the millenarian hopes of seventeenth-century Protestants, see note 14 of Chapter 9.

5 The prefatory poem in Philip Traherne's manuscript hand has all the character of a public introductory poem, which proposes to the reader that

> thy Soul might see
> With open Eys thy Great Felicity,
> Its Objects view, and trace the glorious Way
> Wherby thou may'st thy Highest Bliss enjoy.

6 For Traherne's affinities with the Cambridge Platonists Peter Sterry, Henry More, John Smith, and Benjamin Whichcote, see Gladys Wade, *Thomas Traherne* (Princeton 1944), pp. 215–38; and Martz, *The Paradise Within*, pp. 35–43. See also 'Thomas Traherne: Mystical Hedonist', in Anthony Low, *Love's Architecture* (New York 1978), pp. 259–91.

6 The devotional adventures of Richard Crashaw

'These poems . . . shal lift thee, Reader, some yards above the ground.' This interesting promise is made in the Preface to Crashaw's *Steps to the Temple* (1646), where the author's friend commends the new volume. Clearly, these poems propose something quite extraordinary and dynamic in an unprecedented way. The Preface becomes more explicit about Crashaw's intentions when it explains that

> as in Pythagoras Schoole, every temper was first tuned into a height by severall proportions of Musick; and spiritualiz'd for one of his weighty Lectures; So maist thou take a Poem hence, and tune thy soule by it, into a heavenly pitch; and thus refined and borne up upon the wings of meditation, in these Poems thou maist talke freely of God, and of that other state.

These, then, are devotional poems, aimed at altering consciousness, intended to liberate the spirit from mundane preoccupations and enrapture it with divine visions. They draw us into a realm where customary patterns of thought and association are superseded by sensational progressions of images and metaphors that proclaim spiritual paradoxes and celestial satisfactions. They speak in holy riddles and are suffused with mysterious joys, and they are written with an intensity that we shall never find again in English religious writing. The Preface assures us that these remarkable poems are invaluable for the reader's own spiritual advancement: they are 'Stepps for happy soules to climbe heaven by.'

The title has obviously been chosen to exploit the popularity of Herbert's book *The Temple*, but there are no resemblances in style, technique or temperament between the two poets. Herbert's shade is invoked, rather, as that of an exemplary Christian poet who had rejected the traditional association of poetry with secular pleasures and had turned its energies entirely to religious ends. Throughout the Renaissance in England there had been intermittent attempts to Christianize the Muse, reaching back to Sidney and Southwell, but

Herbert was the poet generally thought to have succeeded best in this enterprise by his complete devotion to Christian themes and by the creation of a body of verse that was spiritually serviceable to the reader – indeed almost a supplement to the Book of Common Prayer. The Preface to Crashaw's poems confirms that they are published to consolidate this new dominion of the Christian Muse:

> Here's Herbert's second, but equall, who hath retriv'd Poetry of late, and return'd it up to its Primitive use; Let it bound back to heaven gates, whence it came. . . . Our Poet [thought] that every foot in a high-borne verse, might helpe to measure the soule into that better world: Divine Poetry; I dare hold it . . . to be the Language of the Angels; it is the Quintessence of Phantasie and discourse center'd in Heaven; 'tis the very Outgoings of the soule.

The language of the angels is rarely heard today, and imperfectly understood. In order to develop some sympathetic responsiveness to Crashaw's exceptional sensibility, and to the climate of religious feeling in which these poems were produced, we need to know something about Crashaw's religious education and poetic development, and about the modes of worship evolving in the Church of England during the critical decades of the 1630s and 1640s. Crashaw was born into a family where religion was energetically professed: his father William Crashaw had been a prominent Puritan divine, whose post as preacher at the Temple afforded excellent opportunities for influencing the young intelligentsia of London. Like most Englishmen of his generation, William Crashaw was a settled enemy of Rome, being convinced that the Pope was the living Antichrist and the Roman Church a fatal impediment to salvation. His relatively early death prevented him from imposing his convictions on his son Richard, who was educated at the Charterhouse and who entered Pembroke College, Cambridge in 1631. Pembroke at this time was a distinctively High Church institution, still living in the afterglow of its saintly and intellectual master Lancelot Andrewes, so to enrol there was virtually an act of allegiance to the ceremonious Anglicanism that Andrewes had encouraged. The scholarship that Crashaw held there required him to compose Greek and Latin epigrams on New Testament themes for every Sunday (the poems were displayed on the College notice board each week, a detail which offers us an interesting glimpse of the social function of this kind of verse) and in 1634 Crashaw brought together his many exercises in this genre in *Epigrammata Sacra*, published by the university press. Few readers today are likely to browse among these pious trifles, but part of their significance for us is to show that from an early stage Crashaw was drawing his inspiration from continental rather than English models, for the vogue for these Latin sacred epigrams came primarily from Italy and was especially associated with the Jesuits who had developed the genre for the concentrated expression of religious paradoxes as an aid to devotion.[1]

During his Pembroke years Crashaw also composed a fair body of conventional verse of the kind that any talented undergraduate poet was expected to produce. One of the pleasures of undergraduate life in the seventeenth century was that it provided so many opportunities for occasional verse, and the many collections of verse in both manuscript and printed form that issued from Oxford and Cambridge did much to strengthen the corporate identity of the institutions and the personal vanity of the contributors. There was no shortage of topics: university deaths, in an age of high mortality, ensured that every poet was an elegist; the waxing and waning of the royal family – Crashaw compliments the Queen that her annual childbed keeps well-wishing poets regularly employed; commendatory verses for new books to help the author get the maximum send-off from his intellectual circle; poems to one's incomparable mistress (usually imaginary), *jeux d'esprit* and translations. Crashaw's secular verse from the 1630s was published as *The Delights of the Muses* and tucked away at the back of *Steps to the Temple*. It is dominated by one astonishing poem, 'Musicks Duell', where a new and original poetic voice asserts itself, but it is notable that this work is a free translation of the Latin poem by the Jesuit writer Famianus Strada, which had been published in 1617, once again suggesting that Crashaw's powers responded favourably to the extravagant neo-classic verse of the Italian *seicento*. The subject is a musical contest between a lutenist and a nightingale, the familiar Renaissance topos of art versus nature. Each fantasia of the lute player is challenged by the nightingale in a crescendo of brilliant sequences until the bird, attempting to scale the highest reaches of musical invention, over-exerts herself and dies. Crashaw far exceeds his poetic model in the evocation of the rival virtuosi, translating musical effects into verbal terms with prodigious facility:

> her supple Brest thrills out
> Sharpe Aires, and staggers in a warbling doubt
> Of dallying sweetnesse, hovers ore her skill,
> And folds in wav'd notes with a trembling bill,
> The plyant Series of her slippery song.

Then starts shee suddenly into a Throng
Of short thicke sobs, whose thundring volleyes float,
And roule themselves over her lubricke throat
In panting murmurs, still'd out of her Breast
That ever-bubling spring; the sugred Nest
Of her delicious soule, that there does lye
Bathing in streames of liquid Melodie;
Musicks best seed-plot, whence in ripend Aires
A Golden-headed Harvest fairley reares
His Honey-dropping tops, plow'd by her breath
Which there reciprocally laboureth
In that sweet soyle. It seemes a holy quire
Founded to th'Name of great Apollo's lyre.
Whose sylver-roofe rings with the sprightly notes
Of sweet-lipp'd Angell-Imps, that swill their throats
In creame of Morning Helicon.

The rush of metaphors out-runs rational coherence, yet the sequence of impressions evokes the rhapsodic splendour of the nightingale's song through images of lusciousness, fertility, sweetness and riches that are so sustained that the meaning is enforced by intensity and musical colour. This is perhaps a sample of 'the language of the Angels'. It is also a foretaste of the mature Crashaw. Besides being a *tour de force* of musical illusionism, 'Musicks Duell' penetrates into states of feeling that will become familiar terrain in later works. In the additions that Crashaw liberally made to Strada's original poem, both the nightingale and the lutenist are transported, by their total devotion to their art, into states of transcendent delight:

Her little soule is ravisht: and so pour'd
Into loose extasies, that shee is plac't
Above her selfe, Musicks Enthusiast.

The excited measures of the lute carry

Their Masters blest soule (snatcht out at his Eares
By a strong Extasy) through all the sphaeares
Of Musicks heaven; and seat it there on high
In th'Empyraeum of pure Harmony.

What is here an aesthetic sensation will deepen into a religious experience in the later poetry, but the method of intense, insistent exploitation of a theme will remain the same.[2]

The most powerful influence on Crashaw during the 1630s was that of the contemporary Italian poet Giambattista Marino, a name little honoured today, but an exciting phenomenon in his time. He excelled in a brilliant, witty, paradoxical poetry, heavily rhetorical, that strained invention towards its limits. His subjects tend to be overburdened with an excess of description in which sweetness, colour and extreme sensations mix to form a compound repugnant to modern taste yet stimulating to a large body of seventeenth-century admirers all across Europe. He touched secular and religious themes with equal virtuosity, and Crashaw found his manner peculiarly congenial for several reasons. It was in keeping with the sophisticated cleverness of the Latin epigrams that Crashaw enjoyed writing, and it showed how wit and sensationalism could be brought together to illuminate Christian subjects in a new way. From Marino, Crashaw learnt how to build up a long devotional poem by an accumulation of striking and often bizarre images that induce a fine sense of the marvellous. There was evidently an affinity of temperament between the two poets, and Crashaw's translation in 1637 of *Il Sospetto d'Herode*, the first book of Marino's brief epic on the Slaughter of the Innocents, was at once a tribute to Marino's art and the culmination of his apprenticeship to foreign masters.

Crashaw's unusual position among the poets of seventeenth-century England is to a large extent the consequence of his pursuit of continental models for style and content. Unlike most of his contemporaries, he was not disposed to model himself on the older generation of English poets, represented by Spenser, Donne, Jonson or Herbert (although some of his secular poems, such as the epitaphs, show that he experimented with the Jonsonian manner; and even in the translation of Marino there are some lapses into the Spenserian mode); nor was he drawn to the conventional classical poets. This turning away from the familiar paths indicates in fact that Crashaw was an *avant-garde* poet who tried to extend the range of expressiveness attainable in English by learning from Renaissance Latin and Italian developments. Moreover, he wanted an expressiveness of a very special kind, for during the 1630s, as his religious vocation became more urgent, he was moved to forge a style that would respond to his passionate adoration of sacred mysteries and also permit the exercise of a special sort of religious wit that was essential to his devotions. English poets had traditionally enhanced their imaginations by association with Italian poets: Petrarch had inspired generations of writers, Ariosto and Tasso had brought a new spirit to later Elizabethan verse, and now Marino helped liberate Crashaw. Nor was Crashaw alone, for other poets of the time were attracted to Marino: minor figures admittedly, who lacked the poetic personality that would enable them to assimilate his influences and then present their own distinctive experience to their age; figures such as Crashaw's friend Joseph Beaumont, or William Randolph, or Stanley. Marino and the Latin Jesuit poets of modern Italy offered a poetry that was flamboyant and ingenious, serious and intense, in a fashion that the English tradition could not match; Crashaw alone was able to exploit it fully during a few years of exotic creativity. The novel style that he developed from foreign sources was a complement to and a medium for the novel devotional exercises, which also had a foreign inspiration, that he wanted to practise and communicate.

Crashaw's religious life entered a more fervent phase in 1635, when he was elected to a fellowship at Peterhouse, a college even more High Church than Pembroke, thanks to the successive ministrations of two masters, Matthew Wren and John Cosin. Cosin was the leading supporter at Cambridge of Archbishop Laud's policies in religion, and he did his utmost to make his college a place where 'the beauty of holiness' might flourish. He attracted to Peterhouse fellows and students who favoured the high formal modes of devotion that he believed were the fittest forms of worship. Wren had built a new chapel for the College; under Cosin it was furnished with many of those images and aids to prayer that had been absent from English churches since the Reformation: carved angels, crucifixes with the image of Christ, religious paintings, stained-glass windows, incense and an organ – even a picture of the Virgin Mary. Crashaw is listed in the College records as one of those who helped embellish the new chapel. Cosin had written *A Collection of Private Devotions* (published in 1627) which was now used in the College services: this was a book of prayers for the different hours with a litany and penitential psalms, all of which gave a ritual shape to the religious day in a fashion reminiscent of the pre-Reformation Church. Order, dignity, beauty, these were the accompaniments to devotion at Peterhouse. In the later 1630s, through Cosin and through his pupil Colet Ferrar, Crashaw became an intimate of the Anglican community at Little Gidding, some 30 miles away in Huntingdonshire, where the Ferrar family had instituted an intensive devotional regime which has already been mentioned in connection with George Herbert. The constant practice of piety there, the keeping of the fasts, feasts and vigils of the Church, accorded well with Crashaw's desire for a life of continual worship.

There was a shared connection between Peterhouse and Little Gidding, for Cosin's *Private Devotions* was one of the sustaining books of both the College and of the community.

Soon, Crashaw acquired what was in effect his own oratory, for he was made curate of Little St Mary's Church, which adjoins Peterhouse, and there in his private domain he lived a life of austere religious fervour, spending his nights in vigil and meditation, in praise and adoration of the Divine Name, in the fellowship of the saints. There he gave 'those thronged Sermons on each Sunday and Holiday, that ravished more like Poems, . . . scattering not so much Sentences as Extasies',[3] and there also, according to his biographers, he composed many of his poems as part of his devotional exercises.[4] When we look at the range of Crashaw's subject matter, his preoccupation with Mary Magdalene and St Teresa, with saints and martyrs and the blood of Christ, it seems easy now to type these concerns as the expression of a spirit naturally Catholic. Yet these poems were written when Crashaw was firmly in the Anglican communion, a member of a prominent, disciplined High Church community. His religious practices, his choice of subjects and the remarkable tone of his poetry should be understood rather as part of the process, which Laud had promoted, of enlarging the devotional terrain available to the Church of England. The Tudor period had been the primitive age of the Anglican Church, when it was young and defensive, determined to survive; but with the Stuarts, it became the Church militant and triumphant, assured and confident. It considered itself a catholic and universal Church, doctrinally superior to Rome and infinitely purer in faith. Large numbers of Anglicans wanted to see their Church repossess some of those rich areas of piety that had been forfeit at the Reformation. Under the Elizabethan settlement of the Church there had been no provision for the meditative life; instead, an active communal life of preaching, Bible-reading and prayer was enjoined. The need for a fuller, more imaginative life of spiritual exploration was widely felt, with the result that by the early seventeenth century, English Protestants of all shades were making use of the Jesuit manuals of meditation imported from the continent to discipline, intensify and dramatize their understanding of the Christian mysteries. With Laud at the head of the Church in the 1630s, and with the King behind him, the movement into a warmer and more fertile devotional climate grew bolder; to the Puritan element in the Church this was an encroachment into Catholic territory, but to the Laudians it was a proper expansion of the Anglican Church into the traditional domain of Christian worship, undertaken in the fresh spirit of a pure faith. Religious images returned to help stimulate and concentrate meditation, and veneration of the saints was again permitted for their perfect faith and exemplary piety; the figure of the Virgin could again be contemplated as 'a transcendent Creature' who inspired a special kind of tender affection long denied to Protestants;[5] angels reappeared in the Anglican heavens. The Laudian wing of the English Church was kept from falling into the Roman Church by the safeguards of the Thirty-Nine Articles, by deep division of doctrine over such questions as the intercession of saints, purgatory, indulgences and the status of the sacraments, and above all by vigorous anti-papal sentiment. Laud eventually fell victim to his Puritan antagonists in 1641, but the evolution of High Church sentiment continued in many places until its adherents were dispossessed, exiled or imprisoned during the Civil War. Crashaw's poems remain as the most adventurous expression of this unusual phase of English Church history. The invocation of George Herbert's memory in the title and Preface of *Steps to the Temple* in 1646 emphasized to readers how much these poems belong within an Anglican context, and the publication of a second edition in 1648 suggests that they could attract a fairly large audience in adverse times.

What did the reader of the 1646 volume find? What sort of religious experience was he offered, and what were the poetic and pious satisfactions he might receive from Crashaw? One notices first the author's motto, 'Live, Jesus, live, and let it bee / My life to dye, for love of thee', a profession of complete dedication to the Holy Name, and the suggestion of a willingness to court martyrdom for his faith. It sets a high pitch. The opening poem is 'The Weeper', which either repels or attracts depending on one's temperament. Its function at the beginning of the volume is surely to identify a 'fit audience' for the kind of worship offered in Crashaw's *Temple*. The subject is a meditation on the tears of Mary Magdalene, and as such it belongs to an extensive literature of tears that flowed through the seventeenth century, having its source in the cult of tears encouraged by the Catholic Counter-Reformation to direct the affections and emotions to a holy end: tears were the consequence of the faithful soul's infinite sorrow at the sufferings of Christ, and infinite joy at the miracle of salvation made possible by Christ's sacrifice. Because the tears sprang from a spiritual source, they were qualitatively superior to tears shed for human misfortunes and delights. Some devotional exercises incited weeping as a high emotional surrender to the great mysteries of the faith; where the intellect could no longer proceed, feelings and intuitions advanced to a profounder understanding, and the visible expression of this state of faith was tears. The pattern of tearful devotion was Mary Magdalene, who is depicted in the Gospel of St Luke as a repentant sinner who came to Jesus offering a box of precious ointment, 'And stood at his feet behind him weeping, and began to wash his feet with tears, and did wipe them with the hairs of her head, and kissed his feet, and anointed them with the ointment.' Jesus declared that 'Her sins, which are many, are forgiven; for she loved much . . . and he said unto her, Thy sins are forgiven . . . . Thy faith hath saved thee; go in peace' (Luke 7:38, 47–50). The Magdalene's tears, therefore, could be interpreted as an expression of her sins, of her love for Jesus, the insatiable love of the human for the divine, and as a free and sublime act of worship. For long after the Reformation in England, Mary Magdalene was one of those saints whose adoration was unthinkable for Protestants, but whose significance as an exemplary figure in the New Testament was inescapable. In particular, the High Anglicans looked favourably on her (we may remember George Herbert's mother was named Magdalen). The popularity of the Jesuit Robert Southwell's prose meditation *Marie Magdalens Funeral Teares* (for the death of Christ), which went through eight editions in England between 1591 and 1636, shows that the Magdalene had a considerable following, for she could so well represent the passionate love and sorrow of the faithful Christian. Protestants could benefit from the Catholic cult of the Magdalene by imitating her devotional conduct, without worshipping her as a saint and intercessor and without according to a mortal, no matter how worthy, the praise and glory which should be Christ's alone. This is Crashaw's approach to his poem. He concentrates on the tears, not on the personality of the weeper, for Mary has been reduced to a figure whose sole function is to weep. Because Christ forgave her her sins, her tears are an efficient means of grace: they are waters of salvation, infinitely precious. As such, they are worthy of endless study, because these falling tears lead us paradoxically upward to heaven – the first of the poem's many spiritual ascents.

Crashaw's method has sometimes been described as Marinist: that is to say he employs the rhetorical devices he learnt from Marino to create a mood of sensuous, enraptured devotion. The energy of the poem is generated by the 'concetto' or conceit, the elaborate, ingenious image that exploits every imaginable aspect and suggestive property of the subject, in this case the pious tear.

Upwards thou dost weepe,
Heavens bosome drinks the gentle streame.
Where th' milky rivers meet,
Thine Crawles above and is the Creame.
Heaven, of such faire floods as this,
Heaven the Christall Ocean is.

Every morne from hence,
A briske Cherub something sips
Whose soft influence
Adds sweetnesse to his sweetest lips.
Then to his Musicke, and his song
Tastes of this breakefast all day long.

The 'concetto' has a bizarre logic all of its own: it is supra-rational, developing here according to the paradoxes and improbabilities of the spiritual life. One could say, indeed, that because of its freedom from the normal conventions of association, because of its capacity for the unexpected perception, it is a peculiarly suitable medium for conveying the marvels of a world where all the topography and all the action is spiritual. The underlying idea of these stanzas is not hard to grasp: the Magdalene's tears fly upwards to mingle with the Milky Way, which in classical and later in Christian poetry was traditionally the glorious pathway to heaven; because they are of such rich spiritual substance, the tears super-naturally become cream in this setting. Since the tears are faith in liquid form, one can truly say that heaven is composed of such 'faire floods', which constantly refresh the celestial inhabitants and enhance the everlasting praise of God. The ingenuity owes much to Marino, and so does the sensuous tone, but the special quality of the sensuousness, the indulgence in softness and sweetness, and purity of colour, this is distinctively Crashavian. There is much wit here and a certain irreverent humour: there is musicality and an imaginative absorption in a wholly religious world. Moreover, the poetry radiates a strong sense of pleasure at its own success.

In the revised version of the poem published in 1652, Crashaw greatly increased the length, and introduced many new conceits, including the notorious sequence that depicts the faithful Magdalene following Christ in a remarkably picturesque state of tearfulness:

And now where're he strayes,
Among the Galilean mountaines,
Or more unwellcome wayes,
He's follow'd by two faithfull fountaines;

> Two walking baths; two weeping motions;
> Portable, & compendious oceans.

These lines may be dismissed as grotesque or preposterous, or as an extraordinary failure of taste or tone, and they have often been so ridiculed. They can, however, be regarded appreciatively, for as the excitement of the recreated poem rises, Crashaw's images multiply and become more urgent, so that he cannot linger to unfold them, but he begins to use that shorthand notation of the seventeenth-century religious poet, emblem writing. The walking baths, the portable and compendious oceans, have the character of those detached images that are conventional in emblem books, and Crashaw expects the reader who shares his own imaginative excitement to sense the coherence of these images, and register them as rapid understandings of the tumult of emotions. The Magdalene's response to Christ is a complex of love, grief, hope, fear – infinite feelings in a shower of tears. Already in the previous stanza, Crashaw has moved on to this elevated plane where he expresses himself elliptically in compact images, as he realizes with a sudden immediacy that the Magdalene's outpourings spring from a mystical contact with Christ, the moment that Crashaw and every devout reader yearns for:

> Twas his well-pointed dart
> That digg'd these wells, & drest this Vine;
> And taught the wounded Heart
> The way into these weeping Eyn.
> Vain loves avant! bold hands forbear!
> The lamb hath dipp't his white foot here.

A passage such as this only makes sense when read as a series of emblems that have to be interpreted by reference to biblical texts, whereupon the stanza becomes comprehensible as an account of Christ's transfiguring love for the sinful soul. This extreme and cryptic writing does not often appear in Crashaw; it tends to occur more in his later poetry, and is an accelerated technique for noting complex religious states. Like most advanced techniques, it finds few sympathetic readers.

The original 'Weeper' has no discernible structure: it is an accumulation of images that are offered to 'a worthier object, our Lord's feet' – the humblest part of the deity, yet the limit of the devout man's aspirations for the Magdalene's act of washing Christ's feet with her tears is the symbol of the highest desires of unworthy mankind. The rewritten version shows no marked improvement in organization, although some critics have argued otherwise.[6] Its significance as the opening poem of *Steps to the Temple* lies in the atmosphere of wonder it creates, for wonder is the natural element of Crashaw's muse, and it is the mood most conducive to spiritual glory. The paradoxes, the impossibilities and excesses of 'The Weeper' lead us marvelling into a realm where holy mysteries abound.

A collection of divine epigrams follows 'The Weeper', English examples of a genre in which Crashaw had already established a reputation. There is much concern with the blood of Christ and of the martyrs, and this preoccupation culminates in a group of witty meditations on the wounds of Christ. Christ's blood has always been venerated as one of the great wonders of religion. As the blood that redeemed mankind, its nature is inconceivable except as an act of faith. Institutionalized as the wine of the eucharist, its significance can be controlled by the order of the mass or the communion service, but when exposed to adoration in its own right, it can provoke the most extreme manifestations of ecstasy or morbidity. For the private meditator on the mysteries of the Crucifixion, it was essential to realize the actuality of Christ's blood in order to feel the immensity of the sacrifice and to astonish the soul with this miracle of the redemption. Devotional exercises current in the seventeenth century encouraged the vivid recreation of Christ's sufferings as a preparation for dwelling on the mysteries of atonement and redemption. Crashaw returns again and again to the spectacle of Christ's bleeding wounds, often as a spiritual lover views the body of the beloved Christ, whose wounds are the token of his love for mankind.

O These wakefull wounds of thine!
  Are they Mouthes? or are they eyes?
Be they Mouthes, or be they eyne,
  Each bleeding part some one supplies.

Lo! a mouth, whose full-bloom'd lips
  At too deare a rate are roses.
Lo! a blood-shot eye! that weepes
  And many a cruell teare discloses.
  ('On the wounds of our crucified Lord')

Blood itself is the object of his adoration. It flows irresistibly, as purple rivers, a double Nilus, a Red Sea, a general flood, until it streams through the Crashavian universe. Crashaw finds it immensely satisfying to contemplate the blood of redemption: it thrills and staggers his spirit. He cannot gaze enough. But sometimes, in the presence of so immense a theme his imagination can lapse into bathos:

> Water'd by the showres they bring,
> The thornes that thy blest browes encloses
> (A cruell and a costly spring)
> Conceive proud hopes of proving Roses.
> ('On the bleeding wounds of our crucified Lord')

Even the well-known epigram 'On our crucified Lord Naked, and bloody' fails for some readers because the wit of the 'purple wardrobe' may be too trifling for its subject:

> Th'have left thee naked Lord, O that they had;
> This Garment too I would they had deny'd.
> Thee with thy selfe they have too richly clad,
> Opening the purple wardrobe of thy side.
> O never could bee found Garments too good
> For thee to weare, but these, of thine owne blood.

Yet it is precisely the image of the purple wardrobe that awakens one's response. The King of Kings is clothed in the purple robe of his own blood, which alone is rich enough for such a service, and his body has stored this garment until it is needed; but Christ has magnanimously volunteered to clothe all men with his blood, so his body may be considered, metaphorically, as a great wardrobe. (There is probably also a pun here on the Royal Wardrobe, where the King's clothes were kept at Whitehall.) How successful is this conceit? A function of wit is to enable the poet and the reader to manoeuvre into a position which gives a novel perspective on a traditional subject, and thereby to enjoy new insights, often shocking or surprising, into familiar themes. Thus wit keeps devotion fresh and alert, providing a stream of stimuli that produce a delight in new understandings of even the most grievous subjects. We often find, therefore, a seventeenth-century poet expressing intellectual and emotional pleasure in circumstances which to us may be inappropriate or unseemly – but here we come up against the great change in sensibility that separates us from that age. Crashaw's sacred wit probably gave immense satisfaction to his readers – why else would his poems go into seven editions in the seventeenth century?

One of the minor literary consequences of the broad Counter-Reformation movement that worked to renew the zeal of the Catholic world had been the encouragement of the exercise of wit in religious matters, and through the Jesuits the witty style of devotion and preaching and prayer had spread around Europe. This style had proved so attractive and effective that it had been adopted by many Protestants as well, in England especially by those of a High Church disposition, whose most articulate representatives were Andrewes, Donne, Herbert and Crashaw; learned men like these found the witty style a valuable aid to a more strenuous religious life.[7] Conceits, emblems (and we must remember that the Jesuits had been responsible for many of the early emblem books) and all manner of witty devices helped to disclose the hidden meanings of biblical events and spiritual transactions. Until the Civil War and the victory of the men of plain religion, this intellectual ingenuity had flourished in the Church of England: wit was the salt of devotion and the spice of prayer. Its exponents might have maintained that wit could never diminish the seriousness of subjects whose grandeur was beyond question, it could only sharpen faith. Crashaw combined this witty manner with a sensationalist temperament in a way which often alienates modern readers. Yet he was not unique, for his poetry shares many similarities with that of Robert Southwell, Giles Fletcher and Joseph Beaumont, though these poets are scarcely read today.

Even his deep passion for martyrs and martyrdom was not exceptional. Englishmen were nourished on the blood of martyrs, for Foxe's *Book of Martyrs* was in every church and in many homes, detailing the sufferings of Protestants under Marian persecution in horrible detail. The Church of England had been founded on their blood, and their memory was kept fresh by Foxe. It was an age of martyrs: the Roman Church celebrated those who had died and were still dying for the faith in the Americas, the Indies, China and Japan, and their steadfastness moved Christians everywhere to admiration. Crashaw's enraptured acclaim of the martyrs in the Hymn 'To the Name of Jesus' is a vision for the times: at the very height of heaven in a blood-red radiant bank of fire they stand, the 'flaming-brested Lovers', whose defiance of torture and death was the impetuous means of the soul to embrace Christ.

An acquaintance with the historical background may diminish our distaste for Crashaw's apparent excesses, but even the most well-disposed modern reader may find it difficult to respond to the cult of the Holy Innocents, which evidently enthralled Crashaw. These infants killed by order of Herod in his search for the Christ-child are honoured by the Church as the first to die for Christ. Their innocence, their precociousness, and their involuntary sacrifice naturally made them targets for the witty poetry of the Italian *seicento*, and Marino had even written a brief epic on the subject. Crashaw began to translate this, giving up before he reached the massacre itself, but he published the lengthy preliminaries in *Steps to the Temple*. In addition, he wrote several epigrams in English and Latin that reveal his relish for the theme. These latter were presumably composed as devotional exercises for the Feast of the Holy Innocents, celebrated on 27 December. One example will suffice:

> To see both blended in one flood
> The Mothers Milke, the Childrens blood,
> Makes me doubt if Heaven will gather,
> Roses hence, or Lillies rather.
> ('Upon the Infant Martyrs')

This poem today could be accused of perversity or grotesque bad taste. However, if we assume that the poem celebrates the martyrs on their feast day, a day of rejoicing, then the tone is more understandable: the blood is the mark of their martyrdom, the milk of their innocence, their felicity is certain, so the buoyant sense of pleasure radiated by the poem is part of its festive character. But why was Crashaw particularly attracted to the Innocents, when the calendar is red with martyrs? Here one is on difficult ground, approaching the area where psychological solutions become tempting, yet since we know so little about the poet's private self, speculation is bound to be unreliable. Crashaw certainly experiences a frisson of pleasure at the thought of the tenderness of children, and of the tenderness of breasts, for he had a highly sensuous nature. Blood stimulates him, and the idea of martyrdom definitely excites him. (In the opening of the 'Hymn to . . . Sainte Teresa' his fantasies coalesce in a rapturous speculation that she might fall an infant martyr to the Moors.) This excitability has to be acknowledged in Crashaw, though whether it was fostered by overmuch devotion or whether religion provided a socially accepted stimulus to certain neurotic proclivities is difficult to say. Whatever its origins, this preoccupation with martyrdom was not untimely in the 1640s. In 1645, the Archbishop of Canterbury, William Laud, was executed, and in 1649 came King Charles's turn. Both men were widely considered as martyrs, and King Charles's death immediately inspired a cult of relics of the sacred monarch. The supreme governor of the Church of England and its spiritual head perished, and the tide of persecution was rising against the High Anglicans. Martyrdom was in the air, and was a not inconceivable destiny for Crashaw and his co-religionists.

We encounter a more attractive aspect of Crashaw's art, when we turn to the 'Hymne of the Nativity, sung by the Shepheards'. This is a poem that shows to advantage Crashaw's musical talents, which tend to be overshadowed by his startling subject matter. Crashaw was, after all, one of the most melodious of English poets, and his rhythms, metrical pauses, repetitions and assonances form no small part of his art. Most of his finest poems are hymns of praise, a genre which favours musicality and enraptured description, and exempts him from analysis or introspection, qualities which are not among his strengths. The 'Nativity' Hymn is set as a sacred oratorio with a choir alternating with two soloists, Tityrus and Thyrsis. The names of these shepherds are taken from Virgil's pastorals; since Virgil had from ancient times been regarded as an honorary Christian (because of his prophecy in the Fourth Eclogue of the Virgin and Child who would bring about a new golden age), it is a happy stroke of Crashaw's to have these Virgilian shepherds sing of the realization of that prophecy. As with most of Crashaw's major poems, there are two versions, and as usual the alterations for the 1648 edition of *Steps to the Temple* represent an improvement both poetically and theologically. The 1646 version is a fairly conventional piece which uses the meditative technique of 'composition of place' to recreate the scene of the Nativity with vividness and immediacy, so that the reader may have the impression of participating in the divine event. The shepherds proclaim the traditional paradoxes of the Incarnation – such as the spiritual light that is born in the midst of winter, which far outshines the light of nature – and they conclude with the offering of gifts: first the flowers of spring, but then more significantly they offer the gift of their own souls to the King of Love: 'At last, in fire of thy faire Eyes, / Wee'l burne, our owne best sacrifice.' The attractiveness of this first version lies in its delightful buoyancy of tone, and in the tenderness and intimacy of the shepherds' affection for the Child. The later version is much more fully orchestrated, richer in sound, strengthened by choric repetitions, and devotionally more intense. Christ is now the incarnation of divine love whose presence kindles an immediate response in the shepherds. A remarkable new stanza presents the theological mystery, the radiant complexity that lies behind the simple pastoral scene:

Proud world, said I; cease your contest
And let the Mighty Babe alone.
The Phaenix builds the Phaenix' nest.
Love's architecture is his own.
The Babe whose birth embraves this morn,
Made his own bed e're he was born.

The phoenix was traditionally an image of the uniqueness of Christ; here the image transforms the scene in the manger into something miraculous, where we sense the pre-ordained rightness of the moment, and glimpse the immense spiritual structure that is taking shape in this humble room. It is as if the shepherds in a moment of vision had penetrated to the redemptive energies released by 'this starry stranger'. The language and rhythms show Crashaw's rare art of suggesting the inconceivable, of carrying us to the threshold of a new order of experience; one begins to understand why his poetry might be a valuable aid to devotion.

Divine love was the power that much of Crashaw's poetry was set to catch. The intellectual knowledge that God's love for mankind is the cause of the Incarnation, and that the soul's love of Christ is the natural reciprocity of that great act of love is insufficient for Crashaw. He must feel the effects of that love in himself. This is the chief end of all his meditations: to direct his highly emotional nature, by dwelling on suggestive images and responsive themes, to attain a state of consciousness where the mutual love of Christ and the soul is known as a personal experience. Emulation of those whose love was fulfilled is a part of his practice: the shepherds knew an instinctive love of the Christ child at his first appearance in the world; Mary Magdalene was as ardent with love for her Saviour as she was tearful at her inadequate means of loving him, and the tension between the two states accounts for much of the emotional turmoil of that poem. Above all, however, Crashaw was attracted to a near-contemporary who had known the mystic union of her soul with divine love, and who had recorded her exalted flights in a remarkable spiritual autobiography, St Teresa of Avila. Crashaw wrote three poems in her praise, and such a preoccupation might suggest a strong Catholic bias in the writer, for Teresa was a leading figure in the Counter-Reformation Church. Yet it is probably fair to believe that in the first two poems published in 1646 Crashaw still took the view of an Anglican admirer, seeing her as an exemplary figure whose experiences were heavenly currency for all Christians; he addresses her not as a saint of the Roman Church but as the 'Vertuous and Learned Lady Madre de Teresa that sought an early Martyrdome.' To a man of Crashaw's special propensities, the appeal of a woman who had sought martyrdom as a child by preaching Christianity among the Moors, and who lived to experience the mystic love of Christ, can hardly be overstated. She had realized the dreams of Crashaw's own spirit, in effect. The affinity he feels with his subject is complete, and results in the most resounding start of any poem he wrote: 'Love thou art absolute, sole Lord / Of life and death.' Love is, of course, divine love – it could not be anything else in Crashaw – and it so influences the infant Teresa that she is consumed with a passion to die for Christ as a sign of her devotion:

> Love toucht her heart, and loe it beats
> High, and burnes with such brave heats:
> Such thirst to dye, as dare drinke up,
> A thousand cold deaths in one cup,
> Good reason for shee breaths all fire,
> Her weake breast heaves with strong desire.

At the age of 6, a miracle of piety, she leaves to convert the Moors: the elation of the octosyllabic verse expresses Crashaw's delight at the thought of another infant martyr: 'Farewell house, and farwell home: / Shees for the Moores and Martyrdome.' The poem is already filling with blood before Crashaw checks his imagination, and turns to the different fate that awaited her, for this poem is truly a spiritual biography of the Saint, depicting the extraordinary attainments of her inner life. The divine love that controls her does not wish her to die at the hands of enemies; rather she is reserved for a more mysterious fate, to undergo a death of love for God. Crashaw draws directly from Teresa's autobiography, which had been translated into English in 1642 as *The Flaming Heart*, to describe the ecstatic visions of the Saint, especially the vision in which an angel of great beauty struck her repeatedly through the heart with an arrow of fire, kindling in her a passionate love of God. Teresa's own account of her ecstasies is erotic, and Crashaw doesn't hesitate to follow suit.

> O how oft shalt thou complaine
> Of a sweet and subtile paine?
> Of intollerable joyes?
> Of a death in which who dyes
> Loves his death, and dyes againe,
> And would for ever so be slaine!

> And lives and dyes, and knowes not why
> To live, but that he still may dy.
>
> How kindly will thy gentle heart,
> Kisse the sweetly-killing dart.

However, to read this sequence, as it is sometimes read, as an indulgence in eroticism under the cloak of religion, is to misread it entirely. For Crashaw, as for so many pietists, the senses and passions are susceptible of a lower or a higher animation, depending on whether they are concentrated on the world of nature or on the realm of grace. It would be unthinkable for people of the spiritual calibre of Teresa or Crashaw to gratify their senses with the ephemeral satisfactions of the natural world: all their faculties are consecrated to spiritual ends, to the exclusion of all mundane distractions. To employ the senses for spiritual profit was part of the discipline of the meditative exercises that conditioned the lives of devout people, and for Crashaw, to write as sensuously as he does in this poem is to vindicate his intentions to make poetry serve the love of God, and not the love of sundry mistresses. This poem, too, is a 'stepp for happy soules to climbe heaven by', for through the imaginative excitement of poetry, Crashaw participates in Teresa's rapture, and he is able to fly beyond it in the spectacle of the beatific vision on the occasion of Teresa's ultimate entry into heaven (lines 110–82). Crashaw rarely attains these moments of vision, most of his poetry being a steady upward beating that then hangs lark-like in loud praise, with a sudden cease. That this poem to St Teresa enters such a rarefied element is its true tribute to the Saint's value as a spiritual director.

The succeeding poem, 'An Apologie' for writing of Spanish Teresa to Englishmen, scarcely needs to make its case, for her merits are already justified. Sincere devotion renders differences of allegiance irrelevant.

> Christs Faith makes but one body of all soules,
> And loves that bodies soule; no Law controules
> Our free trafick for heaven.

The poem proceeds to describe the state of divine inebriation that Crashaw shared with Teresa, for both were by temperament God-intoxicated souls, and Crashaw freely admits that he is drunk with 'richer blood than blush of grape / Was ever guilty of'. Their temperamental affinity is sealed in the final tribute to the Saint, 'The Flaming Heart', which first appeared in the 1648 volume. It begins as a meditation on the picture of the Saint and the seraphim, and then, in one of those bewildering transformations that seventeenth-century poetry specializes in, the Saint is metamorphosed into a flaming heart and she becomes her own emblem, an object for rapt contemplation. The effect of that contemplation is revealed in the impassioned coda that Crashaw added to the poem at the end of his life, lines of gratitude to a luminary who by that time had effectively become his patron saint, whose example had taught him the annihilation of self in a total surrender to divine love.

> By all thy dowr of Lights & Fires;
> By all the eagle in thee, all the dove;
> By all thy lives & deaths of love;
> By thy larg draughts of intellectuall day,
> And by thy thirsts of love more large then they;
> By all thy brim-fill'd Bowles of feirce desire
> By thy last Morning's draught of liquid fire;
> By the full kingdome of that finall kisse
> That seiz'd thy parting Soul, & seal'd thee his;
> By all the heav'ns thou hast in him
> (Fair sister of the Seraphim!)
> By all of Him we have in Thee;
> Leave nothing of my Self in me.
> Let me so read thy life, that I
> Unto all life of mine may dy.

In Crashaw's spiritual life, books were channels of grace as much as prayer. Teresa's life came to him in a book, and it was another, the Book of Common Prayer, that inspired an ode that stands among his finer works as the record of the progress of a soul towards divine illumination. Addressed, like most of his poems of spiritual advice, to a woman (the unknown Mrs M. R.) the ode moves through a series of unremarkable similes of a military nature, then in a sudden change of tone (which often accompanies Crashaw's shifts to the confession of personal experience) describes the figure of Christ as the lover of souls advancing through the prayer book – the pages grow luminous and transparent, and phenomena unknown to the average Anglican reader of the Book of Common Prayer occur:

> Amorous Languishments, Luminous trances,
>   Sights which are not seen with eyes,
> Spirituall and soule peircing glances.
>   Whose pure and subtle lightning, flies

Home to the heart and setts the house on fire;
And melts it downe in sweet desire:
Yet doth not stay
To aske the windowes leave, to passe that way.

Delicious deaths, soft exhalations
Of soule; deare, and divine annihilations.
A thousand unknowne rites
Of joyes and rarifyed delights.

Crashaw specifically counsels an unrestrained love for Christ as against any human engagement of the affections. Human love is seen as a potential danger to salvation, but

O happy and thrice happy shee
. . .
Whose early Love
With winged vowes,
Makes haste to meet her morning spowse:
And close with his immortall kisses.
. . .
And every day,
Seize her sweet prey;
All fresh and fragrant as hee rises,
Dropping with a balmy showre
A delicious dew of spices.

The Christian lover's day outranks a dull sublunary lover's life in amorous delights because the former is enveloped in an infinity of love.

Happy soule shee shall discover,
. . .
How many heavens at once it is,
To have a God become her lover.

In the 1640s Crashaw's own life, so long led in the privileged shelter of the Cambridge colleges, was disrupted by the arrival of the Parliamentary Commissioners, rooting out the Laudians. He was dispossessed of his fellowship in 1644. Aware of their coming, he had already gone abroad to Leyden, and now began a time of wandering, common to many victims of the Civil War, which continued until his death. He came back to England, and seems to have attached himself to the Court at Oxford, and then to have gone into exile with the Queen to Paris in 1645. Some time in this year he converted to the Roman faith, impelled one would assume by the ruin of the Church of England, and the impossibility of finding any other setting for his devotional ardour which was his essential life. It is very likely the execution of Archbishop Laud in 1645 was the critical moment for Crashaw. In September 1646 Queen Henrietta Maria wrote to the Pope requesting an occupation for Crashaw at Rome; after much delay he was taken into the suite of one of the Cardinals, and finally nominated to a post of canon at the Cathedral of the Santa Casa at Loreto. This was a wonderfully apt appointment, for the Santa Casa was believed to be the house where Mary had been born and where she had received the Annunciation. Transported by angels from the Holy Land in the thirteenth century, it had been piloted by stages to Loreto, where it became one of the great shrines of Christendom. In this aura of the miraculous, amid the memory of angels and the veneration of the Virgin, Crashaw lived out the brief remainder of his life, until August 1649. He appears to have died of spiritual over-exertion, the 'holy ardor of his soul overheating his body',[8] rather after the fashion of the nightingale in 'Musicks Duell'.

His last volume, *Carmen Deo Nostro*, was published posthumously in Paris in 1652, seen through the press by his friend Thomas Car, an expatriate Catholic priest, to whom Crashaw had presumably entrusted the poems before he went to Italy. *Carmen Deo Nostro* offers a selection of poems from the 1646 and 1648 editions, some of them revised, but the character of the new book is more intensely devout than the earlier volumes, partly through the exclusion of all secular poems. The title means 'A song for our Lord', and the collection is dominated by a series of hymns and meditations on the life of Christ, the mystery of his incarnation and death, the power of the sacraments and the expectation of the Last Judgement, which Crashaw confidently foresees as a man who has no fear of death, only a certainty of finally meeting Christ as 'my Judge, my Friend'. The volume is dedicated to Susan, Countess of Denbigh, who must have been Crashaw's patron in his last years, and who was now in exile in Paris at the Queen's Court. She was the sister of the Duke of Buckingham, and as her brother had been the favourite of King Charles, so she exercised a considerable influence with Queen Henrietta Maria, being her close companion and First Lady of the Bedchamber. Her husband the Earl of Denbigh had died fighting in the King's service in 1643. Crashaw was probably introduced to her by John Cosin, her spiritual adviser, who had dedicated his *Private Devotions* to her in 1627. Cosin's presence and advice had succeeded in maintaining the Countess in the Anglican faith, a considerable achievement in view of the

Queen's firm attachment to the Roman Church: in Court circles there was always a discreet struggle to secure the souls of the great courtiers for one of the rival faiths, for when such eminences converted, a train of dependent spirits would be sure to follow. When Crashaw himself turned Catholic, he tried to win over his patron as well, addressing to her the memorable verse letter that opens *Carmen Deo Nostro*, 'Perswading her to Resolution in Religion, & to render her selfe without further delay into the Communion of the Catholick Church.'

This poem is not in fact notable for its Catholic arguments, for Crashaw was no great debater or reasoner in verse; instead, it speaks to the affections, urging the heart to yield to the entreaties of the divine lover, Christ. Indeed, so little doctrinal content is discernible that an extended version was reprinted the next year, 1653, in London, now entitled, 'A Letter Against Irresolution and Delay in matters of Religion'. The existence of this reprint suggests that the poem was regarded as a universally valuable exhortation to lukewarm souls to seek for grace; it also offers an interesting indication of the tolerant climate of Commonwealth England, in that a poem by a known Catholic could be published and freely circulated. The various merits of the two versions may be long contested; the latter unfolds more spaciously, and brings more illustration to persuade, while the former has a greater urgency against delay and a more pressing sense of Christ's love that must be answered. The earlier version gains strength from the curious little emblem that Crashaw drew to preface the poem, showing a hinged heart closed by a combination lock, with the motto 'Non vi' – 'Not by Force' (Plate 6). The lock displays a sequence of letters that must represent the successful combination for opening the heart: RCDMAVI. These letters presumably stand for 'Ricardus Crashaw Deum Amavi': 'Richard Crashaw: I have loved God', a testimony of his own spiritual experience that he now proposes to share with the Countess. This ingenuous confession of faith should alert us to recognize that Crashaw here is writing from the fullness of his own knowledge: he is offering spiritual counsel on a matter of vital significance to any Christian, the urgent need of reciprocating Christ's love for the soul. That experience of this nature should be communicated by means of a verse epistle points up once more the versatile uses of poetry in the seventeenth century. Differences of rank between the poet and the Countess fall away, to be replaced with a relationship between spiritual guide and hesitant disciple.

The poem belongs to a well-established emblem tradition, that of the 'School of the Heart', popular throughout Europe since the 1570s,

NON VI.

'Tis not the work of force but skill
To find the way into man's will.
'Tis loue alone can hearts vnlock.
Who knowes the WORD, *he needs not knock.*

Plate 6 Prefatory emblem to the 'Letter to the Countess of Denbigh'

and represented most prolifically in England by Francis Quarles and Christopher Harvey.[9] A product of the Jesuit cult of the sacred heart, this line of emblems describes the spiritual history of the human heart in its transactions with divine love or in its struggle with sin, all rendered into visual images and explicated by means of a short poem. This Counter-Reformation genre provided the descriptive psychology of the heart for an age accustomed to thinking in images. Donne's sonnet 'Batter my heart', Herbert's 'The Altar' and Crashaw's own poems, 'The Flaming Heart' and 'The Weeper' all belong in their different ways to this same tradition.

Crashaw's verse letter begins with a simple if faintly bizarre image, characteristic of the emblem genre, of the heart resisting the entreaties of heavenly love, unable to make the decisive act of commitment to a full religious life:

> What heav'n-intreated Heart is This?
> Stands trembling at the gate of blisse;
> Holds fast the door, yet dares not venture
> Fairly to open it, and enter.

The function of the poem is to move the affections to a joyful yielding, and as part of his strategy Crashaw discloses that he too has been acquainted with the phases of indecision and timidity in matters of faith, so he is able feelingly to describe that region of wavering uncertainty in which he fears the Countess now wanders. He knows also the dangers of delay and the mysterious inability of the soul to surrender itself to Christ. Writing in the shorthand of the emblem tradition, he tactfully chides the Countess for her lack of resolution, alerting her to the dangers ahead, rising to a memorable image of the spiritual ice that imperceptibly freezes the soul:

> Ah linger not, lov'd soul! a slow
> And late consent was a long no,
> . . .
> What fatall, yet fantastick, bands
> Keep The free Heart from it's own hands!
> So when the year takes cold, we see
> Poor waters their owne prisoners be.
> Fetter'd, & lockt up fast they ly
> In a sad self-captivity.
> The'astonisht nymphs their flood's strange fate deplore,
> To see themselves their own severer shore.

The final couplet that so condenses the process of freezing and infuses it with the conscious dismay at the limitation of freedom is a marvel of imaginative expression and ingenuity. To liberate the Countess's soul, Crashaw offers a prayer to the divine power that must conquer her and so remove her from the region of mutability to the fixed sphere of heaven: 'Allmighty Love! end this long warr, / And of a meteor make a starr.' Then he turns again to the Countess, pleading with her to respond to the shafts of love that fall incessantly on her heart, in language which recalls both the 'Hymn to St. Teresa' and the 'Ode on the Prayer Book'.

Meet his well-meaning Wounds, wise heart!
And hast to drink the wholsome dart.
That healing shaft, which heavn till now
Hath in love's quiver hid for you.
O Dart of love! arrow of light!
O happy you, if it hitt right,
It must not fall in vain, it must
Not mark the dry regardles dust.
Fair one, it is your fate; and brings
AEternall worlds upon it's wings.
Meet it with wide-spread armes; & see
It's seat your soul's iust center be.

The rapturous experience of these lines – and it must be accounted experience even though it is conveyed with such artifice – is vital to the success of the poem; for here is the assurance from Crashaw's own knowledge. The paradoxes of the spiritual life are tumbled out: the wounds that give life, the dart of love that refreshes the soul, the shaft that heals, the mysterious heavenly lover whose embrace annihilates the world yet reveals eternity, these are truths to the mystic and the saint, but mere confused images to outsiders. After such assurances, delay is wilfully perverse: therefore, 'Yield quickly. Lest perhaps you prove / Death's prey, before the prize of love.'[10]

Even before the poem began, the remedy for the Countess's plight was known, for the verses to the prefatory emblem proclaim ''Tis love alone can hearts unlock. / Who knowes the Word, he needs not knock.' The Word for all who seek salvation in the true faith is Jesus, the synonym of Love, and the magic of the divine name forms the subject of the long ecstatic meditation that follows the Letter to the Countess of Denbigh, the Hymn 'To the Name of Jesus', in which name

A Thousand Blest Arabias dwell;
. . .
And ten Thousand Paradises
The soul that tasts thee takes from thence.
How many unknown Worlds there are
Of Comforts, which Thou hast in keeping!
How many Thousand Mercyes there
In Pitty's soft lap ly a sleeping!
Happy he who has the art
    To awake them,
    And to take them
Home, & lodge them in his Heart.

Clearly for Crashaw love is the element in which he lives; its omnipresence explains the confidence of his poetry, powers his happiness and delight, and accounts for the absence of sinful convictions and spiritual conflict, thus distinguishing him among the major religious poets of the century.

It is usual to describe Crashaw as a poet of the baroque. Crashaw's baroque, however, is not a matter of architectural or pictorial analogies, but it depends on the exploitation of the same subjects that gave rise to the new dynamic style in the visual arts on the continent. The baroque style was above all the medium for expressing the spirit of the Counter-Reformation in the arts. In reaction to the growth of Protestant doctrines and simpler, more austere forms of worship, the Church of Rome intensified the appeal of religion to the senses, stimulating human faculties to a sensational awareness of the divine presence that permeates the world, and insisting on the miraculous phenomena of religion to astonish the soul into transcendent states where faith finds certainties beyond the reach of reason. The Church proclaimed a new age of saints and heroes, it celebrated the martyrs dying for the faith in foreign lands who had rekindled the zeal of the early Church under persecution, it glorified the spiritual adventurers who were finding new ways to heaven by their meditative practices and their lives of utter piety. The mystery of the sacraments was enhanced by their presentation in settings of dazzling splendour, beneath ornate and gilded canopies, before golden sunbursts scattering cherubim. Painting, sculpture and architecture combined to create theatrical scenarios where the delighted spirit could revel in an atmosphere of wonder. The rhythmic vitality of baroque architecture buoys the worshipper into illimitable *trompe l'oeil* vaults where the saints and martyrs swirl and jostle in the cherub-crowded air. The tumultuous marble of baroque sculpture heaves with all the force of pent-up spirit demanding release from the flesh, or glistens with a sleek vitality. Baroque paintings of the death of martyrs crush us with the magnitude of their sufferings, exalt us with the meaning of their sacrifice. All is energy and aspiring movement, rapture of pain and spiritual joy, all advancing towards the sacred mystery of the divine name whose cryptogram gleams in the empyrean of so many Jesuit churches. It was above all the Jesuits who promoted the new arts, who developed the powerful new disciplines of meditation, and who fostered the spiritual heroes. The movement that they led was by far the richest and most creative development in the religious life of the age, and, as we have seen, many Protestants ventured into the new spiritual perspectives opened up by the Counter-Reformation. Crashaw was among the foremost. His temperament and his religious needs must have driven him forward, and in responding unrestrainedly to the new modes of worship he assimilated the extravagant new style that gave them such dramatic expression. Most of his subject matter belongs to the Counter-Reformation ethos: Mary Magdalene and the cult of tears, St Teresa and the ecstasies of divine love, the preoccupation with saints and martyrs and the mystery of the Holy Blood and the sacraments, the adoration of the Holy Name. The high artifice of his style, the emblematic habit of mind, also derive from the same source. His characteristic religious states, a confident wondering delight at the spiritual treasures prodigally offered by Christ to his saints and followers, and a rapturous awareness of divine love, are achieved under inspiration from continental guides to meditation. The Counter-Reformation therefore made possible the distinctive character of Crashaw's worship and art, even though he exercised both in the setting of the Laudian Church for most of his life. The result of these exceptional circumstances is that rarest of phenomena, an English baroque poet.

His lifelong integrity was remembered in the elegy for Crashaw by his friend Abraham Cowley, who had exchanged poems with him back in his Cambridge days: 'Poet and Saint! to thee alone are given / The two most sacred Names of Earth and Heav'n.' He praises Crashaw for having retrieved poetry to devotional uses in an age overmuch given to the idolatrous poetry of carnal love, then speaks of the perfect piety of his life which places him far beyond doctrinal criticism. Cowley writes as an Anglican reflecting on his friend's late apostasy to Catholicism:

Pardon, my Mother Church, if I consent
That Angels led him when from thee he went,
For even in Error sure no Danger is
When joyn'd with so much Piety as His.

. . .

His Faith perhaps in some nice Tenents might
Be wrong; his Life, I'm sure, was in the right.
And I my self a Catholick will be,
So far at least, great Saint, to Pray to thee.

Such appreciation of Crashaw's holy life does much to explain the esteem in which his poetry was held in the seventeenth century, when for all the rancour that religion generated in public life, there were still many men who recognized true saintliness wherever it appeared, and found in Crashaw a rare 'Exalted Man'. Crashaw's Catholic friend in Paris, Thomas Car, also remembered him in similar terms, as an austere man entirely given 'to heavenly exercise', whose 'onely part / Is God and godly thoughts', and who through continual devotion had 'Wholly called / His thoughts from earth, to live above in th'aire / A very Bird of Paradise.'

Notes

1 For a discussion of the background of the Epigrams, see Ruth C. Wallerstein, *Richard Crashaw* (Madison, Wisconsin 1935), pp. 56–72.

2 At least ten other translations of Strada's poem into English exist, so Crashaw's attraction cannot be considered eccentric; but the florid splendours of his translation are nowhere paralleled in other versions.

3 From a memoir (1668) by D. Lloyd, quoted in *The Poems of Richard Crashaw*, ed. L. C. Martin (Oxford 1957), p. 416.

4 The chief biographical documents for Crashaw's life are conveniently gathered together in Martin's edition of the poems, pp. 415–24.

5 Of all poems in the 1646 edition, only one, 'On the Assumption', could be considered as standing outside the pale of Anglican doctrine. Yet it has been pointed out that in the spacious atmosphere of the Laudian Church, even this doctrine, of the assumption into heaven of the Virgin at her death, was finding acceptance. The publication of Anthony Strafford's *The Femall*

Glorie in 1635, with the approval of Laud, marked the change to a much warmer climate of acceptance for the Virgin Mary in the Church of England. She was still not accorded powers of intercession, nor should she be an exclusive object of worship, but much of her old pre-eminence was restored to her.

6 See Austin Warren, *Richard Crashaw* (Ann Arbor, Michigan 1939), p. 128; S. Manning, 'The Spiritual Meaning of "The Weeper" ', *ELH* 22 (1955), pp. 34–47. Also G. W. Williams's edition of the *Complete Poetry of Richard Crashaw* (New York 1972), pp. 120–1.

7 Mario Praz has written extremely well of the vogue for this witty manner in Europe and its effect on Crashaw in 'Crashaw and the Baroque', in *The Flaming Heart* (London 1958). Louis Martz's *Poetry of Meditation* (New Haven 1954), traces the process of transition from Jesuit writers to English poets in what has become the classic study of these influences.

8 Warren, *Richard Crashaw*, p. 60, citing Lloyd.

9 See Rosemary Freeman, *English Emblem Books* (London 1948), for a detailed account of the genre.

10 The Countess of Denbigh did ultimately enter the Roman Church in 1651, but unfortunately too late to give satisfaction to Crashaw, who had died in 1649.

7 Robert Herrick and the ceremonies of innocence

Robert Herrick made his bid for poetic immortality with a single volume of poems, *Hesperides*, published in 1648. For a poet who wrote much about the auspicious moments of life, the timing of the volume was singularly unfortunate, falling in that tense period between the Civil Wars and the trial and execution of King Charles. The strong royalist sympathies of the verse were hardly in accord with the time, and the evocation of a world of ceremony and ritual was inappropriate to the present mood of Puritan victory. The title *Hesperides* must have sounded ironic to a nation that had just experienced several years of civil war, and in addition the sheer number of the poems – nearly 1400, with no principle of organization – ensured that the fruit of the collection was copiously shaded with leaves.

These unfavourable circumstances were not untypical of Herrick's life at large. Apprenticeship as a goldsmith, then training as a lawyer had both proved false starts; after he finally took orders in 1623 he managed to gain a place in the Duke of Buckingham's household, served as a chaplain on the expedition to the Isle de Rhé, that disastrous attempt to relieve the besieged French Protestants of La Rochelle in 1627, then had his prospects ruined by the assassination of his patron in 1628. Although a man of great conviviality who delighted in the society of literary wits, and regarded the circle of poets around Ben Jonson as the rose of paradise itself, he was dispatched to a living in remotest Devonshire and spent the greater part of his life in that rural exile. Dispossessed on account of his royalism in 1647, he came to London where he presumably saw his poems through the press, lived through the Commonwealth on the goodwill of relatives, and at the Restoration was reappointed to his living at Dean Prior, where he remained until his death in 1674. Such was the unsatisfactory shape of his career, yet one suspects that the vital impulses of Herrick's life were given to the creation of an imaginary golden world where experience and conduct were conditioned by the precedents of the Roman poets. The very name *Hesperides* indicates the nature of Herrick's design: it alludes to the paradisal garden of classical mythology, set in the west of the world, where the golden apples sacred to Juno grew. The western setting may be a humorous reference to the poet's long residence in Devonshire, where much of his verse was written, but essentially Herrick wishes to suggest that the collection as a whole is a poetic garden, with the individual poems as the golden apples that will grow for ever. The frontispiece, as usual, provides some additional visual information about how the reader should approach the work (Plate 7). We see the mythological landscape of the world of poetry, with Pegasus, the winged horse of the Muses, taking flight from Mount Helicon, from which the fountain of Hippocrene, or poetic inspiration, flows. Nine cherubic figures, who presumably represent the Muses, cavort in this pastoral scene, two of them bearing wreaths to garland the bust of the poet. This bust, which is the most striking feature of the page, presents an insensitive-looking man, a vigorous, beefy figure with a mass of short curled hair and a military moustache, utterly at odds with the mythological fantasies that surround him. However, this robust image projects something of the strength and freshness that we shall find in the poetry, which may seem precious and exceptionally artificial at first, yet on acquaintance proves to have great firmness and power. We notice that Herrick chooses to be portrayed in Roman dress, for a toga frames his bust, and the bust itself stands on a classical altar. Even his unusual hairstyle may be a classical allusion, referring to the crisped and oiled hair that some Roman poets, especially Martial, affected. The image of the poet here may illustrate the third stanza of 'To live merrily, and to trust to good verses', a poem that expresses Herrick's sense of affinity with the ancient writers:

> Now raignes the Rose, and now
> Th'Arabian Dew besmears
> My uncontrolled brow,
> And my retorted haires.

We can see the roses 'raining' in the sky around the poet, for the engraver has invented a visual pun of a kind that contemporary taste enjoyed. The Latin verses of the inscription explain the two wreaths of the picture, one of laurel for poetic genius, the other of olive for a poet of peace, and acclaim Herrick for his achievement: '*Admisces Antiqua Novis, Iucunda severis*' ('You mingle ancient things with new, grave matters with gay').

More than any other of his contemporaries except Jonson, Herrick regarded himself as a poet in the absolute sense. For most seventeenth-century writers, poetry was ancillary to some vocation or role, as clergyman, mystic, masque-writer or dramatist, social observer or wit – even Milton used poetry primarily as an expression of Christian prophecy or philosophical reflection. Herrick, however, presents himself as a poet whose experience is largely conditioned by a knowledge of classical poetry, and who is prepared to treat his own life and that of his friends, and their society, as if all existed to be turned into song and celebrated in the timeless manner of antiquity. Life is not real for Herrick until it has been assimilated into the artifice of poetry, and for him the consummate fictions had been perfected by the poets of the Augustan age: Horace, Catullus, Tibullus, Ovid, Propertius and the later Martial. Herrick endeavours to shape and ennoble the life of his times by associating it with Roman life as selectively represented by the ancient poets. Hence the constant enactment of rituals in Herrick's verse, the preoccupation with ceremonies, the love of formalized behaviour and the careful evocation of classicized landscapes, because all these devices emphasize the affinity between the societies of Augustan Rome and Stuart England, imaginatively perceived, and they show off the poet's faculty for dignifying life by giving order to high moments of human experience: love, marriage, worship, feasting, death. Although the subject matter of Herrick's poetry comes from seventeenth-century England, he excludes virtually all contemporary detail, so that one is left with a sense of the seamless continuity of ancient and modern culture when seen in the light of the poetic imagination. Occasionally a detail of costume or a game is mentioned that betrays the seventeenth century, but for the most part Herrick refers only to the enduring features of human and natural description so that one is rarely conscious of the modern world. This impression remains true even of the epigrams scattered throughout the collection, which being satirical ought to have a strong flavour of contemporary realism, yet manage to remain unlocalized in time and place while delivering a pungent judgement on characters. These harsh epigrams remind the reader that even when the poet sees his society in terms of an antique model, it still contains a large number of unsavoury figures. To classicize does not require the exclusion of what is gross and vulgar: it involves treating such subjects in conformity with ancient models of satire. Ben Jonson had originated this romanization of English life through poetry, asserting thereby his belief that Stuart England could attain a classical level of civilization, and Herrick had been thoroughly conditioned by

Plate 7 The frontispiece of *Hesperides*, published in 1648

that example when he mixed with Jonson's circle in the 1620s. Jonson habitually modelled his role as a social poet on Horace or Martial, yet he never classicized his position to the degree that Herrick did. The consequence of Herrick's practice is that many readers feel his poetry is lacking in vital experience, generated out of engagement with living emotions and issues, or that it is too precious, too decorous and too formal. Enjoyment of Herrick depends on an acceptance of the classical conventions of his art, and a recognition that these conventions can contain a beautifully ordered expression of the pleasures and disciplines of the good life as understood by the social poets of antiquity.

We can form a helpful impression of Herrick's sense of his place in the classical tradition from the poem already mentioned, 'To live merrily, and to trust to good verses' (H–201),[1] which is something of a poetic credo and shows to advantage his easy way of mixing Latin reminiscences with English verse. The phrase 'trust to good verses' echoes the '*Carminibus confide bonus*' of Ovid's elegy on the poet Tibullus (*Amores* III.9), a poem that exerts a significant influence over Herrick. In Ovid, the phrase is immediately followed by the reflection that good verses cannot save one from the grave, for here lies Tibullus dead. Herrick seizes on the optimistic tenor of the words before Ovid's irony has soured them, and uses them to set the mood for a euphoric drinking song that is itself an inheritance from the Greek poet Anacreon. The opening stanza:

> Now is the time for mirth,
> Nor cheek, or tongue be dumbe:
> For with the flowrie earth,
> The golden pomp is come

begins with an echo of Horace's festive ode '*Nunc est bibendum*' (*Odes* I.37) ('Now is the time for drinking'), and closes with a phrase translated from Ovid's *Amores*, '*aurea pompa venit*' ('the golden pomp is come'). In Ovid's poem the words refer to the splendour of a procession in the circus, but Herrick changes the function of the phrase from straightforward description into a grand haunting metaphor: the pomp now is that of the fertile earth and of the fulness of life. The richness of the time is caught in the line from Martial, 'Now raignes the Rose' ('*nunc regnat rosa*'), that introduces the self-portrait of Herrick as Roman poet that we have already looked at. The Arabian dew (myrrh) lavished on the poet's hair is another touch from Ovid, this time from the *Heroides*. We become aware that Herrick's memory is full of myriads of classical phrases in suspension, that crystallize into English at a thought. He very rarely translates a whole poem from the Latin, but his verse is charged with verbal echoes from that ancient world of which he was a naturalized citizen, and very often the context in which he reuses an image or a phrase is richer than the original in which it first appears. Allusion confers complexity, learning and pleasure.

The introduction over, Herrick proceeds to the business of the poem: the drinking of toasts to the great poets he admires. These as one would expect are entirely classical – Virgil, Ovid, Catullus – all Roman except Homer, and the toasts grow more copious and intoxicating until he attains to a divine frenzy, yet there follows no loss of metrical control or neatness of wit. The poem develops a stamping rhythm, full of whirling delight which rapturously increases his joy in those old poets who have given his life its golden hours:

> Round, round, the roof do's run;
>   And being ravisht thus,
> Come, I will drink a Tun
>   To my Propertius.

Tibullus's turn comes next, and at the mention of his name the memory of Ovid's elegy surfaces and the shadow of death falls across the poem, the death not merely of Tibullus, but of all poets, including Herrick. He now paraphrases an elegiac line of Ovid into an epitaph which in its concern for neatness and smallness is quintessentially Herrick: '*Jacet ecce Tibullus. Vix manet e tanto parva quod urna capit.*'

> Behold, Tibullus lies
>   Here burnt, whose smal return
> Of ashes, scarce suffice
>   To fill a little Urne.

Death takes the poet, then, but the poetry lives on; Herrick returns to the sentiment of the title, a sentiment that Ovid had despondently regarded as a futile preservative against death, and optimistically asserts that familiar theme of the perdurable nature of poetry:

> Trust to good Verses then;
>   They onely will aspire,
> When Pyramids, as men,
>   Are lost, i'th'funerall fire.

Poetry will last as long as there are men to read it, and even at the destruction of the world will 'aspire', or fly up to the heavens, for good verses are themselves a kind of virtue, welcome to the gods. The poetry that outlasts pyramids is an allusion to Horace (III.30) (the ode that has the famous phrase '*non omnis moriar*' ('I shall not wholly die'), which may be evoked in an act of secondary recollection by Herrick's reference) and the allusion falls aptly, for Horace was the most eloquent of the Roman poets who were convinced of the triumph of poetry over death. Herrick concludes on a note of assurance that the life dedicated to the creation of good verse is the summit of felicity and secures a certain kind of immortality:

> And when all Bodies meet
> In Lethe to be drown'd;
> Then onely Numbers sweet,
> With endless life are crown'd.

The whole poem propels itself by impulses from Roman authors, and gains a particular force from its submerged interaction with Ovid's elegy for Tibullus. Classical sentiment and classical knowledge permeate the poem and help define Herrick's place in a tradition, and his special values as a poet, yet no one would deny its self-sufficiency as an English poem for its beauty, verve and wit are completely persuasive.

It may seem strange that in a poem about his tutelary gods Herrick does not mention Horace, the closest of his literary ancestors. The Horatian mode of life with its mixture of stoicism and gaiety, gravity and wit, was immensely congenial to Herrick and there are more borrowings from Horace than from any other source in *Hesperides*. One might argue that in 'Trust to good verses' Herrick, romanized and inspired, has become imaginatively transformed into Horace. A poem that opens with a recollection of a Horatian ode and closes with a Horatian sentiment is presumably being sung by a persona of Horace, and part of the function of this poem may be to reveal Herrick's sense of his own poetic character.[2]

This identification can be confirmed in some measure by turning to a lengthy poem of Herrick's which is an imitation of a Horation ode (although considerably enlarged from the original): 'His age, dedicated to his peculiar friend, Master John Wickes, under the name of Posthumus' (H–336). This is based on the 14th Ode of the Second Book, where Horace marvellously evokes for his friend Posthumus the insidious passing of the years and the inevitability of death, made tolerable only by the pleasures of friendship. If Weekes is Posthumus, then Herrick by analogy must be Horace. Capturing the mood of pleasurable regret for the fading of life and stoical acceptance of an implacable fate, Herrick guides his large thoughts through the complicated stanza form that he has constructed as the English equivalent of an ode:

> W'ave seen the past-best Times, and these
> Will nere return, we see the Seas,
>   And Moons to wain;
> But they fill up their Ebbs again:
>   But vanisht man,
> Like to a Lilly-lost, nere can,
> Nere can repullulate, or bring
> His dayes to see a second Spring.

As in so many seventeenth-century poems, the elaborate structure that the thought has to negotiate is a deliberate, self-imposed challenge, and the impression of ease in overcoming it is an act of wit. The pauses enforced by this scheme contribute a significant colouring to the piece, as does the melancholy repetition in this stanza of 'nere can, nere can', while the placing of that exotic Latinism 'repullulate' (to grow again) on the crest of the metrical movement of the line is a typical specimen of Herrickian bravura. He takes a jeweller's delight in setting splendid polysyllabic words in a foil of plain English so that their brilliance shines all the brighter.[3] The fiction of Herrick and Weekes as two cultivated Romans is maintained, and the flow of Horatian sentiments keeps in touch with the original, but where Horace ends his ode with a disparaging preview of the thoughtless heir draining the wines that Posthumus has so carefully preserved, Herrick diverges into territory untouched by Horace as he foresees his old age redeemed by the reading of his verses written in youth. Those verses contain the spirit of his youth distilled into poetry and preserved there, so they may serve to reinvigorate his old age, and confirm that the chief value of his life has been the creation of poetry, an art which is not simply the capturing of fine moments in fine language but the concoction of an elixir whose virtue improves with age. The long dead Horace has contributed pleasure and knowledge to the mature years of Herrick and Weekes, and enabled them to develop a profitable attitude towards growing old; the youthful poetry of Herrick also gives delight and dignity to his aged self, and it will, he hopes, survive to gratify future generations in the same way that

Horace's art has done. Truly, 'No lust there's like to Poetry', and since

> We must be made
> Ere long, a song, ere long, a shade.
> Why then, since life to us is short,
> Lets make it full up, by our sport.

As one might expect of a man deeply affected by Horace, a cult of friendship lies at the centre of his life. Like Horace, Herrick was unmarried, devoted to the art of poetry and the moderated pleasures of the good life. The friendship of like-minded spirits provided the emotional mainstay for this style of living, so predictably we find that with Herrick, as with his master Ben Jonson, who was similarly placed, verse epistles to his close friends form an important group of poems in which the virtues of sociability and self-sufficiency are praised and the shared values of Herrick's circle expounded and confirmed. This is one of the standard social functions of poetry, and the fact that the values in question were largely conventional, derived from the Augustan poets of Rome, does not render them any less real, for educated men in civilized times to draw their values from a literary or historic past, and this traditional community of values is what makes the past of continuing relevance to the present.

'The Country Life' addressed to Endymion Porter, 'A Panegerick to Sir Lewis Pemberton', 'The Hock-Cart' to Mildmay Fane, 'A Country life: To his Brother, Master Thomas Herrick' and 'A New-yeares gift sent to Sir Simeon Steward' can be grouped together at the centre of a large body of friendship verse in *Hesperides*. These are fairly lengthy poems, written under the influence of Jonson's epistles to his friends (particularly 'To Sir Robert Wroth') and ultimately descended from the same source in Horace's Epodes and Epistles in praise of rural life. Endymion Porter was a leading courtier at Charles I's Court, and had been a close associate of Buckingham – at which point he might have become friendly with Herrick. He had a reputation as a connoisseur of the arts, and he was a patron of poets and artists on a modest scale. His milieu was definitely the Court (although he did possess a manor house, at Aston in Gloucestershire) so the poem on the delights of country living provides an example of the elegant fictions that Caroline poets wove around themselves and their friends. This poem, based on Horace's second Epode and Virgil's second Georgic, in effect pays tribute to a shared taste in poetry rather than to any notable fondness for rural ways on the part of

Porter. One is convinced that Herrick genuinely relished the country life, for he returns to it often as a subject, and his observations of natural detail and rustic society are vivid and appreciative, whereas one suspects that Porter would soon grow restless if confined to his estates. Nevertheless, Porter as a cultivated gentleman would admire Horace, and that admiration entailed a conventional approval of the superior pleasures of the country over urban life. These shared values, as we noticed before, are vital to the perpetuation of a cultural milieu in which educated men can exchange messages of admiration, congratulation, warning, censure or advice. Herrick's friends include courtiers, clergymen, lawyers, antiquaries, artists and politicians; many of them wrote poetry themselves and they communicated with each other on formal occasions or on slight pretexts across a great network of relationships that had been evolving since the last decade of Elizabeth's reign, when a sufficiently large number of people had been educated in the classics and had discovered the attractions of imaginative writing for a widespread literate culture to be created throughout the country. Dedications, epigrams, verse letters, marriage songs and elegies bound together individuals of various interest groups: acquaintances in Court, college or Church circles, or members of the far-flung kinship groups of the age talked to each other through poetry and consolidated their sense of community, and Jacobean and Caroline England resounded with this engaging chatter. The quality of the poetry was not that important: the gentlemen who flocked to offer their good wishes to a new book of poetry or plays, travel or philosophy, often turned in lamentably poor verses; what mattered was that they were willing to use poetry for the enhancement of intellectual and social life. The Civil War when it came did not disrupt this habit: rather it intensified it, often of course making it more partisan, and gave it an even more animating range of subject matter. Herrick happened to be one of the better players in this national game, but his skills should not conceal the fact that he was but one of a very numerous class whose combined efforts upheld the literary culture of Caroline England.

So, when Herrick commends the country life to Porter, he does so as an act of friendship to a fellow-Horatian: such a poem is part of the common currency of their culture. No matter that he begins by dismissing attendance at Court as oppressive, for doubtless Porter would agree that in the best of worlds the good life would be pastoral, and one function of the poem is the complimentary suggestion that Porter belongs to this ideal dimension. In conventional poems such as this, expectation waits on how the author will give the subject, which is basically predictable, a distinctive colouring in style or emphasis. Here Herrick's characteristic sensibility soon comes into play: his love of small objects sensuously described, as in

> Thou never Plow'st the Oceans foame
> To seek, and bring rough Pepper home:
> Nor to the Eastern Ind dost rove
> To bring from thence the scorched Clove.
> (H–662)

Herrick likes to handle an object rather than work an idea, the smaller the object the better, as if his early training as a goldsmith had given him a permanent delight in miniaturist art. In these lines too the setting of magnitude against minuteness adds a neat touch of wit.

When day breaks,

> now the Cock (the Plow-mans Horne)
> Calls forth the lilly-wristed Morne.

'Lilly-wristed Morne' is typically Herrick. Presumably the adjective is formed by analogy with Homer's 'rosy-fingered dawn', the youthful white flesh of a maiden's wrist being suggestive of the fresh perfection of the day personified, the wrist being singled out because it creates an idea of graceful gesture introducing the idealized country scene. The sensuous immediacy of the cattle is arresting:

> And smell'st the breath of great-ey'd Kine,
> Sweet as the blossomes of the Vine.
> Here thou behold'st thy large sleek Neat
> Unto the Dew-laps up in meat

– much more powerful than Horace's '*mugientium / Prospectat errantes greges*' ('he surveys the herds of his lowing cattle'). To the list of country sports and pleasures in Horace, Herrick adds a specifically English touch:

> Thy Wakes, thy Quintels, here thou hast,
> Thy May-poles too with Garlands grac't:
> Thy Morris-dance; thy Whitsun-ale;
> Thy Sheering-feast, which never faile.
> Thy Harvest home; thy Wassaile bowle,
> That's tost up after Fox i'th'Hole.

Thy Mummeries; thy Twelfe-tide Kings
And Queenes; thy Christmas revellings:
Thy Nut-browne mirth; thy Russet wit;
And no man payes too deare for it.

These entertainments that marked the cycle of the rural year exerted an enduring fascination over Herrick throughout his career.[4] The ritualization of life answered to some deep-seated instinct in him, an instinct that was very likely conditioned by his familiarity with the ceremonious forms of ancient life as transmitted by the poets, and affected also by his desire to impose form and order on to the flux of life. The discipline of poetry was his personal way of controlling life, but he was appreciative too of the customs and observances that regulated the annual movement of his society. There is a beauty equally in order imposed and order percevied. We shall return to this preoccupation with ritual shortly, but here it is sufficient to remark that these country sports and feasts are all part of the Horatian ideal of the happy life where pastimes are harmless and the daily round productive and free from care. Such is the good fortune wished by Herrick to his friend Porter.

One other poem addressed to Porter deserves notice: 'An Eclogue' (H–492), in which Herrick exploits the mythological overtones of his friend's name in a pastoral fancy, casting himself as Lycidas Herrick, the companion of the shepherd Endymion. In the dialogue Lycidas complains of Endymion's fondness for the court, urging him to return to the countryside and its simple pleasures. Endymion agrees to return before long and Lycidas promises he shall be received 'like young Apollo'. It is a slight piece, but once again it shows how social relationships were served by poetry at the time. Pastoral enjoyed a considerable vogue at the Court of King Charles during the 1620s and 1630s. Masques and Court plays were frequently in the pastoral mode, and Queen Henrietta Maria sometimes appeared on stage in pastoral romances. Besides literary charm, pastoral had a political utility, for it lent a benevolent and innocent air to a regime that was becoming increasingly absolutist. Most of the leading courtiers were involved in this agreeable fiction as part-time shepherds, so Herrick was merely sounding a fashionable note in his Eclogue. He could hardly have expected that Porter would leave his important and remunerative life at Court for rural seclusion, but it is flattering to Porter to suggest that his true self is all simple, blameless goodness; then the real aim of the poem emerges in the final lines:

> And my most luckie Swain, when I shall live to see
> Endimions Moon to fill up full, remember me.

The feigned equality of shepherdhood drops away, and we discern the old relationship between poet and patron, the age-old need of the poet for help and influence in high places.

The poem to his brother Thomas Herrick on the virtue of the country life (H–106) has many similarities with that addressed to Endymion Porter, using the same model from Horace, but it is remarkable in Herrick's work for its seriousness of tone and its ethical gravity. This philosophical mood is probably the result of its closeness to Jonson's moral epistles: the tone is virtually indistinguishable from that of Jonson's 'Penshurst' or 'To Sir Robert Wroth':

> Thrice, and above, blest (my soules halfe) art thou,
> In thy both Last, and Better Vow:
> Could'st leave the City, for exchange, to see
> The Countries sweet simplicity:
> And it to know, and practice; with intent
> To grow the sooner innocent:
> By studying to know vertue; and to aime
> More at her nature, then her name:
> The last is but the least; the first doth tell
> Wayes lesse to live, then to live well.

The slow movement, the air of reflection and moral approval, the plain language, are all pure Jonson, and we imagine that this is one of Herrick's earlier performances and an example of Jonson's influence over the younger generation of poets. We know that Herrick's brother did actually leave a commercial life in London to settle in the country, so for once the literary ideal has been realized: this fact may help to explain the resonant conviction of the conclusion and the sharply realized detail of the poem. Given its model, the poem has to negotiate between a Roman ideal and an English practice, and it does so with assurance. Thomas Herrick begins the day in a spirit of primitive piety:

> but with the Dawne dost rise
> To work, but first to sacrifice;
> Making thy peace with heav'n, for some late fault,
> With Holy-meale, and spirting-salt.

His attitude towards life is one of stoical equanimity:

> But thou liv'st fearlesse; and thy face ne'r shewes
> Fortune when she comes, or goes.
> But with thy equall thoughts, prepar'd dost stand,
> To take her by the either hand:
> Nor car'st which comes the first, the foule or faire;
> A wise man ev'ry way lies square.
> And like a surly Oke with storms perplext;
> Growes still the stronger, strongly vext.
> Be so, bold spirit; Stand Center-like, unmov'd.

His simple fare, 'To taste boyl'd Nettles, Colworts, Beets', is undoubtedly English provincial cooking. And yet, over the actions of his just life a classical spirit, the good Genius, exerts a kindly influence.

Occasionally the sober manner of Jonson gives way to what we recognize as the personal style of Herrick – buoyant, smiling and pert, full of sharp detail and wit – and we feel we are watching the emergence of the younger poet from the stylistic confines of the elder:

> Yet can thy humble roofe maintaine a Quire
> Of singing Crickits by thy fire:
> And the brisk Mouse may feast her selfe with crums,
> Till that the green-ey'd Kitling comes.
> Then to her Cabbin, blest she can escape
> The sudden danger of a Rape.

There is a vivacity and an immediacy about that description that stand out in the serious sententious mood of the poem as a whole. Otherwise, one may say that Herrick has thoroughly assimilated the Jonsonian manner of writing a moral poem, and what he has learnt will be of permanent value to him: the setting of an English life in a Roman context, the well-disguised reference to classical poems to give depth to a contemporary theme, the play of judgement on a subject in such a way as to make the poet an arbiter of morals, the whole management of a social poem, in fact.

The 'Panegerick to Sir Lewis Pemberton' (H–377) shows how well Herrick could adapt Jonson's techniques to honour his own friends. The themes are familiar ones in Stuart literature: praise of hospitality as an expression of magnanimity and praise for the well-ordered country house whose lord is generous, honourable and just. Full of fine phrasing as it is, the poem is perhaps too deeply indebted to 'Penshurst', even to the extent of leaning on the same epigram by Martial for its contrasting scene of niggardly entertainment, for it to achieve any admirable independence. Where Herrick's own poetic character does shine out full in a social poem is 'The Hock-cart, or Harvest home' (H–250), dedicated to his friend Mildmay Fane, the Earl of Westmorland. It celebrates the fertility of the soil and the rustic festivities that accompany the bringing in of the last cart-load of the harvest. What seems now an item of folklore was then the high point of the rural year, and Herrick captures the triumph, the noise and the feasting marvellously well in his deft, fast-moving verse.

> Come Sons of Summer, by whose toile,
> We are the Lords of Wine and Oile:
> By whose tough labours, and rough hands,
> We rip up first, then reap our lands.
> Crown'd with the eares of corne, now come,
> And, to the Pipe, sing Harvest home.
> . . .
> Some blesse the Cart; some kisse the sheaves;
> Some prank them up with Oaken leaves:
> Some crosse the Fill-horse; some with great
> Devotion, stroak the home-borne wheat:
> . . .
> Well, on, brave boyes, to your Lords Hearth,
> Glitt'ring with fire; where, for your mirth,
> Ye shall see first the large and cheefe
> Foundation of your Feast, Fat Beefe:
> With Upper Stories, Mutton, Veale
> And Bacon, (which makes full the meale)
> With sev'rall dishes standing by,
> As here a Custard, there a Pie,
> And here all tempting Frumentie.
> And for to make the merry cheere,
> If smirking Wine be wanting here,
> There's that, which drowns all care, stout Beere;
> Which freely drink to your Lords health,
> Then to the Plough, (the Common-wealth)
> Next to your Flailes, your Fanes, your Fatts;
> Then to the Maids with Wheaten Hats:
> To the rough Sickle, and crookt Sythe,
> Drink frollick boyes, till all be blythe.

Beyond the sheer enjoyment of the scene extends an appreciation of the ritual elements that mark the culmination of the year's fertility in a form of thanksgiving to the spirits of the earth. The poem ends with a recognition that these festivities are a moment of sacred time, snatched from the onrush of ordinary, worldly time, and tomorrow the labour begins again:

> And know, besides, ye must revoke
> The patient Oxe unto the Yoke,
> And all goe back unto the Plough
> And Harrow, (though they'r hang'd up now.)
> And, you must know, your Lords word's true,
> Feed him ye must, whose food fils you.
> And that this pleasure is like raine,
> Not sent ye for to drowne your paine,
> But for to make it spring againe.

The interdependence of the natural and the social worlds is neatly comprehended here. There is a fine sense of a society harmoniously related to the earth and to heaven, all bound together in an endless beneficial cycle of giving and receiving, and essential to this cycle is the generous landowner, the recipient of this complimentary poem.

Yet for all its essential Englishness, 'The Hock-cart' again conceals a Roman original. A glance at the opening of the first poem of the Second Book of Tibullus takes us into the same world in classical times:

> All present, keep holy silence; we cleanse the fields and the harvest,
> To re-enact the ceremony our fathers handed down.
> Come Bacchus, and down from your horns let there be dangled
> Sweet grapes, and, Ceres, bind your forehead with ears.
> Let there be rest for the ground this holy morning, rest too for the ploughman;
> Let the hard labour stop, and hang up the share.
> Untie the traces from the yokes: the bullocks must now stand idle
> By full mangers, with garlands on their heads.[5]

There is nothing new under the sun, and poetry merely confirms the continuity of culture.

Many other shorter poems of Herrick involve his friends in similar innocent rituals. It was his particular way of honouring the men he admired and loved, to see them as persons of an antique simplicity, pursuing virtue and the good life in the unchanging ways of the countryside, possessing a fundamental piety towards the forces that influence the natural cycle. 'This White Temple of my Heroes' is how he describes the complex of poems designed to celebrate his friends and patrons, but they are essentially pastoral heroes or rural saints.

Herrick's habit of looking at life as a round of rituals and observances may well have been conditioned by an admiration for Ovid's *Fasti*, a long poem that describes in elaborate detail the many festivals of the Roman calendar, and how they should be celebrated. It is a book that sees the year as a continuous yet varied festival and conveys a pleasing sense of the harmony of mind induced by the regular and proper performance of the rites and sacrifices due to the gods and spirits that have to be propitiated to assure prosperity and success. Herrick, whose cultural aspiration was, as he admitted, 'to grow to be a Roman citizen', surrounded himself with the fictions of classical piety. For example, when he was dispossessed of his living by the Parliamentarians he wrote the following poem of farewell dedicated to the protective genius of his household, or 'Lar' as the Romans termed it:

> No more shall I, since I am driven hence,
> Devote to thee my graines of Frankinsence:
> No more shall I from mantle-trees hang downe,
> To honour thee, my little Parsly crown:
> No more shall I (I feare me) to thee bring
> My chives of Garlick for an offering:
> No more shall I, from henceforth, heare a quire
> Of merry Crickets by my Country fire.
> Go where I will, thou luckie Larr stay here,
> Warme by a glit'ring chimnie all the yeare.

One imagines that Herrick derived a great deal of satisfaction from such gestures, for classical pantheism fills a need which is not fully met by Christianity in that it assures us of what we may instinctively feel, that there is a spirit of place, that the trees, fields, valleys and lakes have their own special character that can be objectified as a *genius loci* or indwelling local spirit; that there are such things as auspicious days, and that these can be encouraged by offerings and respect paid to the relevant powers; that generally there is a multitude of secondary forces that can be propitiated by due acts of reverence. In a Protestant country where the helpful influence of saints over all aspects of life has been denied or suppressed, there may still remain an emotional need for contact with immediate local spirits and with many people this will result in forms of superstition. In Herrick, although he was an Anglican minister, it takes the form of an imaginative pantheism. His poetry abounds in pantheistic sentiment, so much so that one feels that on a certain level it must have contained a genuine emotional truth for him, although that level could be nowhere near the plane of Christian belief. It was a type of serious game. The making of poetry in the seventeenth century was generally an act of artifice and convention, and did not necessarily bear any relation to personal conviction or belief at all, but when we find Herrick so intent on ritualizing his own life and that of his friends with pagan detail, we may be justified in thinking that some part of his imagination was deeply susceptible to the customs of antiquity.[6] With Herrick we are not simply dealing with another aspect of the recreation of Augustan values in England as pioneered by Jonson – though of course his poetry belongs to that endeavour – but we are in the presence of a mind that is instinctively in harmony with ancient beliefs and that has integrated them into a serene outlook on life. Consider, for example, the poem 'To the reverend shade of his religious Father' (H–82):

> That for seven Lusters I did never come
> To doe the Rites to thy Religious Tombe:
> That neither haire was cut, or true teares shed
> By me, o'r thee, (as justments to the dead)
> Forgive, forgive me; since I did not know
> Whether thy bones had here their Rest, or no.
> But now 'tis known, Behold; behold, I bring
> Unto thy Ghost, th'Effused Offering:
> And look, what Smallage, Night-shade, Cypresse, Yew,
> Unto the shades have been, or now are due,
> Here I devote; And something more then so;
> I come to pay a Debt of Birth I owe.
> Thou gav'st me life, (but Mortall;) For that one
> Favour, Ile make full satisfaction;
> For my life mortall, Rise from out thy Herse,
> And take a life immortall from my Verse.[7]

As a poem of regret for neglecting his proper duties as a son, it owes its strength to the specific detailing of the tributes he has failed to make, and their subsequent enactment by means of verse.

That Herrick saw himself as the poet of 'the ceremonies of innocence' is plain from the introductory poem to *Hesperides*:

> I Sing of Brooks, of Blossomes, Birds, and Bowers:
> Of April, May, of June and July-Flowers.

I sing of May-poles, Hock-carts, Wassails, Wakes,
Of Bride-grooms, Brides, and of their Bridall-cakes.
I write of Youth, of Love, and have Accesse
By these, to sing of cleanly-Wantonnesse.
I sing of Dewes, of Raines, and piece by piece
Of Balme, of Oyle, of Spice, and Amber-Greece.
I sing of Times trans-shifting; and I write
How Roses first came Red, and Lillies White.
I write of Groves, of Twilights, and I sing
The Court of Mab, and of the Fairie-King.
I write of Hell; I sing (and ever shall)
Of Heaven, and hope to have it after all.

It is the consciousness of 'Times trans-shifting' that gives a cold edge to the amiable topics that he lists. The phrase, which is unique to Herrick, would appear to draw together ideas of the transience of life, of mutability, of ages returning again, thus linking by means of an ingeniously invented key-word the themes of the inevitability of death and the renewal of a classical age that are so prominent in his poetry. Much of Herrick's best poetry is an attempt to defeat time or to convert its destructiveness to regeneration. One of his most famous pieces, 'Corinna's going a Maying' (H–178) records a memorable assault against time's power. 'Maying' involved the gathering of may blossom in honour of the spring, and was also a traditional occasion for the betrothal of lovers. The poem also alludes to the Roman festival of May-time in honour of the goddess Flora (mentioned in line 17), a festival described in Book V of Ovid's *Fasti*. Since the Corinna of the title was Ovid's mistress, and also the fictional beloved of the seventeenth-century poet, the poem operates in two dimensions of time, classical and modern, the continuity between which exists because of the willingness of innumerable generations of Corinnas to give up their virginities in the spring. Classical and Christian references are lightly scattered throughout, for the events of the day belong to those aspects of human nature that all religions have to approve and sanctify, for they are the very basis of survival; hence, refusal to participate in the natural cycle must be regarded as 'sin' (for Christians) or 'profanation' (for pagans) against the life force. The sacramental nature of the May-day rites comes across powerfully:

see how
Devotion gives each House a Bough,

Or Branch: Each Porch, each doore, ere this,
An Arke a Tabernacle is
Made up of white-thorn neatly enterwove;
As if here were those cooler shades of love.

The communion feast that features time and again in Herrick's work to set the seal on the high moments of life occurs here too on this busy day of defloration:

A deale of Youth, ere this, is come
Backe, and with White-thorn laden home.
Some have dispatcht their Cakes and Creame,
Before that we have left to dream:
And some have wept, and woo'd, and plighted Troth.

Finally, the poet urges his mistress to take the plunge into the waters of life, as he concentrates the common experience of mankind into an impassioned appeal to outwit time and age, to enjoy youth and beauty by indulging in 'harmless follie' that is also instinctual wisdom.

Come, let us goe, while we are in our prime;
And take the harmlesse follie of the time.
We shall grow old apace, and die
Before we know our liberty.
Our life is short; and our dayes run
As fast away as do's the Sunne:
And as a vapour, or a drop of raine
Once lost, can ne'r be found againe:
So when or you or I are made
A fable, song, or fleeting shade;
All love, all liking, all delight
Lies drown'd with us in endlesse night.
Then while time serves, and we are but decaying;
Come, my Corinna, come, let's goe a Maying.

In this verse biblical echoes mingle with the classical poets. 'The Wisdom of Solomon' (from the Apocrypha) colours the final stanza, along with Persius and Catullus, as the optimism of the ages outsoars death.[8] The past lends hope to the seventeenth-century lover, for as any reader of Latin poetry would know, Ovid's Corinna was a girl of notoriously easy virtue. There is promise in the May-morning air . . . .

Herrick's marriage songs are central to his achievement as a poet, for they exhibit his best qualities in profusion: they are acts of friendship, celebrations of ritual, triumphs of life. They offer the chance to praise love and beauty, to pile on the imagery of fertility and sensuous pleasure. His masterpiece is the 'Nuptiall Song' (H–283) to the splendidly named Sir Clipseby Crew, a close friend who was married in 1625. Herrick's art excels itself here as he invents new poetic graces to adorn the ceremony, for his rapturous delight in the event causes him to break through the conventional limitations of verse in daring expansions that match the overflow of his feelings, yet all is subjected to the larger order of the elaborate stanza form.

> she paces on,
> Treading upon Vermilion
> And Amber; Spice-
> ing the Chafte Aire with fumes of Paradise.
> Then come on, come on, and yeeld
> A savour like unto a blessed field,
> When the bedabled Morne
> Washes the golden eares of corne.

Or the ingenious impressionistic effects of:

> On then, and though you slow-
> ly go, yet, howsoever, go.

or

> this the longest night;
> But yet too short for you: 'tis we,
> Who count this night as long as three,
> Lying alone,
> Telling the Clock strike Ten, Eleven, Twelve, One.

The lay-out of the poem, tracing the sequence of the wedding day from dawn to night, follows that which Spenser established as the norm in his *Epithalamion*, and in addition it owes a good deal to Catullus's wedding hymn to Manlius and Lavinia which lies behind most Renaissance examples of this genre, and which accounts for the generally Roman atmosphere of these poems. The epithalamium enjoyed a vogue that lasted from the 1590s until the Commonwealth; it did not revive with the Restoration, perhaps because its tendency to look like a communal fertility rite no longer suited the more sophisticated society of the later Stuarts. The Clipseby Crew poem is undoubtedly the glory of the genre in English. What could improve on the aesthetic eroticism of the bridal bed:

> And to your more bewitching, see, the proud
> Plumpe Bed beare up, and swelling like a cloud,
> Tempting the two too modest; can
> Yee see it brusle like a Swan,
> And you be cold
> To meet it, when it woo's and seemes to fold
> The Armes to hugge it? throw, throw
> Your selves into the mighty over-flow
> Of that white Pride, and Drowne
> The night, with you, in floods of Downe.

The erotic is succeeded by the intellectual as Herrick anticipates the idea of love that the lovers themselves might seek to approach, and not surprisingly, in this speculative area he reaches out for the language and manner of Donne, and yet the buoyant tone and the lightness of touch show that Herrick is still fully in control of this unusual matter:

> The bed is ready, and the maze of Love
> Lookes for the treaders; every where is wove
> Wit and new misterie; read, and
> Put in practise, to understand
> And know each wile,
> Each hieroglyphick of a kisse or smile;
> And do it to the full; reach
> High in your own conceipt, and some way teach
> Nature and Art, one more
> Play, then they ever knew before.

There can be no doubt that Herrick has his own senses fully aroused here: there is an obvious enjoyment in the encounter, and Herrick as master of ceremonies shows every willingness to participate imaginatively in the wedding night himself. The same sensuous involvement occurs in the Corinna poem, and in some of his descriptions of country revelries. Yet, one can say that Herrick indulges in vicarious eroticism only on the proper occasions, when the events he describes are socially approved moments of licentiousness, like weddings or folk festivals – hence his use of the phrase 'cleanly-Wantonnesse' to explain this side of his verse in the 'Argument' to *Hesperides*.[9]

After the euphoria of this poem there may be found a melancholy sequel elsewhere in *Hesperides* in the poem on the death of a Clipseby son, and the elegy for Lady Crew herself dead in childbirth at the age of 30. These were the common realities of seventeenth-century life, which set in such high relief the moments of fulfilment in an uncertain world.

Death did not provoke Herrick to any great outcry against the injustice of fate, nor did it cause his imagination to range along the vast perspectives of sensation and thought that so many of his contemporaries explored. He feels no horror at death, and his characteristic epitaphs are decent exercises in interment, with a greater interest in neatness and wit than in confronting the issues of death. Herrick's manipulation of the classical tokens of mourning, sprigs of yew and cypress, violets and urns, often seems a heartless charade, an evasion of the reality of death, by trifling with the symbols. The poem on the death of his niece is a case in point:

> Sweet virgin, that I do not set
> The pillars up of weeping Jet,
> Or mournfull Marble; let thy shade
> Not wrathfull seem, or fright the Maide,
> Who hither at her wonted howers
> Shall come to strew thy earth with flowers.
> No, know (Blest Maide) when there's not one
> Remainder left of Brasse or stone,
> Thy living Epitaph shall be,
> Though lost in them, yet found in me.
> Dear, in thy bed of Roses, then,
> Till this world shall dissolve as men,
> Sleep, while we hide thee from the light,
> Drawing thy curtains round: Good night.

Behind all the different kinds of poetry we find in *Hesperides*, there is obviously a unifying sensibility. Much has been said about the ceremoniousness of the verse, but there is an accompanying aesthetic that needs attention too. Herrick is in love with small objects and small creatures, and with certain subtle effects of colour, perfume and light. The sprigs of this and that, the chives of garlic, nettle leaves, rosebuds and lilies, grains of wheat, hazel nuts, etc. that are scattered profusely throughout his work are signs of a mind that is fascinated by the symbolic minutiae of a highly formal world. The objects have a beauty of their own, but they are additionally beautiful in that they indicate a certain tidiness in human affairs, the tidiness of gestures properly made, of perfect ritualized responses carried out in any given circumstances. In many cases they become more important than the experiences that they adorn, and frequently in *Hesperides* one feels that Herrick is just going through the motions, telling his poetic beads and murmuring the appropriate incantations. The range of experience credibly communicated in Herrick is not large, and his most powerful emotions congregate around the consciousness of time slipping inexorably away. But while his stock of common experience may be slight, he has a marvellously developed aesthetic sense, which seems to be his special compensation for an inadequate share of the ordinary human emotions: one might say that the motivating passion of *Hesperides* is the communication and refinement of that aesthetic sense. Certainly one would argue that his imagination works most freely in those poems where there is no experience to control, only description of sensitive perceptions to be fixed in verse, as, for example, in his fairy poems, where he achieves some unique effects. The many fanciful poems about transactions in the world of roses and lilies have a perfection of form and wit of an entirely artificial kind: they are quite devoid of emotion, or the emotion is totally factitious, as in the exquisite 'Funerall Rites of the Rose' (H–686). The Julia poems, too, have little to do with love: instead they provide occasions for brilliant aesthetic observations.

The fairy poems are memorable for their perfect consistency of scale and curious registration of eerie and grotesque beauty: they are microscopic visions recorded with the delicacy of an Elizabethan miniature painter. There was a tradition of fairy poetry stretching back to the 1590s to which Shakespeare and Drayton had made notable contributions, so Herrick's pieces such as 'Oberon's Feast', 'Oberon's Palace', and 'The Faerie Temple' are not novel inventions but part of a well established genre. A collection of fairy verse by various hands came out in 1634, and it was in this volume that the first version of 'Oberon's Feast' appeared. Herrick's lawyer friends Thomas Shapcot (to whom 'Oberon's Palace' and the second version of 'Oberon's Feast' were dedicated) and John Merrifield (the dedicatee of 'Oberon's Chapel') were both fairy-fanciers, as was Sir Simeon Steward, another close friend. The genre encouraged fantasy, folklore and whimsy, offered occasion to invent scenes of wonder and ingeniousness to gratify contemporary taste in such matters, and allowed poets to develop a particularly delicate kind of beauty, specializing in effects of moonlight, fleeting images and miniscule detail. All this suited Herrick's sensibility ideally, and his achievements in this minor genre have pleased generations of readers.

'Oberon's Feast' (H–293) typically introduces us to the rarefied delicacies: 'A Moon-parch't grain of purest wheat', 'the hornes of paperie Butterflies', and culminates in an orgy of gastronomic curiosities:

> Gladding his pallat with some store
> Of Emits eggs; what wo'd he more?
> But Beards of Mice, a Newt's stew'd thigh,
> A bloated Earewig, and a Flie;
> With the Red-capt worme, that's shut
> Within the concave of a Nut,
> Browne as his Tooth. A little Moth,
> Late fatned in a piece of cloth:
> With withered cherries; Mandrakes eares;
> Moles eyes; to these, the slain-Stags teares:
> The unctuous dewlaps of a Snaile;
> The broke-heart of a Nightingale
> Ore-come in musicke.

We encounter aesthetic effects of a quite different order when we turn to the Julia poems. These, scattered throughout *Hesperides*, are, superficially, complimentary verses to an imaginary mistress, written with a gallantry that usually attracts the term 'Cavalier'. Essentially, however, they are a means for Herrick to convey some of the sensations that especially pleased and titillated a cultivated Stuart audience in matters of amorous style. 'Delight in Disorder' (H–83) captures best the mood of appreciative delight that shimmers around this group of poems.

> A Sweet disorder in the dresse
> Kindles in cloathes a wantonnesse:
> A Lawne about the shoulders thrown
> Into a fine distraction:
> An erring Lace, which here and there
> Enthralls the Crimson Stomacher:
> A Cuffe neglectfull, and thereby
> Ribbands to flow confusedly:
> A winning wave (deserving Note)
> In the tempestuous petticote:
> A carelesse shooe-string, in whose tye
> I see a wilde civility:
> Doe more bewitch me, then when Art
> Is too precise in every part.

Stuart panache, rather than Elizabethan formality, one might say. This care not to be over-precise in fashion, these calculated lapses from perfection, are the flourishes of an extremely refined culture – even one that may be about to decline into decadence, and there was undeniably a touch of decadence about the Court of Charles I with its *préciosité*, its cult of platonic love, the high mannerism of its verbal wit. Herrick's poetry has a brightness, a crispness that prevents it from becoming effete, but the potential for decadence does exist in the concern for artifice rather than for experience. The slight negligence of manner is something that Van Dyck gives us in many of his relaxed aristocratic portraits; it occurs in Caroline garden design with the admission of small areas of 'wild' nature to offset the formal pattern of the rest; we see it superbly expressed in Inigo Jones's costume designs for the masques of the 1620s and 1630s which were created to please the very senate of good taste, the Court. These beguiling airs were part of the style of Caroline culture, and they receive their finest verbal expression from Herrick, although he certainly was no innovator here: Jonson occupied that position, for in the famous song 'Still to be neat, still to be drest' from *Epicoene* (1609) we find

> Give me a look, give me a face,
> That makes simplicity a grace;
> Robes loosely flowing, hair as free:
> Such sweet neglect more taketh me
> Than all the adulteries of art:
> They strike mine eyes, but not my heart.

Even that lyric derives from a poem in the Latin anthology that Jonson reworked. Herrick has given the consummate touch to this theme, for one cannot imagine any advance on the brilliant perceptions of 'Delight in Disorder'. The thrilling verbs, phrases such as that 'winning wave' of 'the tempestuous petticoat', the 'wild civility' of the shoe-string are superb: language and idea fuse completely together.

Many of the Julia poems elaborate on these sensations, as 'Upon Julia's Clothes' (H–779):

> When as in silks my Julia goes,
> Then, then (me thinks) how sweetly flowes
> That liquifaction of her clothes.
>
> Next, when I cast mine eyes and see
> That brave Vibration each way free;
> O how that glittering taketh me!

or 'Art above Nature, to Julia', or 'Upon Julia's Haire', and 'Her haire fill'd with Dew'. Her voice creates miraculous effects: 'Melting melodious words, to Lutes of Amber' (H–67). Her restless petticoat (H–175) drives the poet into erotic raptures:

> thereupon,
> 'Two'd make a brave expansion.
> And pounc't with Stars, it shew'd to me
> Like a Celestiall Canopie.
> Sometimes 'two'd blaze, and then abate,
> Like to a flame growne moderate:
> Sometimes away 'two'd wildly fling;
> Then to thy thighs so closely cling,
> That some conceit did melt me downe.

Julia is also an exhibition ground for various experiments in colours and scents. The strange perfumes whose exoticism Herrick tries to suggest by their stirring names hint at the varying moods of love that a mistress yields:

> Tell, if thou canst, (and truly) whence doth come
> This Camphire, Storax, Spiknard, Galbanum:
> These Musks, these Ambers, and those other smells
> (Sweet as the Vestrie of the Oracles.)
> Ile tell thee; while my Julia did unlace
> Her silken bodies, but a breathing space:
> The passive Aire such odour then assum'd,
> As when to Jove Great Juno goes perfum'd.
> (from 'Upon Julia's unlacing her self' (H–414)

Sometimes jewels have a similar function. In 'To Julia' (H–88) his mistress becomes a composite of moving jewels:

> About thy neck a Carkanet is bound,
> Made of the Rubie, Pearle and Diamond:
> A golden ring, that shines upon thy thumb:
> About thy wrist, the rich Dardanium.
> Between thy Breasts (then Doune of Swans more white)
> There playes the Saphire with the Chrysolite.
> No part besides must of thy selfe be known.
> But by the Topaz, Opal, Calcedon.

The charms of his mistress are invariably partially concealed in a tantalizing and coquettish way: half-glimpsed through gossamer, gleaming by twilight, or shimmering through translucent streams.

> So looks Anthea, when in bed she lyes,
> Orecome, or halfe betray'd by Tiffanies:
> Like to a Twi'light, or that simpring Dawn,
> That Roses shew, when misted o're with Lawn.
> Twilight is yet, till that her Lawnes give way;
> Which done, that Dawne, turnes then to perfect day.
> ('To Anthea lying in bed' (H–104))

Innumerable permutations of red and white, the heraldry of love, are worked out on the field of his mistress's body. Poets and their audiences seemingly never tired of these colour games, which probably survived so long because the simple subject matter of the complexion of love represented a standing challenge to the ingenuity of poets to execute yet more remarkable turns of fancy on a conventional theme. (After 1625, with the marriage of Charles and Henrietta Maria, there was the added attraction of political compliment, as the rose of England and the lily of France occupied the centre of the national scene in a much publicized love match.) These exercises aim above all at subtlety of tone and delicacy of perception; they achieve too a certain conventional eroticism that befitted a complimentary love poem. 'Upon Roses' (H–78) may serve as a fine specimen:

> Under a Lawne, then skyes more cleare,
> Some ruffled Roses nestling were:
> And snugging there, they seem'd to lye
> As in a flowrie Nunnery:
> They blush'd, and look'd more fresh then flowers
> Quickned of late by Pearly showers;
> And all, because they were possest
> But of the heat of Julia's breast:
> Which as a warme, and moistned spring,
> Gave them their ever flourishing.

Such phenomena as roses in snow gave Herrick a frisson of delight that he endeavoured to register in poetry, but his intellectual and sensuous pleasures were stimulated to extremes by the sight of – or the thought of – 'The Lilly in a Christal' (H–193). In an unusually reflective poem, Herrick analyses the nature of the attraction of the flower imprisoned in a cylinder of rock-crystal.

You have beheld a smiling Rose
When Virgins hands have drawn
O'r it a Cobweb-Lawne:
And here, you see, this Lilly shows,
Tomb'd in a Christal stone,
More faire in this transparent case,
Then when it grew alone;
And had but single grace.

. . .

You see how Amber through the streams
More gently stroaks the sight,
With some conceal'd delight;
Then when he darts his radiant beams
Into the boundlesse aire:
Where either too much light his worth
Doth all at once impaire,
Or set it little forth.

Put Purple Grapes, or Cherries in-
To Glasse, and they will send
More beauty to commend
Them, from that cleane and subtile skin,
Then if they naked stood,
And had no other pride at all,
But their own flesh and blood,
And tinctures naturall.

. . .

He observes that on occasions such as this, the enhancing dimension of the crystal is like the imagination transforming the natural world of the senses: there is a mystery, a lustre, a subtle atmosphere of beauty occasioned by the crystal modifying the lily. The formal conclusion is that transparent intermediaries create a finer passion in love.

So though y'are white as Swan, or Snow,
And have the power to move
A world of men to love:
Yet, when your Lawns and Silks shal flow;
And that white cloud divide
Into a doubtful Twi-light; then,
Then will your hidden Pride
Raise greater fires in men.

But the unspoken implication is that Herrick has here glimpsed one of the secrets of the art of poetry, for the poetic imagination heightens and enhances the scenes it plays upon, and on things already beautiful confers an additional beauty. Confirmation of this reading may be drawn from the long personal poem 'His Age' (H–336) in which he specifically mentions these verses as ones that will most revive him in old age:

> Then shall he read that flowre of mine
> Enclos'd within a christall shrine.

Most of Herrick's poetry belongs to the 1620s and 1630s, as almost all the datable poems on marriages and deaths indicate, and the collection would have seemed a fashionable addition to the literary scene had it been published in 1640, when it was first mentioned in the Stationers' Register. For all his remoteness from London, Herrick's value and taste were essentially those of the Court circle. That exquisite sensibility, neatness of wit and gallantry of compliment are all characteristic of the Cavalier mode of Caroline times, just as the classical framework of his social poetry was part of the Augustanism that flourished at Court. Behind both these modes of poetry lay the example and inspiration of Ben Jonson, whom Herrick honoured as his poetic father. Jonson is virtually the only contemporary poet whom Herrick mentions in his many poems about poetry, his tributes ranging from a recreation of those brilliant 'lyric feasts' of the Jonson circle in 'An Ode for Him' (H–911) to a final vision of the poet 'in a Globe of Radiant fire' in Herrick's 'Elizium' (H–575).[10]

We do not know why publication of *Hesperides* was delayed from 1640 to 1648, but during those years Herrick added a considerable number of pieces celebrating Royalist victories or mourning the Royalist dead. Throughout his career he had written occasional poems to the King and Queen, or complimented them on the arrival of offspring: the titles of several of his poems, sacred and secular, indicate that they had been set to music to be sung in the royal presence at Whitehall. The dedicatory poem of *Hesperides* is addressed to Prince Charles (the future Charles II) and one may assume that Herrick had intended the publication of the volume in 1640 to coincide with the creation of Charles as Prince of Wales. All the signs point to Herrick's desire to find favour and advancement at Court, but frustration was his only reward. His loyalism during the Civil Wars only resulted in his expulsion from his living, nor did the Restoration bring recognition, for he was merely sent back to the country. Although he complained that 'the untuneable times' of the Civil War had silenced his harp (H–210), it is difficult to believe that so fertile a poet as Herrick could cease to write poetry, but whatever he wrote in the years up to his death in 1674 stayed in manuscript and has perished.

There remains his religious poetry, the *Noble Numbers* (published with *Hesperides*), which has never attracted much admiration. In a great age of devotional poetry, Herrick had no private vision to relate. He did not use poetry for meditative purposes, he had no stimulating consciousness of sin, or terror of death; he was not moved to wonder by the Passion of Christ or by the miracle of the Resurrection. Much of his output took the form of divine epigrams, witty little exclamations that attempt to encapsulate religious mysteries in pithy words, a popular seventeenth-century devotional exercise. As a Laudian, Herrick must have enjoyed the formal ritualistic celebration of the Christian offices; poems which reflect this formal manner of worship include 'The Dirge of Jephtha's Daughter' and 'The Dirge of Dorcas', both of which provided Herrick with congenial occasions to work through the customs of Old Testament mourning.

A number of his poems on Christmas themes – 'A Christmas Caroll', 'A New Year's Gift' and 'The Star-Song' were set to music by Henry Lawes (who composed the music for *Comus* and for other pieces by Milton), and sung before the King at Whitehall in the ceremonious setting of the Chapel Royal. They may well have been acted out by members of the royal family in tableaux vivants, with costume as well as musical accompaniment. If Herrick had lived nearer to the Court, or if the Court had lasted longer, he might have contributed to a modest revival of simple religious drama in the Chapel Royal.[11] Herrick's 'Rex Tragicus', a meditation on the Passion, already views the Crucifixion as a purely theatrical event.

> The Crosse shall be Thy Stage; and Thou shalt there
> The spacious field have for Thy Theater.

The latent dramatic possibilities of the royal services were not developed, however. Herrick in any case seems to have preferred ritual action in which he himself could participate. As an example, we might take 'The Parasceve, or Preparation', where he and his soul prepare themselves to take communion.

> To a Love-Feast we both invited are:
> The figur'd Damask, or pure Diaper,
> Over the golden Altar now is spread,
> With Bread, and Wine, and Vessells furnished;

The sacred Towell, and the holy Eure
Are ready by, to make the Guests all pure:
Let's go (my Alma) yet e're we receive,
Fit, fit it is, we have our Parasceve.
Who to that sweet Bread unprepar'd doth come
Better he starv'd, then but to tast one crumme.

This is essentially an appreciation of the external forms of religion, and one feels that Herrick is gratified by the order and beauty of the service, but reluctant to reveal his response to the mystery of the Eucharist. Comparison of this poem with Herbert's final poem, 'Love', shows up the relative shallowness of Herrick's Christian experience, and helps to explain why his religious poetry tends to be neglected.

The most memorable and attractive of the *Noble Numbers* is the simple 'Thanksgiving to God, for his House', the nearest Herrick gets to autobiography in a collection not noted for self-revelations. This poem of gratitude for small mercies is almost secular in content, being in effect another enumeration of the wholesome pleasures of the country life, with all the fond details of his modest estate, yet done with an engaging skill in the alternation of long line and short line, of metrical movement and pause, to produce an appropriately devotional tone:

Lord, Thou hast given me a cell
Wherein to dwell;
And little house, whose humble Roof
Is weather-proof;
Under the sparres of which I lie
Both soft, and drie;

. . .

Lord, I confesse too, when I dine,
The Pulse is Thine,
And all those other Bits, that bee
There plac'd by Thee;
The Worts, the Purslain, and the Messe
Of Water-cresse,
Which of Thy kindnesse Thou has sent;
And my content
Makes those, and my beloved Beet,
To be more sweet.
'Tis thou that crown'st my glittering Hearth
With guiltlesse mirth;

And giv'st me Wassaile Bowles to drink,
Spic'd to the brink.
. . .

The providence that furnishes the wassail bowl inspires more heartfelt gratitude in Herrick than the maker of Heaven and Hell.

Notes

1 The H numbers refer to the numbering of the poems in modern critical editions of *Hesperides*. The edition used here is *The Complete Poetry of Robert Herrick*, ed. J. Max Patrick (New York 1963). The numeration holds good for the edition of L. C. Martin (Oxford 1956).

2 In this context see G. Braden, 'Herrick's Classical Quotations', in *'Trust to Good Verses'*, ed. R. Rollin and J. Max Patrick (Pittsburgh 1978).

3 For example

Then, then (me thinks) how sweetly flowes
That liquefaction of her clothes.
(H–779)

or

Each hieroglyphick of a kisse or smile
(H–283)

or

To see my Lines Excathedrated here.
(H–168)

4 The frequent emphasis on country sports in Herrick's poetry has a political and religious significance, as it demonstrates Herrick's support for the policy of Charles and Laud as formalized in the 'Declaration . . . Concerning Lawful Sports' of 1633, that encouraged traditional sports after Church on Sundays as a form of harmless amusement. Puritans were outraged by the Declaration.

5 *The Poems of Tibullus*, Penguin translation by Philip Dunlop.

6 Shortly after Herrick's death John Aubrey began to compile his *Remaines of Gentilisme and Judaisme*, a collection of folklore customs intended to show how many pagan rituals had survived into seventeenth-century England, either openly or under disguise. Not surprisingly he uses Ovid's *Fasti* as a basic reference point for Roman customs, and the very large number of survivals that he instances confirms that Herrick was right in detecting a

continuity between the ancient and modern worlds in the countryside. Here, for example, is Aubrey on 'Harvest Home' (cf. 'The Hock-Cart'), which he opens with a quotation from Virgil's *Georgics*, then:

> Home Harvests are observed [more or lesse] in most Counties of England: e.g. South-Wilts. Heref. &c: When they bring home the last load of Corne: it is donne with great joy and merriment: and a Fidler rides on the loaded Cart, or Wayne, playing: a Barrell of good Beer is provided for the Harvestmen, and some good Rustique Cheer. This Custome (no doubt) is handed downe to us from the Romans: who after this manner celebrated their Cerealia [Sacra Cereris] instituted by Triptolemus.
> (in *Three Prose Works*, ed. John Buchanan-Brown (Fontwell 1972), p. 143)

7 We do not know the circumstances that prevented Herrick from visiting his father's grave for so long, but there was a suspicion that Nicholas Herrick died a suicide in 1592, so the place of burial may not have been made public. A lustre was a period of five years in the Roman calendar. Smallage is parsley or celery, a ritual offering to the dead.

8 *Wisdom of Solomon*, ii.1–8; Persius, V.152; Catullus, V.6.

9 The only unseemly erotic piece that Herrick delivered was 'The Vine' (H–41) in which he dreams that he has been metamorphosed into a vine that comprehensively embraces his mistress. It is a rather ineffectual version of 'the rapture' theme popular in the 1620s, the erotic exploration of a mistress that was inspired by certain of Donne's Elegies.

10 In his lifetime, the poems that appear to have enjoyed most popularity, judging by the frequency with which they were copied out into manuscript collections, were the two in praise of wine that owe much to the Jonsonian cult of wine as the inspirer of good verses and the spirit of the good life, a cult that in turn drew strength from Horace and Anacreon. 'Fare-well to Sack' (H–128) and the 'Welcome to Sack' (H–197) are feats of witty hyperbole, abounding in conceits, and written rather in the manner of Donne's Elegies. In style and content they were certain to appeal to a large audience.

11 See Anthony Low, *Love's Architecture* (New York 1978), pp. 222–32.

8 The Caroline Milton

Milton gathered together his early poems for publication in 1645, when he was 37. At that time the first Civil War was drawing to a close with the Parliamentary armies increasingly successful and the King himself under siege at Oxford. It would be difficult to deduce the crisis of the time from the appearance of the 1645 volume, and even more difficult to believe that for several years the author had been engaged in radical pamphleteering in favour of freedom of conscience and thoroughgoing reform of the Church, for the presentation of the book suggests a conservative and even royalist bias. The title page informs us that 'The Songs were set in Musick by Mr. Henry Lawes Gentleman of the Kings Chappel, and one of His Majesties Private Musick', and the portrait frontispiece shows us a man of indeterminate age with the air of a jaded Cavalier (Plate 8). Here Milton has long curled hair, displays a quantity of lace, and sits in front of falling drapery usually associated with courtly portraiture. Milton was evidently displeased with the portrait, for he made the artist-engraver, William Marshall, add a malicious Greek epigram damning the work. We can assume that Marshall did not understand the language he painstakingly copied out:

> You would say, perhaps, that this picture was drawn by an ignorant hand, when you looked at the form that nature made. Since you do not recognize the man portrayed, my friends, laugh at this rotten picture by a rotten artist.[1]

The engraver seems originally to have been copying an earlier portrait of the poet, for he transcribes Milton's age as 21; yet the sitter is obviously older, so perhaps Marshall tried to up-date the face to correspond to the Milton of 1645.

Yet however the face may have been misrepresented (and Marshall was a competent artist by the standards of the time), the accumulation of details in the frontispiece characterizes a poet who appears to be in the mainstream of the Caroline courtly tradition. The view beyond the

Plate 8 Frontispiece to Milton's *Poems* of 1645

portrait opens on to a rural scene with shepherds piping and dancing, suggestive of the pastoral fictions of Caroline poetry, but indicating too that the poet's principal mode is pastoral (as in *Comus*, 'Lycidas', 'Arcades', and many of the Latin poems). At the corners of the frame are set the images of four Muses intended to indicate the scope of the collection. Urania was the Muse of divine poetry, represented in the volume by the Nativity Ode, the 'Passion' and the translations of the Psalms; Clio, the Muse of history, concerned to secure the immortal fame of distinguished men, may allude to the several memorial elegies printed here.[2] Melpomene with her buskins and sceptre represents tragedy, and was also associated with music and mourning; she has an uncertain relation with the poems, although we know from the Trinity Manuscript, Milton's commonplace book, that he had plans to write tragedy. Finally there is the bare-breasted Erato,[3] the Muse of erotic poetry, a reminder that Milton did write love poetry – though in this volume his amorous poems are all in Italian or Latin.

The impression of Caroline courtliness is strengthened when we find that by far the longest poem in the volume is 'A Mask presented at Ludlow Castle', which we know as *Comus*.[4] The masque was the distinctive courtly form of Stuart times. Moreover, when we read the letter from the Stationer to the Reader commending these poems that 'may renew the wonted honour and esteem of our English tongue', we discover that Milton's name is being coupled with that of Waller, with the suggestion that the reader will find both equally satisfying. Waller's high reputation was based on courtly compliment and amorous address in very smooth and measured language.

It is not too difficult to see how Milton became misapprehended as a courtly poet. At first sight many of the poems seem to belong to conventional current categories: *Comus* and 'Arcades' could be taken as masques, each praising a great family by saluting it as a pattern of exalted virtue; the Nativity Ode, the ecclesiastical ending of 'Il Penseroso' and the Latin poem on the death of Bishop Lancelot Andrewes might indicate sympathy with the High Anglican orientation of the Court; and the various elegies could be construed as Milton's contribution to the Caroline art of the social tear, but this approach stresses the accidental and misses the essential in the *Poems* of 1645. Instead, we should pay attention to the sign given in the unusual epigraph that Milton set on the title page, '*Baccare frontem / Cingite, ne vati noceant mala lingua*', from Virgil's seventh Eclogue: 'Bind my brow with foxglove [a charm against spells], lest an evil tongue harm the rising poet.' The use of 'vati' is telling, for 'vates' was a word of specialized meaning, applied particularly to the inspired prophetic poet of antiquity, best exemplified by Virgil, and it was in this tradition of poetry that Milton placed himself.

We have seen how Jonson, who was the other thoroughly professional poet of the age, was committed to a social mode of poetry which elevated his own personal relationships to form a generous, humanistic conception of civilized living, essentially secular. Milton rose above this level, transforming the convictions of his private self into authoritative impersonal pronouncements of philosophic and religious truth. There is a social, occasional level in Milton's earlier poems, but he will almost always rise from that level to the exploration of God's purposes towards man that Milton sees revealed in some particular event or theme. The peculiar power of understanding and expression that he knew himself to possess encouraged him to believe that he was one of God's chosen agents for interpretation and prophecy in his time. His early poetry and prose allude often to his sense of being set apart for God's special purposes, and confess his ambitions to be the poet of first and last things, of events that transfix the cosmos. In his oration of 1627, 'Hail native Language', he proclaims:

> Yet I had rather, if I were to choose,
> Thy service in some graver subject use.
> Such as may make thee search thy coffers round,
> Before thou clothe my fancy in fit sound:
> Such where the deep transported mind may soar
> Above the wheeling poles, and at Heav'n's door
> Look in, and see each blissful Deity
> How he before the thunderous throne doth lie,
> Listening to what unshorn Apollo sings
> To th' touch of golden wires, while Hebe brings
> Immortal Nectar to her Kingly Sire:
> Then passing through the Spheres of watchful fire,
> And misty Regions of wide air next under,
> And hills of Snow and lofts of piled Thunder,
> May tell at length how green-ey'd Neptune raves,
> In Heav'n's defiance mustering all his waves;
> Then sing of secret things that came to pass
> When Beldam Nature in her cradle was.

He dedicated and rededicated himself to his high calling, by many years of study and preparation, by encyclopaedic learning and religious investigation. In 1629, for example, when he was composing the Nativity Ode, he wrote to his friend Charles Diodati a verse letter in the form of a Latin elegy, in which he declared, through the classical fictions that were second nature to him even when treating Christian subjects, his consecration to the austere high-minded life of the prophet-poet that he wished to become:

> The poet whose subject is . . . the holy counsels of the gods above, and . . . those deep-buried kingdoms where a savage dog barks – let this poet live frugally, like the philosopher from Samos, and let herbs provide his harmless diet. Let a bowl of beech-wood, filled with clear water, stand by him, and may he drink soberly from a pure spring. In addition his youth must be chaste and free from crime, his morals strict and his hand unstained. He must be like you, priest, when, bathed in holy water and gleaming in your sacred vestment, you rise to go and face the angry gods.[5]

Tiresias, Calchas, Orpheus and Homer are then instanced as his great originals.

The *Poems* of 1645 already display a grandeur of conception appropriate to these ambitions. Everywhere there is a heavenward movement, for Milton's subjects are all capable of attaining divinity. Lycidas and the Marchioness of Winchester become saints through death, the Countess of Derby in 'Arcades' is transformed into a goddess by wisdom and virtue. Bishop Andrewes makes a splendid baroque entry into heaven, the melancholy thinker of 'Il Penseroso' penetrates there in a philosophic exaltation. The Spirit in *Comus* leads the pure in mind and body 'higher than the Spheary chime'. The Ode 'On Time' looks forward to the moment when time ends, and the elect of God shall be translated into eternity: 'Attir'd with Stars, we shall for ever sit.' There is a constant process of apotheosis going on in these poems, a sign of the optimism of Milton's spirit in the early years of his career.[6]

The volume opens with the Nativity Ode, on the subject of the Incarnation that has opened heaven to mankind. Milton does not attempt to meditate on the subject in the familiar seventeenth-century manner (imagining himself present at the scene, exercising the affections, raising his devotional mood to a greater intensity with a new understanding of the epiphany in its personal application); here is no cascade of paradoxes or explosion of wonder as in Crashaw's poem, but a panoptic interpretation of the Nativity's significance in the spiritual history of the world. The lofty tone announces a public poem. Milton immediately moves to associate himself with 'the holy sages' of the Old Testament who have foretold the event, and proclaims his own conviction of prophetic power at the end of the introduction when he joins his voice 'unto the Angel Quire / From out his secret Altar toucht with hallow'd fire'. This incident recalls Isaiah's experience of purification and the gift of prophecy in Isaiah 6:6–7, when a seraph touched him on the lips with a live coal as he saw the vision of the Lord. Milton prepares to sing the theological and philosophic mysteries of 'this great birth'. The mode he chooses is Virgilian. Behind the Nativity Ode lies Virgil's fourth Eclogue, the 'Messianic Eclogue', in which he sang of the Virgin who would bring back justice to the earth, and foretold the birth of a Child who would restore the golden age, the first age of innocence, peace and abundance. This pastoral poem had ensured Virgil the status of an honorary Christian prophet throughout the centuries, and Milton follows his lead in acclaiming the Christ-child as the renewer of the golden age, returning man to a state of harmony with heaven.

The stanza that introduces this miracle has often been described as masque-like, employing the devices of masque character and scenery to create an occasion of wonder:

> But he her fears to cease,
> Sent down the meek-eyd Peace,
> She crown'd with Olive green, came softly sliding
> Down through the turning sphear
> His ready Harbinger,
> With Turtle wing the amorous clouds dividing,
> And waving wide her mirtle wand,
> She strikes a universall Peace through Sea and Land.

The subject was appropriate to masque – indeed Jonson and Inigo Jones had produced a masque entitled *The Golden Age Restor'd* for King James in 1615 – and masque was the contemporary vehicle for the revelation of divinity here on earth. The high artifice of the setting and the wonderful transformation scenes were the accepted means of demonstrating to a Stuart audience the presence of a spiritual power of majesty among men. Milton is appropriating a form that had been developed to reveal the divine qualities of Stuart kingship, and applying it to a purer and more exalted end, the revelation of godhead itself in the person of Christ, 'the Prince of Light'. As in a masque, emblematic creatures (here halcyons, the birds of peace) enhance the scene and symbolize the universal peace that prevailed at Christ's birth:

The Windes with wonder whist,
Smoothly the waters kist,
    Whispering new joyes to the milde Ocean,
Who now hath quite forgot to rave,
While Birds of Calm sit brooding on the charmed wave.

The light and music that are so prominent in the Nativity Ode were habitually used in the masques to express divinity, and harmony between earth and heaven; they were also essential means for expressing the neo-Platonic colouring of the Court masques of the 1620s and 1630s, for light and music served to disclose the numinous power that sustained the ideal forms in these symbolic fictions: Davenant's *Luminalia*, for example, began in darkness and developed a steadily intensifying effulgence that whitened into Queen Henrietta Maria, the personification of Divine Energy. We can recognize that in the Ode, Milton is transferring the conventions of masque from the secularized context of courtly performance into a religious setting. The primal light of true divinity intensifies throughout the Nativity Ode, outshining the sun, and the growth of this light is accompanied by a rising harmony that is the music of the spheres. Traditionally, this music made by the planets as they moved in their courses had been audible in paradise, but the Fall had impaired man's ability to hear the celestial concord; it would, however, be heard again when the Earthly Paradise was restored by Christ at the end of time, a conviction given noble expression by Milton in his Ode 'At a Solemn Musick'. Platonically, the music of the spheres communicated the perfect order and proportion of the turning universe. With Christ's birth, heaven and earth unite again, and the poet, transported in imagination by the celestial symphony, anticipates the restoration of the paradisal world, the age of gold:

For if such holy Song
Enwrap our fancy long,
    Time will run back, and fetch the age of gold,
And speckl'd vanity
Will sicken soon and die,
    And leprous sin will melt from earthly mould,

and the imagery of masque is again mobilized to effect the transformation:

Yea Truth, and Justice then
Will down return to men,

Th'enameld Arras of the Rainbow wearing,
And Mercy set between,
Thron'd in Celestiall sheen,
With radiant feet the tissued clouds down stearing,
And Heav'n as at som festivall,
Will open wide the Gates of her high Palace Hall.

This vision is curtailed by the cold realization that Providence has arranged otherwise: that Christ must suffer and die, time must run its course and the Last Judgement must 'thunder through the deep' before 'at last our bliss / Full and perfect is'. The prophetic acclamation of paradise regained gives way to a philosophic understanding of Christ's birth in the process of universal history: the age of the false gods that misled mankind is ended, the regeneration of the world begins, and in that beginning is the promise of a return to a perfect state. The poet settles down to describe the procession of departing gods, who are cast in effect as an anti-masque, the movement of hostile, corrupt or grotesque forces to be dispelled by the action of the main masque. In keeping with this conception, Milton gives the pagan gods the music and dances appropriate to their debased condition in the anti-masque of spiritual history: they leave with a 'hideous humm', 'with hollow shriek', 'with midnight plaint', 'with Timbrell'd Anthems dark', and they move ' in dismall dance about the furnace blue'. Against them rises the music of the main masque of Christ's birth, the 'full consort' of 'th'Angelike symphony'.

Even the penultimate stanza, which has often been singled out unfavourably for its naïvety, properly belongs to the masquing mode in which the Ode is cast: it projects a theatrical scene – stage properties and stylized action are emphasized – and it serves as a final tableau, making a background for the group of the Virgin and Child centred in the bright order of angels. The setting, though a stable, is 'Courtly' and the final image of order assured by divinity is the correct termination of a masque. Milton's own role, that of prophetic interpreter, is equivalent to the presenter of this 'Masque of Christmas'.

The large attention given in the Nativity Ode to the eclipse of the pagan gods puts us in touch with a lifelong fascination of Milton's: the nature of the powers that have imposed their unsanctioned authority over the nations during the long centuries before the Incarnation. There is no doubt that these powers are demonic, and ultimately, in *Paradise Lost*, they will be clearly identified with the fallen angels who tyrannize over unenlightened men as gods. Although Milton here paints the Greek and Roman gods in soft colours (for his classical spirit responded to their character and operations), nevertheless they are regretfully called 'deceiving' and are joined with the brutal gods of Egypt and Palestine that Milton always detested and rejected as a 'damned crew'. Even the fairies, so tolerantly entertained in Herrick's poems of the 1620s and 1630s, are consigned to the darkness where they belong, for Milton seems to regard them as manifestations of the least harmful fallen angels, and judges that their allegiance is with evil.[7]

The poem on 'The Passion' that Milton seems to have started shortly after the Nativity Ode confirms our sense of the earlier poem as a miniature masque. He recalls it in the first lines –

> Ere-while of Musick, and Ethereal mirth,
> Wherewith the stage of Ayr and Earth did ring,
>
> . . .
>
> My muse with Angels did divide to sing

– and he explicitly remarks, 'O what a Mask was there, what a disguise!' 'The Passion', written probably for Easter 1630 (the Nativity Ode had been written for Christmas 1629) seems intended as a meditation, but the subject frustrated him. He takes care to assert his prophetic status, and declares himself inspired: 'There doth my soul in holy vision sit / In pensive trance, and anguish, and ecstatick fit', but the vision blanks out, Milton becomes over-absorbed in a mournful conceit, and the rushing chariot of his imagination fails to take off. The poem has interest in that it discloses some of Milton's techniques for getting a poem moving; it also interestingly reveals his inability to contemplate the suffering of Christ; but the weakness of the poetry makes one doubt Milton's judgement in publishing the fragment.

The initial sequence of poems in the 1645 volume shows Milton's apprenticeship as a Christian prophet, associating himself with Isaiah in the Nativity Ode, with Ezekiel and his fiery chariot in 'The Passion', with David in his translation of the Psalms, with St John in 'At a Solemn Musick', where the poet ascends by earthly music to hear the everlasting music around the throne of God (described in Revelation). He describes the divine mysteries of Christ's life, and is their interpreter; he gazes into illimitable eternity in the poem 'On Time'. Other poems, and these include *Comus*, show a philosophic escalation that is complementary to his prophetic art. Milton's intense years of encyclopaedic study are forming the philosopher-poet, the *magister arti*, the Renaissance Magus, whose knowledge of the secrets of nature, the wisdom of the Ancients and the high providence of God raises him to the summit of intellectual and moral power, as near divinity as a man might reach. We are familiar with the type in Prospero, and Prospero is a dramatic projection of an ideal of human development that fascinated educated men in those countries where the revival of classical learning had enlarged the sense of the attainable. The ideal of universal knowledge and philosophic enlightenment exercised its greatest appeal in the late fifteenth and throughout the sixteenth century, when the influence of its prime exponents, the Italian neo-Platonists, was still vigorous. Pico della Mirandola, Marsilio Ficino and their associates had synthesized a vast range of material harmonizing the mysteries of the Jewish Cabala (the secret wisdom believed to have been transmitted orally from Moses, who had talked with God) with the mysteries of the Greek understanding of the spiritual world that were believed to be allegorized in the structure of their mythology. Later elaborators of this extraordinary system, which drew on philosophy, magic, mathematics, music and theology, were Cornelius Agrippa in Germany, and Giordano Bruno, who evolved an astoundingly complex system of universal knowledge, and who came to England in the 1580s.

With the late development of Renaissance methodologies in England, caused by the all-consuming issues of Church doctrine and reform, there was a slow response to the spacious liberal possibilities of Christian neo-Platonism. Spenser ventured into its currents, as did Chapman, but their achievements remain locked up in the esoteric mythological codes of their poems. Milton was a late, perhaps even the last such aspirant in England.[8] The ambition of these mystagogues was to liberate the soul from its earth-bound limitations and permit it to ascend ecstatically through the planetary spheres until it verged on the regions of divinity and acquired angelic knowledge of virtue and power. The soul could refine itself through strict discipline and unremitting contemplation of ideas that lay beyond the phenomenal world. The Florentine neo-Platonists were inclined to believe that the key to the profound philosophic attainments of the Greeks, and to the accumulated wisdom of the ancient world that they inherited, was in the system of mythology they had elaborated. The secrets of Greek mythology, once understood by the initiate, could furnish a revelation of spiritual regeneration compatible with and complementary to Christian revelation itself.[9] It was in this direction that Milton's studies during the 1630s pointed, by learning, by meditation and by the practice of virtue, to attain a supernatural wisdom that only the most elevated spirits might experience. He confesses these ambitions in the Latin verse letter to his father, published in the 1645 *Poems*, in the 'Elegia Sexta' addressed to his close friend Diodati, and most eloquently in his Cambridge speech, known as the 'Seventh Prolusion', that he is thought to have delivered in 1632 as part of the requirements for his Master's degree. But he refers to them more engagingly, with a wonderful lightness of touch, in 'L'Allegro' and 'Il Penseroso', the companion poems of the early 1630s that optimistically disclose his hopes.[10]

The landscapes of these poems with their many vignettes have long been admired and enjoyed, and so have the contrasting themes: the pleasures of the day and of the night, the attractions of the active and of the contemplative life, lightness of spirit set against gravity; yet behind these evident contrasts the serious development of Milton's poetic character is concealed. The two poems should be read as complementary rather than antithetical to each other: 'Il Penseroso' represents a philosophic advance over 'L'Allegro', but does not invalidate it. The mythological figures that function as symbolic images marking the stages of advancement in experience and power are important clues here. The high-spirited man of 'L'Allegro' consorts with Euphrosyne, or Mirth, one of the Three Graces fabled as the offspring either of Venus and Bacchus (or Dionysus) or of Aurora, goddess of the dawn, and the wind Zephyr, often understood as a divine spirit animating the natural world. Both parentages suggest the divine origin of the poet's guide. She sharpens his sense of social pleasure and increases his delight in the beauty of the natural world, as the succession of pastoral scenes confirms. Moving now to the city, the pleasures become more elevated and complex:

> There let Hymen oft appear
> In Saffron robe, with Taper clear,
> And pomp, and feast, and revelry,
> With mask, and antique Pageantry.

A nobility of spirit fostered by pleasure is developing here, intensified by the experience of the theatre of comedy and romance. There, the combined power of poetry and music playing over life that has been significantly ordered by the dramatist's art arouses in Milton a sense of the divine potential in man, and of the heights that the individual soul may scale in these moments of poetic furor:

> Then to the well-trod stage anon,
> If Jonsons learned Sock be on,
> Or sweetest Shakespear fancies childe,
> Warble his native Wood-notes wilde,
> And ever against eating Cares,
> Lap me in soft Lydian Aires,
> Married to immortal verse
> Such as the meeting soul may pierce
> In notes, with many a winding bout
> Of lincked sweetnes long drawn out,
> With wanton heed, and giddy cunning,
> The melting voice through mazes running;
> Untwisting all the chains that ty
> The hidden soul of harmony.

The final image in 'L'Allegro' is of Orpheus, the father of poetry, responding to these English strains as a new magic capable of restoring and re-integrating fallen human nature, here symbolized by the lost Eurydice.

Orpheus was a cult figure for Milton as for many Renaissance poets, who saw their art as a search to know the secret ordering of the world. Orpheus is central to the account given by the Florentine neo-Platonist Marsilio Ficino of the poet-philosophers of remote antiquity, who preserved and transmitted the secret knowledge of the faculties of the human soul – its means of harmonizing itself with the nature of the Godhead, and of understanding the mysterious language of the natural world – so that a right harmony might prevail in man's control of nature. (Again, Prospero's philosophical sublimity and his power over nature through Ariel illustrates this theme for the modern reader.) Here is the 'genealogy of wisdom' as given by Ficino – and we should remember that Milton was a close student of Ficino as well as of his colleague in the Florentine Academy, Pico della Mirandola. The great original was Hermes Trismegistus, the Egyptian magus who was coeval with Moses.

> He is called the first author of theology: he was succeeded by Orpheus, who came second amongst ancient theologians: Aglaophemus, who had been initiated into the sacred teaching of Orpheus, was succeeded in theology by Pythagoras, whose disciple was Philolaus, the teacher of our Divine Plato. Hence there is one ancient theology (prisca theologia) . . . culminating in the Divine Plato.[11]

In this line, Orpheus is the only poet, and as one might deduce from his proximity to Pythagoras, numbers, proportion, harmony and music are aspects of his art. His fabled exploits exhibited his mysterious knowledge: his descent to the underworld to bring back Eurydice to life revealed a power over death exceeded only by Christ's; his ability to make trees, streams and rocks move to his music showed his miraculous power over nature, a divine power of animation. Milton aspired to be a poet of the Orphic type.[12]

In the voluble, optimistic confession of the Seventh Prolusion, Milton assures his audience that hard study of philosophy, religion and poetry can let a man overleap the limitations of his humanity:

> The delights that are the secret of study and learning . . . easily surpass all others. How much it means to grasp all the principles of the heavens and their stars, all the movements and disturbances of the atmosphere . . . and – finally – [penetrate] into the divine powers and faculties of the spirit, and whatever knowledge may be accessible to us about the beings that are called household gods and genii and daemons. . . . When the cycle of universal knowledge had been completed, still the spirit will be restless in our dark imprisonment here, and it will rove about until the bounds of creation itself no longer limit the divine magnificence of its quest. Then most happenings and events about us will become obvious so quickly that almost nothing can happen without warning or by accident to a man who is in possession of the stronghold of wisdom. Truly he will seem to have the stars under his control and dominion, land and sea at his command, and the winds and storms submissive to his will. Mother Nature herself has surrendered to him. It is as if some god had abdicated the government of the world and committed its justice, laws and administration to him as ruler.[13]

The figure that presides over the culmination of this Prolusion is Orpheus, who attained and exercised these 'mysterious powers'. The modern reader may be bewildered by these limitless aspirations and dismiss them as manic delusions of Renaissance grandeur, or he may by a sympathetic act of the historical imagination acknowledge the presence in Renaissance England of a supremely confident strain of humanist thought which believed in the supernatural potential of the fully extended intellect.

'Il Penseroso' describes that process, the solitary enterprise of intellectual transformation that Milton undertook in the 1630s. The stillness at the centre of the poem is the ecstasy of the mind:

> Or let my Lamp at midnight hour,
> Be seen in som high lonely Towr,
> Where I may oft out-watch the Bear,
> With thrice great Hermes, or unsphear
> The spirit of Plato to unfold
> What Worlds, or what vast Regions hold
> Her mansion in this fleshly nook:
> The immortal mind that hath forsook
> And of those Daemons that are found
> In fire, air, flood, or under ground,
> Whose power hath a true consent
> With Planet, or with Element.

The visionary form that he hopes to glimpse is Orpheus, his poetic archetype (lines 105–8). The conditions propitious to his hopes are created by Melancholy. Volumes have been written to explicate the Renaissance admiration for Melancholy as the temperament conducive to exalted philosophic thought, the precondition of heaven-piercing contemplation, most of them using Dürer's 'Melencolia' as the classical representation of the type. There can be no doubt that this figure honoured by Milton in 'Il Penseroso' was envisaged as a neo-Platonic guide and mentor. She is derived from the golden age ('Saturns raign') when men's spirits were clear and when men lived in easy commerce with the gods. Under her inspiration, Milton fables, the thoughtful man (Il Penseroso) might regain a large understanding of the structuring ideas of the universe. Melancholy's iconographic pose – '[Thy] looks commercing with the skies / Thy rapt soul sitting in thine eyes' – encourages the initiate, who, tuned by peace, quiet and abstinence, may in his trance hear 'the Muses in a ring / Ay round about Joves Altar sing', and fly with

> Him that yon soars on golden wing,
> Guiding the fiery-wheeled throne,
> The Cherub Contemplation.

Pagan and Christian images coalesce in a typical neo-Platonic fusion.

At this stage Milton still held that Greek mythology was compatible with Hebrew legends and the revelations of the New Testament, that it represented the codified secrets known to the wisest of the ancients, who had intuited the sublime order of creation and the innate capacity of the soul to refine itself into the divine energy that was its source. The visionary ecstasy that Milton anticipates here, as he boldly imagines himself assisting at the central mysteries of creation at 'Joves

Altar', and becoming one of the cherubim distinguished for their 'faculty of seeing God, and of contemplating the beauty of the Supreme Being',[14] recapitulates the high experience of 'At a Solemn Musick' and 'On Time', and looks forward to the ascent at the end of *Comus*. In 'Il Penseroso', the optimism is there, but the experience is still elusive. The poet turns to describe his retired life amid the shadows and forsaken woods, and he finally commits himself hermit-like to the shelter of the Anglican Church, whose aesthetics and spirituality he feels are especially conducive to the enlightenment he desires. (It is the time of 'the beauty of holiness' urged by Laud in the early 1630s.)

> There let the pealing Organ blow,
> To the full voic'd Quire below,
> In Service high, and Anthems cleer,
> As may with sweetnes, through mine ear,
> Dissolve me into extasies,
> And bring all Heav'n before mine eyes.

Philosophic study and religious devotion both further his quest

> Till old experience do attain
> To something like Prophetic strain.

The two poems thus mark ascending stages of philosophic mastery, one concerned with the poet's engagement with sense impressions, the other charged with a potential for transcendent illumination. In both poems the descriptive passages would seem to be interludes 'where more is meant than meets the ear', concealing the studious philosophic quest of Milton's youth.[15]

Milton continued to give poetic shape to his personal ambitions when he was invited to compose a masque for the Egerton family to celebrate their reunion at Ludlow in 1634. John Egerton, Earl of Bridgewater (son of Sir Thomas Egerton, Donne's first patron), had been appointed Lord President of Wales in the previous year, and now his family joined him, so the masque was designed to applaud his new elevation, and to honour his family. Milton had already written the brief masque 'Arcades' for Sir Thomas's wife, the Countess of Derby, but how he came to know the Egertons is uncertain: it may have been through his father, who had had financial dealings with them, or more probably, an introduction had been arranged by Henry Lawes, who was a friend of the Milton family and music tutor to the 'Lady' of *Comus*. One might assume that Milton obliged the Egertons by writing for them, and that he did not actively seek the commission, for his scheme of studious retirement presumably did not envisage the creation of masques; none the less, here was an opportunity to attempt a highly fashionable art form, and the chance to exploit the transcendental character of the genre.

Masque as it had been developed at the Stuart Court under Ben Jonson was a symbolic drama, which revealed, in settings of exceptional splendour, the secret spiritual virtue of the participants. The masquers, always of gentle birth, are engaged in a relatively simple fable which permits them at a critical moment to display their true sublime nature as paragons and powers: they may be elements of Harmony or aspects of Ideal Beauty, Olympian spirits or British Heroes, while the principal masquer, often royal, may be exalted as some controlling force, such as Heroic Virtue, Concord, or Chaste Love. Masque is a triumphal form, in which the masquers by the very potency of their presence expel all negative qualities or hostile agencies. The triumph of their perfections is expressed in lengthy, elaborate dances that sometimes culminate in symbolic patterns, and traditionally at the end of a masque the dancing spread into the audience so that the members of the Court could associate themselves with the honour of the occasion. The music of the masque too had a symbolic function, for it made audible the harmony established between the human and divine realms in the right action of the masque; equally, the music of the anti-masque of negative forces would have an irregular character. The masquers were creatures of light, usually revealed in an incandescent glow expressive of their purity and their semi-divine nature. One other feature should be stressed: Jonson had made the masque into a learned art, as a reading of his printed texts will indicate. There he explains in detail the symbolism of the emblems that his personages carry, the significance of costume, colour, movement and theme, all the details that might have gone unnoticed in the excitement of performance. The masque for Jonson was a theatre of mysteries, showing in a ceremonious way to a carefully chosen audience the higher powers that operate among fine-souled men, and because he was intent on revealing the intellectual and moral grandeur that infused the courts of kings who ruled by divine right, he applied his fairly conventional neo-Platonic learning and mythology to give sublimity to the action. It was important to Jonson that learning should be present in the masque, and that its statements about the nature of Justice, Beauty, Harmony or Love should be made; the philosophic views that were expounded, the secret operation of powers that were hinted at, were true and remained true whether or not they were fully understood by the Court. As he explained in his preface to a wedding masque, *Hymenaei* (1606), the higher meaning constituted the 'soul' of a masque, its vital principle.

This it is hath made the most royall Princes, and greatest persons (who are commonly the personaters of these actions) not onely studious of riches, and magnificence in the outward celebration, or shew; (which rightly becomes them) but curious after the most high, and heartie inventions, to furnish the inward parts: (and those grounded upon antiquitie, and solide learnings) which, though their voyce be taught to sound to present occasions, their sense, or doth, or should alwayes lay hold of more remov'd mysteries.

So, when Milton came to write his 'Mask', now known as *Comus*, there were many elements he could turn to his own advantage, while still honouring Lord Bridgewater, his family and benevolent rule. In terms of masque convention, the 'remov'd mystery' that Milton chose to celebrate in his symbolic action was a Triumph of Chastity. It has been suggested that the theme of chastity was unusually relevant to the Egerton family because they were closely related to the Castle-haven family, which had been involved in a particularly nasty sexual scandal in 1631–2 which resulted in the execution of Lord Castle-haven for encouraging the rape of his wife and the prostitution of his daughter. Did the Egertons request a masque of Chastity in order to distance themselves from their notorious relatives?[16] For Milton too the theme had an immediate relevance, for it formed part of his regime of self-preparation for the vocation of prophetic poet. Strictness of life, chastity and vigorous application to study were all of a piece. We recall what he had written in his verse letter to Diodati, that 'his youth must be chaste . . . his morals strict'; we have seen how in 'L'Allegro' and 'Il Penseroso' he was tuning his mind to a higher pitch; in *Comus* the process continues with the vindication of the chaste, temperate life against a sensuous life of pleasure and indulgence. The animating belief behind *Comus* is close to the conviction expressed by Pico della Mirandola in his *Oration on the Dignity of Man*, a work Milton certainly knew and admired, when he spoke of man's capacity to approach the infinite perfection of God:

So that with freedom of choice, and with honour, as though the maker and moulder of thyself, thou mayest fashion thyself in whatever shape thou shalt prefer. Thou shalt have the power to degenerate into the lower forms of life, which are brutish. Thou shalt have the power, out of thy soul's judgement, to be reborn into the higher forms, which are divine.[17]

The *Comus* fable mythologizes the temptation men may encounter to engross their spirits in the material pleasures of the natural world, and so move towards the life of beasts; against this is set the conscious choice of the philosophic mind to reject that temptation in aspiring to an angelic enlightenment.

As the Attendant Spirit enters, he announces himself to the audience as a spirit of the Platonic hierarchy, a *daemon*, that is an immortal intelligence from the radiant regions illuminated by the divine Mind:

Before the starry threshold of Joves Court
My mansion is, where those immortal shapes
Of bright aëreal Spirits live insphear'd
In Regions milde of calm and serene Ayr,
Above the smoak and stirr of this dim spot,
Which men call Earth, and with low-thoughted care
Confin'd, and pester'd in this pin-fold here,
Strive to keep up a frail, and Feaverish being
Unmindfull of the crown that Vertue gives
After this mortal change, to her true Servants
Amongst the enthron'd gods on Sainted seats.
Yet som there be that by due steps aspire
To lay their just hands on that Golden Key
That ope's the Palace of Eternity:
To such my errand is.

He is the Platonic equivalent of a guardian angel, descended as we learn expressly to help the young aspirant to Virtue, the Lady. The Trinity manuscript of Milton's working drafts calls him specifically 'a guardian angel or daemon', and he also serves as the Introducer of the masque, informing the audience about the action. The fashionable theme of the westward movement of the gods is unfolded, and we learn that Comus has now reached this westernmost region, 'this tract that fronts the falling Sun' guarded by 'a noble Peer of mickle trust'. Comus is not directly described, but defined, as Milton prefers, in terms of his mythological ancestry. Son of Bacchus and Circe, he combines dangerous negative powers: he can offer the ravishing transports of wine, with consequent degradation and bestial metamorphosis; he is dionysiac, seductive, destructive and indestructible.

After the Spirit has descended, he changes his celestial robes for shepherd's weeds, his 'mask' for the action. Pastoral had long been a favourite mode for masque. As the genre furthest removed from Court life with its artifice and corruption, it offered plenty of scope for fables of innocence and simplicity and primitive perfection – also for spiritual allegory. The harmony between divine power, nature and man was implicit in the genre. Moreover, the writers could exercise their skills in pastoral verse, which was universally enjoyed in the seventeenth century. For Milton especially, pastoral brought the greatest satisfaction in his early years, for it allowed him to develop in his poetry the Spenserian character in English and the Virgilian in Latin, at the same time enabling him to evolve a complex intellectual world under a pastoral cover by ordering mythological characters into significant relationships. Milton immediately attributes a favourite character to the Attendant Spirit, who has now disguised himself as the shepherd Thyrsis, equating him with Orpheus:

> Who with his soft Pipe, and smooth-dittied Song,
> Well knows to still the wilde winds when they roar,
> And hush the waving Woods.

Later, we hear more of his music,

> whose artful strains have oft delayed
> The huddling brook to hear his madrigal
> And sweetened every musk-rose of the dale.

The tribute is to Henry Lawes's musicianship, but as an Orpheus figure with power over the natural world through the controlling magic of his music, Thyrsis is, in the intellectual structure of the masque, a neo-Platonic mystagogue, the conductor of souls to a heaven of harmony, and it is he who is the real protagonist against Comus, a spirit who desires to degrade mankind. As a master of music and philosophy, Thyrsis is also a type of the poet that Milton is preparing to be, so that in the action of the masque, Milton's attention is divided between the Lady, whose trials are relevant to his present regime of self-control and chastity, and the Spirit, who represents what he might conceivably become.

When Comus enters with his revellers, his language is so imaginative and beguiling that the reader is readily won over, but we respond today primarily to the language, and do not *see* that he is accompanied by a 'rout of monsters'. Although he claims his own fineness of spirit – 'We that are of purer fire / Imitate the Starry Quire' – the irregular music of his anti-masque would deny it. We may well be persuaded to approve his pleasures as harmless and natural when he claims that his dance echoes the great dance of nature in praise of the Creator, which is led by the 'swift round' of the months and years:

> The Sounds, and Seas with all their finny drove
> Now to the Moon in wavering Morrice move,
> And on the Tawny Sands and Shelves,
> Trip the pert Fairies and the dapper Elves;
> By dimpled Brook, and Fountain brim,
> The Wood-Nymphs deckt with Daisies trim,
> Their merry wakes and pastimes keep.

But the stage directions call for 'a riotous and unruly noise', and we may also recall that for Milton the 'pert Fairies' and 'dapper Elves' belong in the catalogue of fallen spirits, as we saw in the Nativity Ode: their moral colour is mischief darkening into evil, and their rites belong to the 'dun shades'.

That music communicates moral values in the masque becomes evident as the Lady approaches, when Comus cries:

> Break off, break off, I feel the different pace,
> Of som chast footing neer about this ground.

She, lost in her father's forest (which is also for the purposes of the masque the Wood of Error), proclaims her conviction that her active, virtuous soul will soon attract divine guidance. Faith, Hope and Chastity, that distinctly Miltonic triad, will compel protection from above. Chastity is a most self-regarding virtue compared to charity, yet Milton insists on its importance by making it one of the cardinal virtues here. We have speculated that there may have been a premium on chastity in the Egerton family at this time, but we also know that the young Milton held chastity in high seriousness as a prerequisite of the philosophic life. The tradition of the ascetic sage has ancient origins, and the belief that bodily pleasures destroy mental concentration has followers even today. Milton drew on many sources to feed his belief – Hebrew, Christian and Greek – and we should not forget that, like many educated men of his age, he found ancient authorities more compelling than personal experience. Behind the claim in *Comus* that chastity rarefies the soul and prepares it for meditation on divine mysteries, lie the lives of the prophets, the practice of Christ, the strictures of St Paul that 'the body is . . . for the Lord; and the Lord is for the body', and the reading of Revelation 19 that the elect around the Lamb of God in the New Jerusalem shall all be chaste. Plato and Xenophon contributed pagan justifications of chastity that Milton responded to with equal zeal.[18] Chastity in *Comus* seems to comprehend virginity and to exclude marriage, but Milton is not explicit about this, being concerned with chastity more as a state of mind than as a physical condition.[19]

When the encounter between Comus and the Lady takes place, there is essentially no contest. Although Comus delivers a superbly fluent speech enticing her to enter into the fertile cycle of the natural world, the Lady is already so dedicated to the severe ways of virtue that she is never engaged by his temptation. Comus's arguments have an undoubted validity for most men and women, but the Lady is no ordinary woman, but one self-elected to 'the sublime notion and high mystery' of a philosophic quest. She may be captive, but the virtue of her mind cannot be assailed.

Milton contrives her release, which her brothers cannot effect, by the introduction of another spirit figure, Sabrina, the water nymph of Severn. River gods appeared with some regularity in Stuart masques: they introduced local and patriotic sentiment, for as gods of the region they paid homage to the lord through whose lands they flowed, and as servants of Neptune they reminded the audience of England's mastery of the ocean. According to legend, Sabrina had been a maiden who threw herself into the Severn to preserve her chastity, 'And underwent a quick immortal change / Made Goddess of the River', so thematically she is an appropriate figure to rescue the Lady, and also to exemplify the god-like power that chastity bestows. Finally the action moves to Ludlow, so that the fiction is now superimposed on the social occasion; the Lady and her brothers are presented to their father, having proved their virtue and their fortitude, and the masque modulates into a 'triumph in victorious dance / O're sensual Folly and Intemperance'.

But that is not the end. The Attendant Spirit returns for a last round of instruction, and in general in *Comus* his are the words that carry the weight of Milton's thought. He now describes in mythological terms the regions he inhabits, the realm that ultimately, we are to infer, all choice and chaste spirits will inherit. It is the Platonic heaven where the mythological archetypes of Virtue are laid up. Here are the Elysian Fields, the reward of the Blessed Spirits, and of the Heroes of Virtue. The tree with the golden apples of virtue grows in a musical setting of everlasting harmony, now freely accessible, its traditional guardian dragon gone. The Graces (here unspecified, but in neo-

Platonic symbolism indicative of the interaction of qualities whose synthesis in dance prepares the mind for transcendent knowledge)[20] combine with the Hours, also dancing figures appropriate to masque, who represent propitious time, in a perpetual climate of simultaneous spring and summer, promise and fulfilment. Even as he evokes this paradise of spiritual delight that is the reward of the philosophic soul, Milton sounds a call to attention – 'List mortals, if your ears be true' – that marks the movement towards more removed mysteries. Drawing now on images from Spenser's *Faerie Queene*, Book III (the Book of Chastity), from Apuleius's *Metamorphoses* and Boccaccio's *Genealogy of the Gods*, all books noted for their neo-Platonic allegories, he reveals the last two exalted mysteries, those of Venus and Adonis, and of Cupid and Psyche. Esoteric learning is rhymed into the most lyrical tetrameters:

> Beds of Hyacinth, and roses
> Where young Adonis oft reposes,
> Waxing well of his deep wound
> In slumber soft, and on the ground
> Sadly sits th'Assyrian Queen;
> But farr above in spangled sheen
> Celestial Cupid her fam'd Son advanc't,
> Holds his dear Psyche sweet intranc't
> After her wandring labours long,
> Till free consent the gods among
> Make her his eternal Bride,
> And from her fair unspotted side
> Two blissful twins are to be born,
> Youth and Joy; so Jove hath sworn.

Venus and Adonis as the highest types of natural love figure the mystery of earthly fertility, in which death and renewal perform a constant cycle, and where the mortal, wounded Adonis is forever regenerated by the love of Venus, the immortal goddess. The natural cycle, therefore, 'eterne in mutabilitie' (*Faerie Queene* III.vii.47) is sustained by the love of the divine for the mortal. As the archetypes of this phenomenon, Venus and Adonis occupy a high place in the scale of ideal images. Even higher than they, and at the extreme limits of human understanding, already partially engulfed in the light of the divine Mind ('in spangled sheen' – where intellectual and divine light mix) are Cupid and Psyche, who image the soul's ascent to divine fulfilment. Psyche may represent the beautiful form of the earth-bound soul liberated by Cupid as Divine Love, and their union is the climactic merging of the earthly and the divine that the philosophic mind sees as its ultimate consummation. The legend tells how by a premature viewing of her lover, Psyche loses her felicity and has to undertake arduous tasks, 'her wandring labours long', imposed on her by the gods as penance. These tasks disguise the striving of the soul to regain its lost bliss and to retain it by steadfast perseverance and selfless pursuit of divine love. Finally, Psyche is reunited with Cupid in a mystical marriage, the fruits of which, in *Comus*, are Youth and Joy, simple personifications of the regeneration and sublime ecstasy that the soul experiences in its divinely assimilated state. This myth enjoyed considerable currency in the fashionable neo-Platonic circles at Court surrounding the Queen in the 1630s,[21] and would hardly need much explanation by Milton, but whereas in the Court masques, poems and paintings it was largely a decorative fiction that pleased the audience with a semblance of profundity, in *Comus* one feels that Milton has organized an intellectual structure that is seriously intentioned and which reproduces in symbolic form his convictions and aspirations concerning the capacities of the strictly disciplined philosophic mind.

> Mortals that would follow me,
> Love vertue, she alone is free,
> She can teach ye how to clime
> Higher then the Spheary chime;
> Or if Vertue feeble were,
> Heav'n it self would stoop to her.

This verse has a light optimistic air suitable to a festive occasion, just as much of the poetry in the masque has a liveliness that suits it to music and dance; yet the design of *Comus* seems to come from a man who is intent on raising a temple of mysteries within a scene of courtly spectacle and entertainment. The frustration that modern readers may feel will probably be caused by our less than ample conception of the philosophic life that Milton was devoted to, as well as our inadequate response to abstractions such as 'Chastity' and 'Virtue', and our difficulty in dealing with the shorthand code of Renaissance mythology. We lack the necessary knowledge of neo-Platonic texts and systems of thought that sustained the symbolic images. We do not sufficiently understand the nature of the reward for virtue's quest. Had Milton been able to have the opulent facilities of a Whitehall masque with Inigo Jones as designer, he might have used the wonder-working power of the transformation scene and the brilliant effects of intensive lighting to conjure up a vision of the celestial delights that await the transported soul. Instead he had to settle for the verbal description provided by the Attendant Spirit's epilogue, which does not give the climax of wonder that the masque requires.

When the text of *Comus* was first published, anonymously, in 1634, the title page carried this epigram from Virgil's second Eclogue: '*Eheu quid volui misero mihi! floribus austrum perditus*' ('Alas what harm did I mean to my wretched self when I let the south wind blow on my flowers?'). The feeling that he has been forced by circumstances into exposing to view the beauties of his art and the secrets of his mind prematurely, and not in his own time, is strong in Milton.

The sentiment recurs at the opening of 'Lycidas', the elegy he wrote in 1637 for his drowned friend Edward King, and which he placed as the concluding poem of the English section of the 1645 volume.

> Yet once more, O ye Laurels, and once more
> Ye Myrtles brown, with Ivy never-sear,
> I com to pluck your Berries harsh and crude,
> And with forc'd fingers rude,
> Shatter your leaves before the mellowing year.

The pastoral elegy had such a long and complicated literary tradition by the seventeenth century that a poet might spend years preparing to master its art, acquainting himself with its antique and Renaissance developments and the innumerable graces of mood and meaning that were possible within so dense an inheritance. Although in principle the simplest of forms, pastoral had by the Renaissance become an extremely learned and sophisticated art in which the poet delighted to half display and half conceal his recollections of earlier masters, his mythological learning, and his skill in applying the pastoral mode to every aspect of life and death. The pastoral elegy in particular, by conventionally casting its subject as a dead shepherd mourned in sympathetic grief by his fellows and by the natural world, had developed an exceptional emotional power; it was an impersonal form that expressed universal mourning for an individual who had been raised to the status of a type. If the dead person had been a poet or priest, so much the better, as shepherds were conventionally poets and pastors too. In the Greek tradition, the arch-poet Apollo, leader of the Muses, had many pastoral aspects, and in the Christian tradition Christ had from earliest times been the type of the Good Shepherd. Milton's friend had been both poet and priest, so the two streams flow easily and naturally together in the elegy. The name Lycidas itself exemplifies how we are dealing with a tradition running right down from Greek antiquity, for it had been first used by Theocritus, the originator of the pastoral manner as we know it, and had had many poetic lives before Milton chose it to denominate his friend Edward King. Most notably, however, Lycidas is a pastor of the Virgilian plains, the shepherd–poet of the ninth Eclogue, and Milton's poem has an insistently Virgilian quality in the nobility of its movement and in its deep attachment to the beauty of the earth. Virgil's fifth Eclogue also contributes its note, for there the lament for the dead Daphnis, accompanied by the strewing of leaves on his grave, turns from sorrow to a resounding joy as the singers understand that Daphnis has been transformed into a god. Milton's indebtedness to Virgil is scarcely surprising when we remember the Roman's reputation as a prophetic poet and his association with the prophecy of Christ's redemptive mission; the Virgilian stance permits Milton to develop a large classical pastoral sequence that modulates easily into a Christian key towards the end.

In the context of Milton's development through the 1630s that we have been concerned with here, 'Lycidas' introduces some new issues: the premature death of the poet, and the question of religious allegiance. In 'Il Penseroso', *Comus* and the Latin letters to Diodati and his father, the assumption had always been of a lengthy poetic apprenticeship leading to some magisterial work, some sublime achievement that would be 'exemplary to a nation', as well as an act of personal dedication to the highest form of knowledge. What if death should intervene? Edward King's fate could well be Milton's own, and Milton is quick to establish their close identity: 'For we were nurst upon the self-same hill, / Fed the same flock, by fountain, shade, and rill.' As the case of Lycidas seems at first to show, the poet has no special guarantee of protection: his death is arbitrary, inexplicable. Yet Lycidas too, Milton feigns, had been Orphic, with a sympathetic power over nature, moving the trees by the secret harmonies he knew:

> The Willows, and the Hazle Copses green
> Shall now no more be seen,
> Fanning their joyous Leaves to thy soft layes.

In this desolating time when the whole endeavour of the poetic life is in doubt, Milton recalls the terrifying end of Orpheus himself, the dark fate of the father of poetry that Milton had never before dwelt on, torn to pieces by the mad followers of Dionysus:

What could the Muse her self that Orpheus bore,
The Muse her self, for her inchanting son
Whom Universal nature did lament,
When by the rout that made the hideous roar,
His goary visage down the stream was sent,
Down the swift Hebrus to the Lesbian shore.

These lines mark the failure of the large optimism of the earlier poems with their confidence in the poet as a favoured species. The grim remembrance of Orpheus's fate precipitates the crisis of lines 64 to 76, which ask what can justify the hard dedication to poetry when life can be so easily destroyed. The reply of Apollo as god of poetry and music, that the reward of one's fame will be in heaven, seems inadequate: fame is not the real issue for the Miltonic poet, but rather the development of a vast moral power, a wisdom and a skill in art that might raise him to be a demi-god. An answer to Milton's question is never fully given; we must assume that the poet's labours are self-justifying.

The ritual procession of mourners enters to offer tribute and consolation. All the figures come in their watery aspect fitting to the occasion of Lycidas's death at sea. So Cambridge is represented by the River Cam, and the chief mourner, St Peter, is introduced as 'The Pilot of the Galilean lake', a figure of mastery over water. He speaks as pastor, apostle and bishop, the patron of Lycidas the priest. His measured denunciation of the contemporary clergy for their unworthiness, greed, poor faith and neglect of pastoral care intrudes harshly into the poem. It is too strident, and the rough language forces the character of the poem towards satire. The disruption of decorum here suggests the strength of feeling behind the formalism of the elegy: the impersonality of manner is maintained, for the attack remains general, yet one senses that Milton's interests are closely engaged in this passage. The prefatory note to the poem has prepared us for this outburst – 'And by occasion foretels the ruine of our corrupted Clergy then in their height' – presenting it as an example of prophetic writing. These lines of bitter discontent with the Anglican Church under Laud mark a critical change in Milton's career. The various devotional hymns and odes, the elegy to Lancelot Andrewes, the contentment with the 'beauty of holiness' expressed at the end of 'Il Penseroso', perhaps even the vows of chastity in *Comus*, had all been compatible with a vocation as a minister within the Anglican Church. By 1637, however, his suspicion that the Caroline Church was being taken over by the wrong sort of people and becoming a false Church is sufficient to make him summon up St Peter to anathematize it. The long course of Milton's public opposition to the character and efficacy of the established Church begins with this protest in 'Lycidas'.

It is difficult for Milton to recover from the change of mood caused by St Peter's authoritative voice. He does so by falling back on the antiquity of the pastoral tradition, which has rituals to soften death in all ages. He recalls the myth of Alpheus and Arethusa, water nymphs of Arcadia who fled beneath the sea and reappeared in Sicily; thematically it introduces the motif of disappearance and restoration that will be applied to Lycidas: 'For Lycidas your sorrow is not dead, / Sunk though he be beneath the watry floar.' Classical myth and natural phenomena (the setting and rising of the sun, the turning of winter into spring, as marked by the vegetation in the poem) prefigure and allegorize the truth of the Christian promise of resurrection and eternal life. Christ appears in the poem as a deity with power over water – 'the dear might of him that walk'd the waves' – who ensures the translation of the doomed shepherd to a heaven where elements of Greek myth combine with images from Revelation to create the ultimate scene of Lycidas among the life-giving waters, 'Where other groves, and other streams along, / With Nectar pure his oozy Lock's he laves.' In the classical action of the poem, Lycidas becomes a water spirit, a protective 'genius of the shore', but that fiction, required by pastoral convention, glosses the reality of his Christian apotheosis.

So with this resolution the English poems of 1645 end. The shepherd–poet prepares towards new scenes. In the 'Epitaphium Damonis', the pastoral elegy to his friend Diodati that closes the Latin poems of the same volume with a similar fusion of classical and Christian ritual celebrations, and with a similar intention of renewed purpose after a check, Milton promises some epic or romance on legendary British history. The final English and Latin poems both look to new beginnings, and the 1645 volume as a whole represents a finished phase of work, accomplishments in many genres, a grandeur of ambition matched by a strength of achievement.

The Civil Wars unexpectedly cut across Milton's plans for a carefully controlled process of maturation and the due composition of sublime poetry. The scholar–sage discovered he possessed remarkable talents for aggressive disputation in the matters of civil liberties and Church government that fell wide open for debate in the 1640s. Poetry was largely put aside for the business of the State, and it was only when

Milton was excluded from public life after the Restoration that he turned again to the great poetic ambitions he once entertained. *Paradise Lost* was published in 1667, twenty-two years after previous poems, thirty years after the mourner of Lycidas turned to 'pastures new'. *Paradise Lost* is a universal epic, the great philosophic poem he had always desired to write; its action stretches from before the beginning of time to 'the world's great period'. Its vast scale and subject matter put it beyond the limits of this book, but one large theme may be briefly taken up because it relates so closely to the expectations of many of the writers we have examined in both their religious and secular works, and that is the millenarian theme of the restored paradise, which is central to Milton's thinking in spite of the title of his epic.

We have observed how widespread was the belief in this period that men were living in the last phase of history, in the night of time, that Christ would soon return to judge and to re-establish the Earthly Paradise where he would rule over his elect for a thousand years. Donne, Vaughan, Traherne and Marvell all shared this assumption. Milton too became a millenarian in the 1640s, convinced that the extraordinary upheavals in Church and State, culminating in the execution of the King as a tyrant, were signs of the latter days as prophesied in Isaiah, Daniel and Revelation. God was shaking the kingdom with 'strong and healthy commotions to a general reforming'. The innumerable sects that sprang up in the suddenly free atmosphere of the 1640s were clear evidence of the rising of the spirit that marked the reforming of Reformation itself in anticipation of Christ's return. Milton wrote of 'the Eternall and shortly-expected King' in 1641[22] and prayed fervently for the return of Christ:

> Come forth out of thy Royall Chambers, O Prince of all the Kings of the earth, put on the visible roabes of thy imperiall Majesty, take up that unlimited scepter which thy Almighty Father hath bequeath'd thee; for now the voice of thy Bride calls thee, and all creatures sigh to be renew'd.[23]

As Israel had been the scene of Christ's Incarnation, England (so Milton hoped) would be the place of his return, for in this last age God's manner is to reveal himself 'first to his Englishmen'.[24] Under Cromwell (when Milton was an important political figure as Secretary of Foreign Tongues to the Council of State) his expectations of some divine intervention remained high, and Milton, like his friend Marvell, could view Cromwell as a godly harbinger of Christ, preparing the way for his kingdom. But when the political miracle of 1660 occurred, which brought the Restoration of Charles II, Milton's apocalyptic hopes collapsed. Nevertheless the paradisal idea that had been so prominent in the 1640s and 1650s lingered on in the 1660s, fading into literary metaphor and transforming itself into a secularized passion for gardening. Milton's epic on the loss of paradise may be an immense compensation for his unfulfilled political dreams, an explanation by poetic theology of why the human endeavour towards perfection in any sphere will meet with failure. But, on another level, it permits him to make a last lingering discovery of the unfallen world and of the state of innocence, and to realize the deepest fantasies of his generation. The wonderful descriptions of Paradise in Book IV are a revelation of the supreme natural beauty that English poets from the time of Spenser had tried to attain:

Thus was this place,
A happy rural seat of various view:
Groves whose rich Trees wept odorous Gums and Balm,
Others whose fruit burnisht with Golden Rind
Hung amiable, Hesperian Fables true,
If true, here only, and of delicious taste:
Betwixt them Lawns, or level Downs, and Flocks
Grazing the tender herb, were interpos'd,
Or palmy hillock, or the flow'ry lap
Of some irriguous Valley spread her store,
Flow'rs of all hue, and without Thorn the Rose:
Another side, umbrageous Grots and Caves
Of cool recess, o'er which the mantling Vine
Lays forth her purple Grape, and gently creeps
Luxuriant; meanwhile murmuring waters fall
Down the slope hills, disperst, or in a Lake,
That to the fringed Bank with Myrtle crown'd,
Her crystal mirror holds, unite thir streams.
The Birds thir choir apply; airs, vernal airs,
Breathing the smell of field and grove, attune
The trembling leaves, while Universal Pan
Knit with the Graces and the Hours in dance
Led on th'Eternal Spring.
(IV:246–68)

Slowly and with complete authority Milton unfolds the scene. The perfections of Milton's Eden had long been meditated by the author. They are far more than the accumulated memories of other literary paradises, more than the recreations of some fabled golden age; they are the known features of a divinely bright world that could be the millennial future, a world that many men of profound faith believed they might yet live to inherit. Paradise may be the next, last scene of earth, just as it was the first. The dream faded, but the clarity of Milton's vision is a measure of how intensely it had shone for him. Milton's *Paradise Regained* has to be won by the solitary confrontation of Christ with Satan in the wilderness, and instead of the imminent happy termination of history and the communal repossession of a restored paradise by the elect, there is only the cool theological assurance that such repossession has been made possible, by Christ, but that the event is now indefinitely deferred.

With the successful re-establishment of the new regime of Charles II, with its thoroughly worldly concerns and its pleasure-seeking drives, the lofty scheme of *Paradise Lost* seems forlornly out of date. Milton's retirement from public life, no longer chosen as in youth, but enforced by political pressure, is the evidence of the new society's rejection of his noble vision of a Christian commonwealth guided by spiritual heroes and godly men, with an honoured place for inspired prophets like himself. The sublime conception of humanity on which he had modelled himself, the Prospero-ideal of wisdom, poetry and benevolent power, looks very insubstantial in the plain Restoration light.

Notes

1 Translation from *The Poems of John Milton*, ed. John Carey and Alastair Fowler (London 1968), p. 292.

2 Clio is also relevant to the Latin poem 'Mansus' in which Milton honours the Italian poet Manso, whom he met in 1638. See lines 24–8 ('I, a young stranger sent from Hyperborean skies, wish you a long and healthy life in the name of Clio and of great Phoebus').

3 Erato traditionally carries a lyre, for lyric poetry should accompany love. Here the engraver seems to have misread or confused his visual sources, for the lyre and its bow have been turned into a sphere and a set-square, symbols of geometry or architecture.

4 The title *Comus* was attached to the masque in the eighteenth century, against the use of custom, for masques had titles that alluded to the victorious achievement of the action, and were not named after antagonists.

5 Translation from Carey and Fowler, *The Poems of John Milton*, p. 118.

6 This fascination with apotheosis is a reminder that Milton responded enthusiastically to the aesthetics of baroque art. The dynamism of the baroque apotheosis, where the deceased hero is swept up into heaven and rapturously received in a tumultuous chiaroscuro, appealed strongly to him, as did the free mingling of classical and Christian elements it employed, and the host of personifications. He could have seen prints of Rubens's works of this kind before he went to Italy in 1638, when he would have seen the interiors of the Jesuit churches; and of course Rubens's paintings of the Apotheosis of James I were installed in the Banqueting House at Whitehall in 1635. Milton had invented his finest apotheosis as early as 1626 for the death of Lancelot Andrewes, Bishop of Winchester: 'Everything glowed with a rosy light. . . . As I gaze all round me in wonder at the shining spaces and the shadows under the clustering vines, suddenly the Bishop of Winchester appears, close by me. A star-like radiance shone from his bright face, a white robe flowed down to his golden feet and his god-like head was encircled by a white band. . . . The heavenly host clap their jewelled wings, and the pure upper air rings with the blast of a triumphant trumpet' ('Elegia Tertia', translation from Carey and Fowler, *The Poems of John Milton*, p. 53).

7 See the association of the fallen angels with fairies at the end of *Paradise Lost*, I:775–90.

8 John Dee and Robert Fludd were the most active of the English aspirants to universal knowledge, but they wrote in Latin and their great prose works remain scarcely known. *Doctor Faustus* dramatizes the plight of a misdirected magus.

9 See Frances Yates, *Giordano Bruno and the Hermetic Tradition* (London 1964). This book, together with Edgar Wind's *Pagan Mysteries in the Renaissance* (London 1958), offers the most coherent approach to these most involved subjects, Renaissance neo-Platonism and mythography. In the course of the sixteenth century, some components of this system of ideas had been simplified and popularized into emblems that could be used by educated Italians who were aware of the arcane philosophical circles of the great courts, and who wished to gain a superficial proficiency in understanding these exciting developments. In the Court masques of James I and Charles I, Ben Jonson had intro-

duced symbolic figures and images derived from these emblem books to create a theatre of mysteries, but the mysteries were not too profound as they had to be fathomed by the members of a Court audience.

10 The Italian titles may acknowledge the Italian tradition of philosophic inquiry that Milton was indebted to, or may merely indicate that they were dedicated to his Anglo-Italian friend Charles Diodati.

11 *Argumentum* to Ficino's *Pimander*, translated and quoted in Yates, *Giordano Bruno*, p. 14.

12 See Raymond B. Waddington, 'Milton among the Carolines', in *The Age of Milton*, ed. C. A. Patrides (Manchester 1980), pp. 348–51, for a discussion of Milton's Orphism.

13 'Seventh Prolusion', translated in *John Milton: Complete Poetry and Major Prose*, ed. Merritt Y. Hughes (New York 1957), p. 625. cf. the more succinct statement by Cerimon, the magus figure in Shakespeare's *Pericles:*

> I hold it ever,
> Virtue and cunning were endowments greater
> Than nobleness and riches; careless heirs
> May the two latter darken and expend,
> But immortality attends the former,
> Making a man a god.
> (III.ii.26)

14 Note in Carey and Fowler, *The Poems of John Milton*, p. 142, citing a neo-Platonic text on angelology.

15 We might associate with 'L'Allegro' and 'Il Penseroso' Edgar Wind's observation, that 'the Renaissance mystagogues cultivated a combination of gloom and banter', made in a discussion of the comic and tragic aspects of the myth of Apollo and Marsyas, *Pagan Mysteries*, p. 146.

16 See Christopher Hill, *Milton and the English Revolution* (London 1977), pp. 43–4, and Barbara Breasted, 'Comus and the Castlehaven Scandal', *Milton Studies* III (1971).

17 Pico della Mirandola, *Oration on the Dignity of Man*, trans. E. L. Forbes, in *The Renaissance Philosophy of Man*, ed. E. Cassirer, P. O. Kristeller and J. H. Randall (New York 1948), p. 225. See also A. Fletcher, *The Transcendental Masque* (New York 1971), pp. 60–5, for an extended assessment of Milton's debt to Pico.

18 See the passages in *An Apology for Smectymnuus*, where Milton cites the many authorities he respected regarding chastity, in Hughes, *John Milton*, pp. 694–5.

19 Later, after his marriage, Milton revised his views around the ideal of married chastity, i.e. total fidelity to one's partner in marriage.

20 As, for example, in Botticelli's 'Primavera', where the Three Graces have been interpreted as Beauty, Chastity and Pleasure, reconciled in concord that prepares the soul for a heavenward ascent, guided by Hermes. The interpretation of this painting in Wind, *Pagan Mysteries*, ch. 7, provides an excellent introduction to the Renaissance art of argument by mythological images that Milton practised in *Comus*.

21 See Graham Parry, *The Golden Age Restor'd* (Manchester 1981), pp. 196–7.

22 *Of Reformation in England* (1641).

23 *Animadversions* (1641).

24 *Areopagitica* (1644).

9 Andrew Marvell and providential history

Marvell, although a friend of Milton, could scarcely have been more unlike him in character. While Milton habitually sought the light of public attention, and deliberately prepared himself for the role of a public poet, Andrew Marvell was a reticent man, guarded and self-protective. John Aubrey wrote of him that 'He was in his conversation very modest, and of very few words: and though he loved wine, he would never drink hard in company, and was wont to say that, he would not play the good-fellow in any man's company in whose hands he would not trust his life. He had not a general acquaintance.' His letters reveal little about his character or beliefs. His lyric poetry is notoriously ambiguous in tone and meaning, and it is only in his political satires after the Restoration that his position becomes more defined, but even then he preferred to publish anonymously. The great majority of his poems were published for the first time in 1681, three years after his death, in the volume unrevealingly called *Miscellaneous Poems*. So, his literary career is characterized by a secretiveness that has made the interpretation of his poetry in this century a matter of considerable conjecture. Where did Marvell's political loyalties lie? What were his personal opinions about Charles I and Cromwell? What was the nature of his religious commitments? These are obvious questions relating to his public self. Associated with them are matters of cultural or moral choice: whether the active life is to be preferred to the retired life, material ambitions to spiritual, artifice to nature, experience to innocence. Decision does not come easily: a number of his poems take the form of a dialogue that ends in a draw rather than a definite conclusion. Throughout his work, his sophisticated and witty manner makes it difficult to determine the seriousness of his intentions. In short, he is the most puzzling, pleasing, tantalizing poet of his age.

Marvell's poetry has to be read in its historical context, in the setting of the 1640s and 1650s, if we are to find some coherence and consistency in it. The rapidly changing political circumstances of these decades were doubtless a major cause of Marvell's caution: he was not a man disposed to flaunt his allegiances; his sense of discretion was too strong for that. We do not know whom he associated with during his time at Trinity College, Cambridge, and his activities throughout the 1640s, after he left, remain obscure. He appears prudently to have been travelling on the continent for four years during the period of the Civil War.[1] His first appearance in print was by means of a commendatory poem prefixed to Lovelace's volume of Cavalier verse, *Lucasta*, in 1649, a suggestion of Royalist sympathies further indicated by his elegy on Lord Hastings in the same year. The Lovelace poem regrets that the harshness of the present age makes it impossible for a poet to write the generous complimentary verse that the Caroline Court used to encourage, for 'Our wits have drawn the infection of our times.' There is the sense of living after the decline of a golden age of poetry that flourished in a civilized, cultured world engagingly represented by Lovelace; now the old codes of poetry are outmoded, the social confidence has gone, and the easy unforced praise of virtue and beauty is discredited. 'Our Civil Wars have lost the civic crown.' Marvell was born just too late for that 'candid age', and his own poetry reflects the divisiveness of a time of faction. As we have noticed, many of his poems are concerned with setting some quality or person or idea in balanced opposition to another, and there is often a sense of divided loyalties or alternative ways of action. Yet though he responded to the pressures of events in his own time, he was extremely attracted to the Cavalier mode, and in a sense he is its valedictorian.

In the lyric poems that we assume to date from the late 1640s and early 1650s,[2] Marvell seems almost consciously to be tidying up and terminating the Caroline tradition, putting the finishing touches on various conventions, giving them one last perfect and unfollowable performance before the shadows of history close on them. He was very familiar with recent poetry, and his own work is full of memories of Lovelace and Suckling, Carew, Herrick, Crashaw, Cowley and Cleveland, Randolph, and in particular Waller; the phrase 'my ecchoing song' (in the 'Coy Mistress') is an apt one.[3] Time and again he takes some poetic convention of love, gives it a supremely fine and exquisite expression, adds an unexpected twist, and effectively concludes that line of development. Who could persuade a reluctant mistress more urgently or more wittily than Marvell? Who could define love more remarkably or explain its irresistible power? Could more intellectual tears be shed, or cruel mistresses described? The pastoral complaint attains its height of sophistication with Marvell's mowers, the pastoral dialogue with his shepherds. 'Upon Appleton House' terminates the tradition of the country house poem in the seventeenth century. Only Milton's Eden lies beyond the numinous gardens of Marvell. This air of finality derives from his historical moment: it is not that other poets were inhibited by his brilliance from attempting the topics he treated so well, but rather that the subject matter of his poems belonged to a world that had vanished, leaving him the last inheritor. Seen from our own vantage point, he seems to stand at the end of a poetic movement whose living culture, that of the Court of Charles I, he had never experienced, although he was highly appreciative of its consequences for art. Writing outside the social milieu of this kind of poetry, as one assumes he was, he intellectualizes and refines and introduces teasing ambiguities into a manner that was already notably artificial and posed, so that the result is a super-subtle, privately crafted group of poems that seem self-contained and self-absorbed to an unusual degree.

In 'The Definition of Love', for example, Marvell took a subject that had had a long popularity in seventeenth-century philosophic and courtly circles, the attempt to explain the nature of love. Donne had treated the theme in several poems, such as 'The Exstasie' and 'A Valediction: forbidding Mourning'; Lord Herbert had written a well-known poem, 'Whether love should continue for ever'; the Caroline masques frequently explored the question, and it was probably the sort of discussion topic that exercised the wits of men and women in gallant conversations in country houses and at Court. Marvell takes it up, and immediately begins to exploit the ambiguity latent in the title: as he attempts to define the uniqueness of his love, he discovers that an aspect of that uniqueness is its definition, or limitation, by fate. Although his love partakes of cosmic energy, its fulfilment is prohibited by fate lest the new power prove uncontrollable.

> For Fate with jealous Eye does see
> Two perfect Loves; nor lets them close:
> Their union would her ruine be,
> And her Tyrannick pow'r depose.

The nature of his wonderful love is that it should remain restricted, thwarted and in fact defined. Marvell applies a great deal of wit and paradox in the manner of Donne, with a fine display of the geometry and astronomy of love; conceits and spectacular hyperbole abound;

there is a high intellectual spirit, an elegant style of demonstration, that belong to the Cavalier mode. Yet the poem lacks the optimism and the humanity of its forebears. The reader, like the lover, is trapped by that frustrating balance of opposing forces that marks so many of Marvell's poems. The resounding conclusion is an ingenious stalemate:

> Therefore the Love which us doth bind,
> But Fate so enviously debarrs,
> Is the Conjunction of the Mind,
> And Opposition of the Stars.[4]

There is a finality about this ending that seems to preclude any further discussion of the topic. Yet, one leaves the poem with a lingering uneasiness, caused by the disturbing image in the third stanza:

> And yet I quickly might arrive
> Where my extended Soul is fixt,
> But Fate does Iron wedges drive,
> And alwaies crouds it self betwixt.

In a poem largely dealing with abstractions, these 'iron wedges' intrude an unexpected, unpleasant realism. Where do they come from, what do they refer to? They may be a literary memory of Horace, whose Ode I.xxxv depicts pitiless Necessity wielding 'cuneas' or wedges, but their solidity seems to require a more immediate reference, some glance at the iron-clad world of Civil War England, where 'decrees of steel' were enforced.[5] Is there (faintly suggested) some Royalist–Roundhead / Capulet–Montague situation of star-crossed lovers here to give a social basis to the abstract geometry of the poem? Impossible to say: Marvell is a specialist in conjuring up spectral meanings in his verse.

Marvell's most memorable treatment of a conventional theme is 'To his Coy Mistress', where he takes the *carpe diem* topos that was so popular in the Renaissance and gives it the most irresistible statement in English. Jonson in his Celia poems, Herrick to Corinna, are the most successful of a host of such invitations to love, but Marvell's poem out-pleads them all in compliment, wit, argument and urgency. The fantastic hyperboles with which he praises his mistress's beauty carry the tradition of exaggerated compliment so enjoyed by the Caroline poets to unprecedented lengths, the whole of history being imaginatively devoted to the contemplation of her beauty, and their love expanding to fill the world.

Thou by the Indian Ganges side
Should'st Rubies find: I by the Tide
Of Humber would complain. I would
Love you ten years before the Flood:
And you should if you please refuse
Till the Conversion of the Jews.
My vegetable Love should grow
Vaster then Empires, and more slow.
An hundred years should go to praise
Thine Eyes, and on thy Forehead Gaze.
Two hundred to adore each Breast:
But thirty thousand to the rest.
An Age at least to every part,
And the last Age should show your Heart.

The exotic is humorously contrasted with the familiar, the Ganges with the Humber, Marvell's native river (the only personal touch in a thoroughly impersonal poem). The time-span allotted to their love engages with the apocalyptic speculations so strong in the 1640s and 1650s, which Marvell, as we shall see, had a serious respect for; here they are an occasion for wit and compliment, but none the less they add darker tones to the poem. The conversion of the Jews was a prerequisite of the Last Judgement, according to the Book of Revelation; the Flood wiped out the world once, and mankind barely survived, but the Last Judgement will destroy the world entirely. Although the poet's love is miraculously strong enough to endure through the first cataclysm, it will not survive the Final Day. Hence it stops at the conversion of the Jews, when the Judgement is imminent, so there will be just enough time for amorous action before the world ends. This is the 'last age' when the lady herself will yield. Against the vast and amusing scenario of world history is set the drama of the poet's time, brief, fleeting, threatened by death.

But at my back I alwaies hear
Times winged Charriot hurrying near:
And yonder all before us lye
Desarts of vast Eternity.
Thy Beauty shall no more be found,
Nor, in thy marble Vault, shall sound
My ecchoing Song: then Worms shall try
That long preserv'd Virginity:

And your quaint Honour turn to dust;
And into ashes all my Lust.
The Grave's a fine and private place,
But none I think do there embrace.

That chariot is the most famous vehicle of the seventeenth century.[6] The image is one of Marvell's great imaginative inventions, for it is compellingly right, and metre and rhythm combine to intensify the menace of its pursuit. The line 'Desarts of vast Eternity' represents a splendid dismissal of centuries of Christian hope: eternity, the golden dream of the ages, nullified into a desert for lack of his mistress's love.[7] The hope of eternity and the despair of the grave are equally horrendous without love, which is proposed as the only value that can counteract time, and change its character from destructive to regenerative, an idea that is already prefigured by the contrast between the Flood (destructive time) and the conversion of the Jews (regenerative time) in the first section. This transformation of the quality of time by love looks forward to the triumph of the final section when the lovers will outpace time, escape beyond 'the Iron gates of Life' – and whatever these may be, they are strongly expressive of limitation and sorrow – into a new dimension of timeless delight left tantalizingly undescribed by the poet.

The brilliant qualities of the poetry of the 'Coy Mistress' have been vastly admired in this century: the suppleness of the octosyllabic couplets, the variety and verve of the rhythm, the argumentative structure, the accelerating pace of the appeal, all these help to give the poem its unusual power. The central section quoted here must be one of the high moments of seventeenth-century expression, with its command of immensities, the personal urgency heard amid so many emotional tensions, the aural and tactile power of the language which causes the reader's response to be so complex. Note how that little word 'try' (with all its meanings of test, experience, sample) is set delicately, provocatively, ironically on the end of the line to make the horror of the situation more immediate. 'The Grave's a fine and private place' is an ingenious observation on the part of the lover, but it includes the ambiguity of 'fine' meaning narrow and terminal, and 'private' suggesting that one is 'deprived' of all sense in the grave. The quizzical 'I think' reminds one of the intellectually speculative character of the poet–lover and allows the shadow of necrophilia to fall across the verse. Things happen by suggestion in Marvell's poetry, so that secondary colonies of meaning often develop that are at odds with the primary meaning. For example, we hear the love song echoing in the tomb, even though we are told it will never sound there, just as the possibility of love in the grave is raised even as it is denied. These ambiguities are characteristic of Marvell's method of proceeding, making the reader conscious that diverse experiences are accessible within a poem, as the nominal subject raises various possibilities of interpretation through the subtlety of linguistic usage.

Contemporary issues and dilemmas are never far from the surface in Marvell's poems, even in his most lyrical compositions. In small but significant ways the poems reveal their relationship with the turbulence of the Civil Wars and the uncertain years that followed. The plain statement that opens 'The Nymph complaining for the death of her Faun' describes a sudden irruption of violence into the pastoral world suggestive of the disruption by war of Caroline England, so often characterized in poetry and masque as a pastoral idyll:

> The wanton Troopers riding by
> Have shot my Faun and it will dye.

The sense of unmerited suffering and inexplicable betrayal in that poem reflects the bewilderment (expressed at length in 'Upon Appleton House') that an apparently secure and divinely favoured country should be blighted by Civil War. The impression of innocence destroyed, of Christ killed again by the evil of the world, amplifies the poem's meaning far beyond the conventional lament of a mistress for her pet. The garden that is also a wilderness, the emphatic association of the fawn with roses and lilies (which also happen to be the royal emblems of Charles and Henrietta Maria), the grief that is so much in excess of its nominal object, cause one to suspect that this poignant poem is also a lament for a mortally wounded monarchy and for the 'candid age' before the Civil War.

'The Unfortunate Lover' also seems to be a poem haunted by contemporary allusion: its emblematic tableaux are rich in images of disasters of state and are powerfully suggestive of the passion of Charles I. This seems to be a poem where political events are concealed by a combination of Petrarchan and masque-derived images.[8] The portentousness of its splendid lines again seems to relate to a situation far graver than its explicit subject, which is the characterization of a heroic yet defeated lover. This ability to project material of substance and grandeur from a slight platform is a constant in Marvell's art. 'The ratling Thunder hurl'd, / As at the Fun'ral of the World' compels us to feel that this poem too is an elegy for the age, related moreover to the interest shown in the 'last age' of the 'Coy Mistress', for Marvell's poetry is pervaded by a sense of living at the climactic period of time, when 'angry Heaven' was preparing for the terminal revelation of history.

Further evidence of Marvell's interest in the latter days may be found in his numerous references to mowers. These innocent-seeming subjects commonly figure graver issues. The landscape they inhabit is dark indeed, and though at first hearing their songs are pleasantly forlorn, closer acquaintance may detect undertones of a universal elegy. The mowers are personifications of the destructive energies of war, 'depopulating all the Ground', but also, more ominously still, they are apocalyptic types, agents of the vast desolation of the last days, when 'Flowr's, and Grass, and I and all, / Will in one common Ruine fall' ('The Mower's Song'). They are prefigurations of the coming End: 'For Death thou art a Mower too' ('Damon the Mower').[9] Everywhere Marvell's poetry is marked with signs of the times, though his habitual secretiveness often makes him seem to be handling some mild, conventional subject when he is covertly interested in far deeper affairs.

Marvell first directly addressed himself to the major issues of the day in his 'Horatian Ode upon Cromwell's Return from Ireland', which can be dated by its subject between May and July 1650, and which was soon circulating in manuscript. The Ode represents a shift towards the observation of and commentary on contemporary affairs that characterizes much of his poetry during the 1650s;[10] it also marks the beginning of a long fascination on the part of Marvell with the character of Cromwell and the attempt to assess his place in history. The unexpectedly dispassionate tone of this work may be seen as an indication of his desire to assess objectively an historical process that was taking place at the time of the poem's composition. An understanding of the Ode will be helped by a rapid sketch of the political situation in mid 1650. Cromwell as Lord General, responsible to Parliament, had returned victorious from Ireland, where he had brutally crushed the Catholic–Royalist rebellion, and was about to embark on an expedition against the Scots, who had proclaimed Charles II King and forged a Presbyterian–Royalist alliance. Charles I had been executed in January 1649, the Republic was still young, and it was obvious that Cromwell as military commander had sufficient power to master Parliament if he chose. In order to get some perspective on events, Marvell employs a comparison with Roman history, incorporating various Roman details in his appraisal, and entitling his poem 'An Horatian Ode', a title which invites us to recall Horace's example as a writer of judicious public poems, and also reminds us of Horace's position *vis-à-vis* Augustus after the Roman Civil Wars. Horace had been on the losing side in those wars, yet had managed to appreciate the qualities of the victor, Augustus. Augustus himself had transformed the Roman republic into an Empire, the opposite process to that which occurred in England, where the monarchy was replaced by a republic. Yet Augustus's career may prefigure Cromwell's, for he began 'in the Republic's Hand', where Cromwell then was in 1650, but he went on to take absolute power for himself, as Cromwell might well do. The comparison with Augustus implied in the title concedes this possibility. The discretion with which Marvell hints at his own position and at Cromwell's likely development shows his instinctive dislike of adopting an open political stance in dangerous times, and this guardedness comes across in his balanced treatment of both Charles and Cromwell in the poem. Recent studies of Marvell's politics and allegiance suggest that his sympathies were monarchical rather than republican, and that in matters of religion he was for toleration, a liberty of conscience man, an Independent like Cromwell. Toleration in the seventeenth century, however, did not extend to Catholics, for whom Marvell had a lasting detestation. He also was a life-long opponent of the system of episcopacy, which he saw as a variant of Catholicism. He admired King Charles as a man, yet believed that Charles's cause was ruined by his dependence on the bishops (or 'prelates' as Marvell usually called them), who demanded uniformity and conformity in religion, and in so doing made Charles's regime intolerable to many Englishmen in a way that ultimately led to his downfall.[11] Marvell disliked military rule, and was also fearful of the democracy that was threatening to develop after the execution of Charles. During the 1650s he grew steadily more appreciative of Cromwell's authority as Lord Protector, but in 1650, the moment of the Ode, his view of Cromwell was ambivalent, even as he recognized that a critical point of English history had arrived. What was the nature and destiny of the new power that had arisen in England in the person of Oliver Cromwell? The crisis of the times obliges men to involve themselves in politics and war, even such private men as the young poet of the opening lines, in whom we may see a reflection of Marvell himself: 'The forward Youth that would appear / Must now forsake his Muses dear'. Love lyrics and pastorals, 'his Numbers languishing', have to be abandoned for public themes. The poet under pressure of the time follows in his own fashion the direction of his subject, Cromwell, who has left the retired life of a country gentleman for 'adventrous War' and the vast power of State. As Cromwell acts, the poet judges.

Marvell's ambivalent attitude to Cromwell has frequently been commented on. He characterizes him as a violent force which has ruined 'the great Work of Time', the fabric of Church and State, crushed the 'antient Rights' of monarchy, and imposed a forced power upon the nation. He is described as 'the English Hunter' and as a killer falcon, scarcely favourable terms, yet there is also a strain of admiration in the verse, for his 'industrious Valour' and his 'wiser Art': 'And, if we would speak true, / Much to the Man is due.' Marvell's position becomes clearer when we realize that he views Cromwell as a figure of providential history, just as he sees the events of the time as 'climacteric' – productive of radical change that will effect a transition from one epoch to another. Cromwell is more than a military man, he is a divinely directed force, God's agent for the reshaping of history. Therefore, criticism of his actions cannot hope to judge the man, but must struggle to understand the process of history in which he is a determining factor. In common with vast numbers of his contemporaries, of whom Milton was the most eloquent, Marvell believed in the providential nature of history, that history was a manifestation of God's purposes for men, and that ever since the Reformation, God's hand had been increasingly visible as he went about the purifying of religion and the promotion of his favoured nations in preparation for the last age of the world, fulfilling the prophecies of Isaiah, Daniel and the Book of Revelation. The climactic struggle with Antichrist was at hand, God was calling his elect, events were moving swiftly towards the supreme moments of history, the Second Coming of Christ and the Judgement. Such views were especially strong among Protestants generally, who saw the vast events of the Reformation as evidence that God was intervening in history to an extent unknown since the early days of the Church; they were strongest among English Protestants, who believed that their island had been set apart for God's special purposes at the end of time just as Israel had been the theatre of his designs in an earlier age. God was now moving among 'his Englishmen' as he had once worked through the Jews. The unprecedented tumult of the Civil War leading to the abolition of monarchy and the overthrow of the Church inevitably drove religious speculation to new heights. What was God preparing here? Attention naturally focused on Cromwell as the most remarkable man of the time, whose career was so extraordinary that it seemed to many to be directed by providence. Cromwell himself believed he had a divinely apportioned role to play, and habitually (and as far as one can tell, sincerely) considered his victories as God's triumphs, and his achievements as properly the work of God.[12]

It is in this mood of heightened anticipation that Marvell surveys Cromwell. Cromwell is 'the force of angry Heavens flame', an emanation of 'Fate', whom it would be 'Madness to resist or blame.' The ambivalent tone of the poem can be to some extent explained by this assumption: there are really two Cromwells in the poem, the individual and the providential force. He may not be a good man, but he acts in the interests of a divinely sanctioned power. Marvell had no affection for the man or his actions, for the poet's sympathies lay with the 'Kingdom old' and the 'antient Rights', and he disliked the violent measures that mark Cromwell's advance, but in viewing Cromwell as a providential figure, he had no alternative but to accept that his power was ordained and fateful, and inevitable. King Charles too accepted the inevitability of that power: he did not call 'the Gods with vulgar spight / To vindicate his helpless Right', but he complied with the force of events, acquiescing in his execution as a necessary part of the historical drama. The poem supposes that the Stuart regime has offended the deity, its 'Palaces and Temples' have been rent by 'angry Heavens flame', and Charles is the sacrificial victim. Yet the destruction is for purposes of renovation: the bleeding head portends a 'happy fate' for the nation, Marvell avers, making use of a Roman parallel. God's intentions towards England are favourable, and Cromwell, whether he seize supreme power or not, is destined to be the instrument of vast designs of international scope. England's happiness under Cromwell would seem to be of a religious order, achieved by victories over Catholicism: Ireland has already been crushed, and Marvell looks forward to the extension of militant Protestantism into Italy and France:

> A Caesar he ere long to Gaul,
> To Italy an Hannibal,
> And to all States not free
> Shall Clymacterick be.

Freedom in the context of 1650 would seem to refer to religious freedom, freedom from the power of Antichrist. Scotland is the next target, the home of the Presbyterians that Marvell so much disliked.[13] Cromwell's role is to enlarge the power of England and the Protestant Revolution, moving towards a destiny not yet clearly revealed, but it will be achieved against spiritual darkness, 'the Spirits of the shady Night', and it is a destiny that must be realized by continued force. 'The same Arts that did gain / A Pow'r must it maintain.'

Marvell's next poem about Cromwell, 'The First Anniversary of the Government under his Highness the Lord Protector', shows a remarkable change of heart. It was written and indeed published (anonymously but with official approval) in 1655, a year after Cromwell had been proclaimed Protector, *de facto* head of State. Much had changed in five years. Marvell had moved closer to government circles, and had come to know Cromwell, Fairfax and Milton at close quarters. In 1653 he had been recommended by Milton for the post of Assistant Latin Secretary of State; he did not get the job, but he was appointed tutor to one of Cromwell's wards. He had developed a vast admiration for Cromwell, and the intimations he had first expressed in the 'Horatian Ode' about Cromwell's providential role in history had now become certainties. 'The First Anniversary' is explicitly millenarian in theme, proclaiming Cromwell as the harbinger of the latter days, the divinely appointed hero who is to preside over the elect nation in conformity with God's will and to prepare for the Second Coming of Christ and the Millennium of the Earthly Paradise.[14] The flashes and gleams in Marvell's earlier poetry that testify to his long sympathy with millenarian ideas finally shine out clearly and unobstructed. The opening of the poem is concerned with various modes of time: Cromwell appears as a superhuman activist, forcing time forward as he proceeds rapidly with the enactment of his great designs:

> Cromwell alone with greater Vigour runs,
> (Sun-like) the Stages of succeeding Suns:
> And still the Day which he doth next restore,
> Is the just Wonder of the Day before.
>
> . . .
>
> 'Tis he the force of scattered Time contracts,
> And in one Year the work of Ages acts:
> While heavy Monarchs make a wide Return,
> Longer, and more Malignant then Saturn

The lethargic monarchs of the West are now identified by Marvell with the heads of Antichrist, whose interest lies in impeding the advent of the Saviour. They do not 'build the Temple in their dayes, . . . Nor sacred Prophecies consult within, / Much less themselves to perfect them begin', but they oppose the new age of reformation which will sweep them away. Cromwell, however, displays the activism proper to the last days: 'the Day which he doth next restore' is a direct reference to the Final Day for which his work is preparing. The long process of history is suddenly speeding to an end. The principal business of Cromwell as the forerunner of Christ is to create the true Christian state conformable to God's will and fit for the reception of Christ. This harmonizing of England to heaven's concord is a paramount concern of the Protector:

> While indefatigable Cromwell hyes,
> And cuts his way still nearer to the Skyes,
> Learning a Musique in the Region clear,
> To tune this lower to that higher Sphere.

Marvell devotes a long section of the poem to an imaginative account of Cromwell's construction, in a new time of peace, of the ideal state – the Commonwealth. Here is the creative Cromwell, a far more sublime being than the devastating Cromwell of the 'Horatian Ode'. The verse touches epic notes as Marvell foresees the mystical creation of the Commonwealth, which rises as a perfectly proportioned, circular structure, composed to a divine music which is the harmony of heaven and earth. Cromwell as its builder has now attained Orphic powers, a sign of his superhuman state. All forms of civic tension are resolved within this work, and the whole is mysteriously held together by his strength as Protector (lines 87–98). The building has obvious affinities with the Temple of Solomon – perfectly proportioned, divinely approved – but this is the Temple at the end of time, the Temple of the Lord in England that contains and is the gathered nation before God. Marvell is convinced now that the final days are at hand: he warns 'observing Princes' to make their preparations for the End, and 'Kiss the approaching, not yet angry Son.'[15] Cromwell already offers himself as the leader to those spirits who recognize the signs of the End: 'How might they under such a Captain raise, / The great Designes kept for the latter Dayes!' He is active in converting the Jews, in converting the heathen, but above all in pursuing the monster of Popery, the Beast of the Apocalypse (in Protestant interpretation), which must be overcome before Christ will return. Marvell enthusiastically encourages

> Angelique Cromwell who outwings the wind;
> And in dark Nights and in cold Dayes alone
> Pursues the Monster thorough every Throne:
> Which shrinking to her Roman Den impure,
> Gnashes her Goary teeth.

As he discerns everywhere the signs of Revelation being fulfilled, Marvell exceptionally stands forward to prophesy:

> Hence oft I think, if in some happy Hour
> High Grace should meet in one with highest Pow'r,
> And then a seasonable People still
> Should bend to his, as he to Heavens will,
> What we might hope, what wonderful Effect
> From such a wish'd Conjuncture might reflect.
> Sure, the mysterious Work, where none withstand,
> Would forthwith finish under such a Hand:
> Fore-shortened Time its useless Course would stay,
> And soon precipitate the latest Day.
> But a thick Cloud about that Morning lyes,
> And intercepts the Beams of Mortal eyes,
> That 'tis the most which we determine can,
> If these the Times, then this must be the Man.

The whole poem breathes the conviction that these are indeed the long awaited times when Christ shall return and judge, and gather his elect; this *must* be the man appointed to preside over the final phase of history. The remainder of 'The First Anniversary' is concerned with denouncing the various groups, many of them radical Protestant sects, that delay the onrush of the blest days by their resistance to Cromwell's leadership and by their refusal to recognize that all the final signs are present. The poem reverberates with urgent apocalyptic imagery. To us today it must seem strange that so poised and judicious a poet as Marvell should be carried away by such extremist religious emotions. His enthusiasm, though, is a measure of how widespread were these eschatological expectations at the time, and how they were shared alike by the eminent, the learned and the ordinary people. Milton and Cromwell looked for some marvellous revelation of divinity, as did the Diggers and the Levellers (vulgar sects that were preparing for a new Eden). The times were criss-crossed by prophecies of the great impending event, and when history flowered into the Restoration of Charles II instead of Christ, there was infinite dejection among the millenarians who had so confidently foreseen the Second Coming. Marvell's own hopes foundered with the death of the Protector in 1658, and his long poem on that event, a curious mixture of heroic and intimate recollections, is a farewell to his religious hopes as well as a tribute to Cromwell.

Providential history is also prominent in Marvell's most elaborate poem, 'Upon Appleton House', the most remarkable of the poems he wrote while in the congenial service of Thomas Lord Fairfax from late 1650 to 1652. Fairfax had been General of the Parliamentary armies until July 1650, but he had disapproved of the execution of the King, and he refused to lead the English army against Scotland as Parliament wished. He resigned his command, being replaced by Cromwell, whose new fortune provoked the speculations of the 'Horatian Ode'. Fairfax retired to his estates at Nun Appleton near York, where Marvell joined the household as tutor to his 11-year-old daughter Mary Fairfax. How Marvell came to be recommended to this position we do not know, but it was probably the consequence of Yorkshire connections. Fairfax was a highly cultivated man, interested in antiquities, engravings and books, and was himself a poet of modest ability. His estates provided the stimulus, and he himself the immediate audience, for 'Appleton House', 'Upon the Hill and Grove at Bill-borow', 'The Garden' and the Mower poems. 'Upon Appleton House' is generally considered as a country house poem, in the tradition of Jonson's 'To Penshurst' and Carew's 'To Saxham', for like them it surveys the house, the estates, the history and lifestyle of the family, but its scope is far larger than its predecessors', for it extends into national history and ultimately into apocalyptic events, although all is managed in a light and witty manner which is a mark of its composition in the intimate setting of the Fairfax family. It is an informal poem, for all its resonant subject matter. It is also the last of the country house poems of the seventeenth century, for the Civil Wars disrupted the culture based on the country house, and when society re-grouped after the Restoration, its London orientation devalued the country life and was largely indifferent to the self-contained rural economy of the country estates.[16]

The poem initially concerns itself with complimenting Fairfax on the modesty of his house and of his bearing: all things relate to the golden proportions of his life, the proportions of true humanism. His modesty deserved praise, for here was a man who had just relinquished the highest power of state for a country retirement, and Marvell honours Fairfax by his comparison with the primitive exemplar of Roman virtue, Romulus. The exercise of virtue has already made Appleton House a 'sacred place', but as Marvell unfolds the history of the family, we come to realize too that the Fairfaxes are heroes of the Reformation, saints of Protestantism. The history of their house is the recent history of England in miniature: long a Catholic institution (a nunnery), it is now the home of a militant

Protestantism: ' 'Twas no Religious House till now.' The family is characterized by a resolute anti-Catholicism; they have enacted their own Reformation by the overthrow of the nunnery and defeated the Catholic conspiracy to 'intercept' their 'great Race' when William Fairfax liberated 'the blooming Virgin Thwaites' from her enforced vows.

> Is not this he whose Offspring fierce
> Shall fight through all the Universe;
> And with successive Valour try
> France, Poland, either Germany;
> Till one, as long since prophecy'd,
> His Horse through conquer'd Britain ride? (ll. 241–6)

This is a family of destiny that moves in an atmosphere of prophecy and acts in accordance with fate: the Fairfaxes have made 'their Destiny their Choice', and their martial exploits have extended through Europe and ultimately will reach 'through all the Universe'.

It is not long before Marvell introduces the matter of universal history into the poem, with particular reference to England. The tone of the poem deepens in stanza 41 as Marvell turns from the peace and innocence of the Fairfax gardens to the larger 'garden' of England.

> Oh Thou, that dear and happy Isle
> The Garden of the World ere while,
> Thou Paradise of four Seas,
> Which Heaven planted us to please,
> But, to exclude the World, did guard
> With watry if not flaming Sword;
> What luckless Apple did we tast,
> To make us Mortal, and Thee Wast? (ll. 321–8)

The question of the Civil War is raised in the form that most worried contemporaries: why had God, who seemed so favourable towards England, permitted this peaceful island, which had been preserved from all the terrible wars of Europe, to be devastated by civil war? Heaven has been profoundly offended in some way, but the true cause of heaven's severity remains unknown, though it must be related to the spiritual condition of the nation. Marvell does not try to supply any specific answer to the question here. The war was universally interpreted in a religious context, and frequently in an apocalyptic one, and the great men of the time were assumed to have providential parts to play in God's drama. Fairfax has played out his part, one that seemed to promise wonderfully well for England, for he appeared to be a man who could have led the country out of war to a lasting final peace. By presenting him as a man who turned from war to gardening, Marvell shows in metaphor what Fairfax could have done for the nation at large: transform England into an earthly paradise under the benevolent aspect of God. England would have become the paradise at the end of time for the acts of the world's last scene. Marvell remarks that Fairfax seemed destined by his race and by his saint-like conscience to usher in the earthly paradise:

> And yet there walks one on the Sod
> Who, had it pleased him and God,
> Might once have made our Gardens spring
> Fresh as his own and flourishing. (ll. 345–8)

But it did *not* please God to proceed thus. For his own reasons, God has set Fairfax aside, and the General has acquiesced in his fate by retiring in good order. We have seen that at this time Marvell began to look to Cromwell as the new instrument of God's designs in the latter days. God has determined to shake England further before he smiles on her, as he used to frown on his Israelites long ago, and so Marvell leads us to the violent scenes in the Appleton fields that act as metaphors of the events of the Civil War, and also introduce dark strains of an apocalyptic kind into the poem.

I am inclined now to stress the apocalyptic aspects of 'Upon Appleton House' and pay little attention to the surface wit and fantasy, because I believe that the reading of the poem as providential history is not sufficiently appreciated, and that such a reading reveals an underlying structure to a poem often thought to be a collection of disparate incidents.[17] The wit of the surface is readily enjoyed (if not entirely understood) by today's reader, but under the surface there are religious and historical currents that are no longer easily recognized.

As Fairfax is a national and providential figure, so his estates can be used to allegorize national and providential events. We may notice that the stanza that precedes the mowing scenes portrays a confrontation between Appleton House and Cawood Castle, the seat of the Archbishop of York across the river: the quarrel between the men of pure religion like Fairfax and religious men of proud ambition like the prelates is at the source of England's troubles.

The meadow scenes have long been recognized as a pastoral re-enactment of the Civil War, but it is an imitation with strong biblical overtones: the tawny English mowers are new Israelites cutting their way to salvation. The mowing of the grass has to be read with the phrase from Isaiah ('All flesh is grass') in mind – the metaphor becomes actual in stanza 50, where the grass suddenly turns into flesh – for the activities in the field are expressive not only of the English Civil Wars, but also of the wars and ravages that are a feature of the last days in the Book of Revelation. Mankind is being mown – here one should remember the words of the angel in Revelation 14:15–16: 'Thrust in thy sickle and reap: for the time is come for thee to reap; for the harvest of the earth is ripe . . . and the earth was reaped.'

> With whistling Sithe, and Elbow strong,
> These Massacre the Grass along:
> . . .
> The Mower now commands the Field;
> In whose new Traverse seemeth wrougth
> A Camp of Battail newly fought:
> Where, as the Meads with Hay, the Plain
> Lyes quilted ore with Bodies slain. (ll. 393–4; 418–22)

The desolation of stanzas 56–7 represents the present state of England, with the appearance of the radical Levellers threatening ominous developments, intensified by mention of 'the Beast' in line 454, which in this charged context may well suggest the Beast of the Apocalypse, whose hour draws near. In fact the new developments of stanzas 59 and 60 seem intended to illustrate future catastrophes of an apocalyptic kind, for a new flood overwhelms the earth, prophetic perhaps of the flood that Daniel foretold would be a sign of the End: 'the end thereof shall be with a flood, and unto the end of the war desolations are determined' (Daniel 9:26).[18] The picture of the world turned upside-down by the flood in stanza 60 is an apocalyptic sign, though humorously figured, of the latter days when gigantic confusions of every kind will prevail.

> Let others tell the Paradox,
> How Eels now bellow in the Ox;
> How Horses at their Tails do kick,
> Turn'd as they hang to Leeches quick;
> How Boats can over Bridges sail;
> And Fishes do the Stables scale.
> How Salmons trespassing are found;
> And Pikes are taken in the Pound. (ll. 473–80)

The flood causes the poet to withdraw into the wood, a place of primitive antiquity (stanza 63), where he reflects on the actions of sin and punishment, mercy and grace, as imaged in the natural world: 'Thus I, easie Philosopher, / Among the Birds and Trees confer' (11.561–2), and he attempts to instruct himself in prophecy (stanza 73). This philosophic meditation is continued until night begins to fall; this is the night of the natural day of the poem, but in the apocalyptic context of figural events it can also be the night of time itself. What happens now is a *parodia* of sacred events: instead of the coming of Christ at the end of time, the revelation towards which all things move, we have the appearance of Maria Fairfax. The poem modulates into an extravagant, delightful compliment to Marvell's pupil. The apocalyptic strains, however, do not die away, for her coming benumbs Nature, and the curious phenomenon of crystallization that she causes ('by her Flames, in Heaven try'd, / Nature is wholly vitrifi'd') surely refers to the sea of glass in Revelation 4:6 that is one of the great transformations of the End. Maria is, moreover, one of the 'great Race' of Fairfaxes and inherits their providential power: she orders and restores Nature (stanza 87) and she may yet have a part to play in the last age of human history, because she grows 'for some universal good'. Her father's role as a divinely ordained leader is passed on to Maria, but more by way of a compliment than in earnest, one must feel.

The poem has a double ending in stanzas 96 and 97; both are related to the spiritual history of the world, but the first offers a concluding compliment to the Fairfax family in keeping with the celebratory nature of the poem, while the final stanza takes us to a shadowy close in the night of time. Here is the farewell to Appleton, which recapitulates the history of the world destroyed by sin and now wasted by the devastations of the latter days, but leaving, in the microcosm of Appleton House, nature restored to its first perfection:

> 'Tis not, what once it was, the World:
> But a rude heap together hurl'd;
> All negligently overthrown,
> Gulfes, Deserts, Precipices, Stone.
> Your lesser World contains the same.
> But in more decent Order tame;
> You Heaven's Center, Nature's Lap.
> And Paradice's only Map. (ll. 761–8)

The auspicious family of the Fairfaxes has renovated its domain and restored the Earthly Paradise in the little world of its own estates, a measure of what it could have achieved for England if

God had permitted the General to be his instrument in the Final Design. That design remains to be completed, but its fulfilment is imminent.

The extraordinary last stanza with its bizarre conceits has always been an enigma:

> But now the Salmon-Fisher's moist
> Their Leathern Boats begin to hoist;
> And, like Antipodes in Shoes,
> Have shod their Heads in their Canoos.
> How Tortoise like, but not so slow,
> These rational Amphibii go?
> Let's in: for the dark Hemisphere
> Does now like one of them appear. (ll. 769–76)

The falling darkness ends the eventful day we have spent at Appleton House, and thus brings the poem to a natural conclusion. If we wish to attribute a religious significance to the stanza, we might feel that the growing darkness refers to the end of time when fantastical creatures make their appearance, inhabitants of an upside-down world that could prevail in the latter days. The startling conceits that make the stanza so unforgettable are delivered as a final blaze of wit in a poem that has maintained an extremely high level of ingenuity throughout. The prominence of this wit is related to the stimulating ambience in which the poem was composed, where Marvell could assume that verbal games and neat allusions would be rapidly picked up. Fairfax must have been a very congenial patron to Marvell, and 'Appleton House' is an enduring tribute to him. The mixture of playfulness and high seriousness that gives the poem its distinct tone probably results from the intimate relationship that underlies the work, for Marvell was writing for an accomplished friend who also happened to be one of the most important men in England at a time of revolution. Small wonder that in viewing the events on the Appleton estate we have the feeling that 'Things greater are in less contained.'

Another poem that was probably written during Marvell's time at Nun Appleton is 'The Garden'. So many critics have crowded into 'The Garden' during the last generation that further comment might seem excessive, but a few observations may provide a helpful context. Virtually no writer of the early or mid seventeenth century could write of gardens without having somewhere in mind thoughts of Eden; Eden is unthinkable without the Fall, and the Fall leads one inevitably to a contemplation of the human condition. The potential of the subject is infinite. Marvell belonged to that generation, which included Milton, Thomas Browne, Vaughan, Evelyn, Cowley and Traherne, whose imagination was aroused by the fervent millenarianism of the revolutionary decades and foresaw as a possibility, at least, the re-establishment in England of the Earthly Paradise. None of the writers mentioned, with the possible exception of Milton, were enthusiasts in the religious sense of the word, but all had assimilated the ideology and were responsive to it. The state of Adam in Eden attracted unusual interest in this ethos because it might be the state to which the elect could be returned in the not very distant future. The state of innocence fascinated Marvell. He constantly tried to reach back to imagine how it might be, in his gardens, his pastorals and his encounters with young children (usually girls). He was equally fascinated by the Fall, just as I have tried to show that he was haunted by premonitions of the End. All in all, man's first state and his last were never far from his imagination.

In 'The Garden', after four stanzas of fanciful wit in praise of hortulan delights, Marvell settles to the main business of the poem, the imaginative retreat into pre-lapsarian consciousness, free from any exercise of will that imposes the self on the scene. (All the fruits offer themselves effortlessly; they do not need to be plucked in an assertion of selfish will, as did Eve's apple.) A fall indeed occurs, but it is a fall without consequence, on to grass. The poet works his art to prolong the state of innocence: the mind itself enjoys the unimaginable pleasures of pre-lapsarian thought, and the soul

> into the boughs does glide:
> There like a Bird it sits, and sings,
> Then whets, and combs its silver Wings;
> And, till prepar'd for longer flight,
> Waves in its Plumes the various Light.

The supreme bliss is paradisal solitude. As the poet emerges from his vision he finds himself by a floral dial, the symbol of time, which began with the Fall, and he observes 'th'industrious Bee' (a symbol perhaps of the work which was the curse of the Fall upon mankind).

> How well the skilful Gardner drew
> Of flow'rs and herbes this Dial new;
> Where from above the milder Sun
> Does through a fragrant Zodiack run;

And, as it works, th'industrious Bee
Computes its time as well as we.
How could such sweet and wholsome Hours
Be reckon'd but with herbs and flow'rs!

Though time and work are imagined pastorally, as befits the subject, they serve to remind us of the fallen world in which we are obliged to live. The poem ends on a note of sweet consolation, but if we want to enlarge its application beyond the confines of the garden where it closes, then we may perhaps think along these lines: the poetic imagination can briefly retrieve the Edenic state of paradise, but if we hope to live again in Garden time as opposed to fallen time, then our hope must lie with 'the skilful Gardner', who is God or Christ (for both are typed as gardeners) and with his drawing of the 'Dial new' or the 'new earth' of Revelation 21, which will be the restored paradise at the end of time. Of course such speculation can only be offered hedged about with reservations. So glancingly oblique is most of Marvell's poetry that the conditioning words are always 'seems' and 'appears'; but the implications of the verse often sound so much greater than the immediate subject requires that one is constantly tempted to search for a larger context.

To conclude, we shall look at 'Bermudas', a poem that brings together the garden interest with the radical religious strain. The poem arose from a Cromwellian connection. When Marvell was appointed tutor to a ward of Cromwell's who was studying at Eton in 1653, he lived for a while in the house of John Oxenbridge, an energetic Puritan minister who had emigrated to Bermuda to escape the Laudian persecution in England in the 1630s.

It was believed by many religious commentators that the discovery of the New World had been purposely delayed by Providence until the last age of history, because it was destined to fulfil a special role in the latter days. As the discovery of the New World coincided with the Reformation, there was inevitably a belief that the purification of the Church begun in Europe in some way related to the revelation of a new world beyond the seas. For many Protestants that word 'new' had a spiritual connotation, as in 'New Jerusalem', for the impression was that the New World was free from the sins and errors of the Old, and may indeed be a promised land set apart for the elect of God as the crisis of history developed; such was certainly the view of many Puritans who emigrated to North America in the seventeenth century.[19] Marvell exploits these convictions in 'Bermudas', with his description of Englishmen who have been guided like latter-day Israelites by God 'through this watry Maze' to this kind isle. (The poem consists of forty lines, which may be a numerological allusion to the years the Israelites spent in the wilderness before their arrival at the promised land.)[20] Everywhere there are evidences of God's special protection for his Englishmen: 'He sends the Fowls to us in care / On daily Visits through the Air', as he once sent quails to his Israelites; he sets them in this special isle which is a foretaste of the Earthly Paradise. The climate here, like that reputed of Paradise, is eternal spring, the nights are not dark but 'green' (frequently in Marvell the colour of spiritual restoration), the fruits, as in Eden (and as also in 'The Garden'), offer themselves voluntarily as God's gift: 'He makes the Figs our mouths to meet; / And throws the Melons at our feet.' The fruits have undoubted symbolic value: the pomegranate, for example, is a traditional symbol of the true Church, its seeds the faithful members close packed within its perfect circle, here applicable to the Puritan English. And just as the true Church is founded on a rock (Matthew 16:18), so that rock is present in line 31, and it forms a natural place of worship where the Lord may be thanked: 'A Temple, where to sound his Name.' When we see it juxtaposed here with the Cedars of Lebanon, we are naturally disposed to think of it as a latter day type of the Temple of Solomon, now infinitely enhanced by the possession of the 'Gospels Pearl' (see Matthew 13:46), the pledge of salvation and the sign of Christ's grace (whereas Solomon only knew the law). The apples that are 'of such a price, / No Tree could ever bear them twice' may be pineapples in fact, but typologically they recollect the fruit of the Tree of Knowledge that stood in Eden, which will reappear as the Tree of Life in the restored Earthly Paradise (Revelation 22:2). The elect have been preserved from their enemies, they are 'Safe from the Storms, and Prelat's rage', and a powerful apocalyptic sign marks their arrival, for to secure his people, God has destroyed 'the huge Sea-Monsters', which in the biblically dense context of the 'Bermudas' surely relate to Leviathan, the image of Antichrist (Isaiah 27:1) that must be slain before the triumph of Christ and his elect can occur. 'Bermudas', then, stands as another poem of providential history; it is both a prophetic poem and a psalm of thanksgiving, for it glorifies the special destiny of reformed Englishmen, foreseeing their imminent victory over present troubles and their attainment of the Earthly Paradise. The events of 'Bermudas' are figurative of impending history. The surface texture is light and colourful, and gives little sense of the depths, but the high finish of Marvell's poem as usual conceals as much as it reveals.

The strange, prophetic strains that are mingled with Marvell's pastoral and political poetry disappear from his verse after the Restoration, as if the new social order had put an end to the religious hopes he seemed to have entertained. He continued to write, but mainly harsh, aggressive satires, fired into the political squabbles that soon made the Restoration scene so acrimonious. He devoted much labour to writing anti-Catholic polemics. He soon became fully engaged in the politics of the Restoration as a Member of Parliament, and this direct involvement in the strenuous affairs of state thoroughly destroyed the detachment and poise that had been such a source of strength in his poetry during the Commonwealth.

Notes

1 The dates of his four-year absence, like so many other details of Marvell's life, are uncertain, but they must lie between 1641 and 1648. There is no record of any participation in the Civil Wars.

2 This assumption is based on the premise that many of the poems of love have close affinities with Cavalier verse of the 1630s and 1640s, indicating that they were written when Marvell was measuring himself against recent achievements in poetry. The Fairfax poems can be dated with some confidence from 1650 to 1652. See the chronology of poems adopted in the Penguin edition, ed. Elizabeth Story Donno (1972).

3 J. B. Leishman's book, *The Art of Marvell's Poetry* (London 1966), examines convincingly and in detail Marvell's affinities with the Caroline poets, and his indebtedness to classical and Renaissance traditions.

4 One of the motifs that Marvell is exploiting in the poem is that of the star-crossed lovers. The phrase in the first stanza, 'begotten by Despair / Upon Impossibility', suggests that Marvell might have begun the poem by playing around with Cowley's poem 'Impossibilities', which has such stanzas as:

> As stars (not powerful else) when they conjoyn,
>   Change, as they please, the Worlds estate;
> So thy Heart in Conjunction with mine,
>   Shall our own fortunes regulate;
> And to our Stars themselves prescribe a Fate.

The connection can never be proved, only felt as a possibility, as so often in Marvell.

5 'Cuneus', like 'wedge' in seventeenth-century English, also means a wedge-shaped body of troops – more likely to 'crowd' than a carpenter's tool. This meaning strengthens the hint of a military allusion here.

6 It is 'winged' because the triumphal chariot of Time in Renaissance pageants was usually drawn by winged horses (e.g. in Petrarch's *Trionfi*).

7 The phrase 'vast eternity' appears in Cowley's poem, 'His Diet', from which Marvell also imitated and improved the arithmetic of love in lines 8–16.

8 Charles's fate is also glancingly alluded to in 'The Gallery', where his collection of paintings at Whitehall is remembered as a vanished glory. Even so slight a poem as 'The Fair Singer' cannot escape from the memories of war: 'It had been easy fighting in some plain, / Where Victory might hang in equal choice . . . .'

9 Perhaps the Mower is even a prefiguration of Christ the Mower, who will gather in the harvest at the Last Judgement (Rev. 14:14–16). Although Marvell's mowers sing of unrequited love, their message is of universal death.

10 These political poems include 'Tom May's Death' (probably late 1650), the Fairfax poems, 'The Character of Holland', 'Bermudas', 'The First Anniversary', 'On a Victory obtained by Blake', and the poem on the death of Cromwell. Also the Latin poems to St John and Dr Ingelo.

11 See in particular John M. Wallace, *Destiny his Choice* (Cambridge 1968), and Warren Chernaik, *The Poet's Time* (Cambridge 1983). Marvell's religious views have to be disentangled from his later prose writings, notably *The Rehearsal Transprosed* (1672), *General Councils* (1676) and *The Growth of Popery* (1677).

12 See Christopher Hill, *God's Englishman: Oliver Cromwell and the English Revolution* (London 1970), *passim*.

13 cf. Milton's phrase, 'New Presbyter is but old Priest writ large.'

14 Discussions of this millenarian excitement may be found in William Lamont, *Godly Rule: Politics and Religion 1603–60* (London 1969); Charles Webster, *The Great Instauration* (London 1975); and Katherine Firth, *The Apocalyptic Tradition in Reformation Britain* (Oxford 1979).

15 The reference is to Psalms 2:2–12: 'The kings of the earth set themselves, and the rulers take counsel together, against the

Lord. Be wise now therefore O ye kings: be instructed . . . . Kiss the Son, lest he be angry and ye perish from the way when his wrath is kindled.'

16 For a study of the genre generally, see W. A. McClung, *The Country House in English Renaissance Poetry* (Berkeley 1977).

17 I am especially indebted here to the interpretation of the poem offered by Margarita Stocker in her doctoral thesis, 'Andrew Marvell: Poet of the Latter Days' (University of York 1981), which documents Marvell's engagement with apocalyptic themes most persuasively.

18 The appearance of the word 'sanctuary' in the same verse probably suggested Marvell's use of it in connection with the flood in line 482.

19 The fact that in known America most of the south was occupied by Catholics was seen as evidence that the struggle with Antichrist would be universal.

20 Or it may be a reference to the forty days that the spies of Moses took to return from Canaan with the grapes, figs and pomegranates of the Promised Land. See P. Brockbank's essay on 'Bermudas': 'The Politics of Paradise', in *Approaches to Marvell*, ed. C. A. Patrides (London 1978). For a poem about the Bermudas close in time and related in subject to Marvell's, but lacking the large religious resonance, see Waller's 'Battle of the Summer Isles'.

Recommended reading

A brief selection of works that bear on the topics discussed in this book.

General

Alvarez, A. A., *The School of Donne* (London 1967)
Aubrey, John, *Brief Lives*, ed. O. Lawson Dick (London 1949)
Corbett, M. and Lightbown, R., *The Comely Frontispiece: The Emblematic Title-page in England 1550–1660* (London 1979)
Firth, Katherine, *The Apocalyptic Tradition in Reformation Britain, 1530–1645* (Oxford 1979)
Freeman, Rosemary, *English Emblem Books* (London 1948)
Hill, Christopher, *Society and Puritanism in Pre-Revolutionary England* (London 1964)
Hill, Christopher, *Antichrist in Seventeenth-Century England* (London 1971)
Hill, Christopher, *The World Turned Upside Down: Radical Ideas During the English Revolution* (London 1972)
Keast, W. R. (ed.), *Seventeenth-Century English Poetry: Modern Essays in Criticism* (Oxford 1971)
Knights, L. C., *Drama and Society in the Age of Jonson* (London 1937)
Knights, L. C., *Further Explorations* (London 1965)
Lamont, William, *Godly Rule: Politics and Religion 1603–60* (London 1969)
Low, Anthony, *Love's Architecture: Devotional Modes in Seventeenth-Century English Poetry* (New York 1978)
Mahood, M. M., *Poetry and Humanism* (London 1950)
Martz, Louis, *The Poetry of Meditation* (New Haven 1954, revised edn 1962)
Martz, Louis, *The Paradise Within* (New Haven 1964)
McClung, W. A., *The Country House in English Renaissance Poetry* (Berkeley 1977)

Miner, Earl, *The Cavalier Mode from Jonson to Cotton* (Princeton 1974)
Parry, Graham, *The Golden Age Restor'd: The Culture of the Stuart Court, 1603–42* (Manchester 1981)
Patrides, C. A. and Waddington, R. B. (eds.), *The Age of Milton* (Manchester 1980)
Ricks, C. (ed.), *English Poetry and Prose, 1540–1674* (London 1970)
Rostwig, M.-S., *The Happy Man* (Oslo 1954)
Stewart, Stanley, *The Enclosed Garden* (London 1966)
Stone, Lawrence, *The Crisis of the Aristocracy* (Oxford 1965)
Stone, Lawrence, *The Family, Sex and Marriage in England 1500–1800* (London 1977)
Strong, Roy, *The Renaissance Garden in England* (London 1979)
Walton, Izaac, *Lives*, ed. G. Saintsbury (Oxford 1927)
Webster, Charles, *The Great Instauration* (London 1975)
Wedgwood, C. V., *Poetry and Politics Under the Stuarts* (Cambridge 1960)

Donne

Bald, R. C., *The Life of John Donne* (Oxford 1970)
Carey, John, *John Donne: Life, Mind and Art* (London 1981)
Kermode, Frank, *John Donne* (London 1971)
Leishman, J. B., *The Monarch of Wit* (London 1951)
Sanders, Wilbur, *John Donne's Poetry* (Cambridge 1971)

Jonson

Barish, J. A. (ed.), *Ben Jonson. A Collection of Critical Essays* (New York 1963)
Leggatt, Alexander, *Ben Jonson, His Vision and Art* (London 1981)
Parfitt, G., *Ben Jonson: Public Poet and Private Man* (London 1981)
Peterson, R., *Imitation and Praise in the Poems of Ben Jonson* (New Haven 1981)
Trimpi, Wesley, *Ben Jonson's Poems: A Study of the Plain Style* (New York 1962)

Herbert

Fish, Stanley, *The Living Temple: George Herbert and Catechizing* (Berkeley 1978)

Summers, Joseph, *George Herbert, His Religion and Art* (London 1954)
Tuve, Rosemond, *A Reading of George Herbert* (Chicago 1952)
Vendler, Helen, *The Poetry of George Herbert* (Cambridge, Mass. 1975)

Vaughan

Durr, R. A., *On the Mystical Poetry of Henry Vaughan* (Harvard 1962)
Hutchinson, F. E., *Henry Vaughan: A Life and Interpretation* (Oxford 1947)
Pettet, E. C., *Of Paradise and Light* (Cambridge 1960)
Post, J., *Henry Vaughan: The Unfolding Vision* (Princeton 1982)

Traherne

Clements, A. L., *The Mystical Poetry of Thomas Traherne* (Cambridge, Mass. 1969)
Grant, Patrick, *Transformations of Sin* (Toronto 1974)
Martz, Louis, *The Paradise Within* (New Haven 1964)
Wade, Gladys, *Thomas Traherne* (Princeton 1944)

Herrick

Patrick, J. Max and Rollins, R. (eds.), *'Trust to Good Verses'* (Pittsburgh 1978)

Crashaw

Praz, Mario, *The Flaming Heart* (London 1958)
Wallerstein, Ruth, *Richard Crashaw* (Madison, Wisc. 1935)
Warren, Austin, *Richard Crashaw: A Study in Baroque Sensibility* (Ann Arbor 1957)

Milton

Brooks, Cleanth and Hardy, John, *Poems of Mr. John Milton* (New York 1951)
Daiches, David, *Milton* (London 1957)
Fletcher, Angus, *The Transcendental Masque: An Essay on Milton's* Comus (Ithaca, NY 1971)

Leishman, J. B., *Milton's Minor Poems* (London 1969)
Patrides, C. A. (ed.), *Milton's 'Lycidas': The Tradition and the Poem* (New York 1961)
Tuve, Rosemond, *Images and Themes in Five Poems by Milton* (Cambridge, Mass. 1957)

Marvell

Carey, John (ed.), *Andrew Marvell: A Critical Anthology* (Harmondsworth 1969)
Chernaik, Warren, *The Poet's Time* (Cambridge 1983)
Colie, Rosalie, *'My Echoing Song'* (Princeton 1970)
Friedman, D. M., *Marvell's Pastoral Art* (London 1977)
Leishman, J. B., *The Art of Marvell's Poetry* (London 1966)
Patrides, C. A. (ed.), *Approaches to Marvell* (London 1978)
Toliver, H. E., *Marvell's Ironic Vision* (New Haven 1965)
Wallace, John M., *Destiny His Choice: The Loyalism of Andrew Marvell* (Cambridge 1968)

Index

Agrippa, Cornelius 197
Anacreon 23, 158, 187n
Andrewes, Lancelot 76, 78, 86, 125, 137, 190, 192, 213, 218n
Anglicanism: Crashaw and 125, 129–31, 151; Herbert and 78–9, 91–3; Herrick and 184–6; Marvell and 229, 237; Milton and 190, 202, 213–14; Traherne and 116; Vaughan and 95, 108–12
Anne, Queen 34, 60
Anti-Christ 66, 230, 231, 232, 243, 246n
Apocalypse 12–13, 74, 112–14, 228, 232–4, 237–40, 243
Apuleius 209
Ariosto 128
Aubigny, Katherine, Lady 34
Aubrey, John 186–7n, 221
Augustanism 11, 156; in Herrick 156, 171; in Jonson 20, 22, 29, 39
Augustus 20, 229

Bacon, Sir Francis 26, 76, 93n
Beaumont, Joseph 129, 137
Bedford, Countess of (Lucy Harington) 34, 54, 58; relations with Donne 60–3, 64, 72n
Bemerton 78, 87
Blake, William 122
Botticelli, Sandro 220n
Bridgeman, Sir Orlando 117
British Heroes 24–6, 32, 203
British history 97, 98, 111
Brooke, Christopher 45, 57
Browne, Sir Thomas 13, 112, 117, 241
Browne, William, *Britannia's Pastorals* 85, 114
Bruno, Giordano 197, 218–19n
Buckingham, Duke of (George Villiers) 37, 76, 145, 154, 162
Burton, Robert 58

Cabala 197
Calchas 192
Cambridge Platonists 123n
Camden, William 23, 25
Car, Thomas 145
Carew, Thomas 222; 'To Saxham' 30, 235
Carlisle, Earl of 52
Casimire Sarbiewski 100
Castiglione 58
Castlehaven, Lord 204
Catullus 35, 156, 159, 173, 174
Cavalier lyrics 35, 95–6, 178–83, 222–4, 244n
Chapman, George 26, 34, 60, 197
Charles I 13, 37, 76, 138, 145, 154, 181, 218n, 221, 227, 228–31; Court of 37, 58, 179, 183, 222–3
Charles II 183, 216, 217, 234
Christian Platonism 116, 120–1
Civil War 98, 137, 155, 163, 183, 188, 214, 222–31, 234–8, 244n, 245n
Cleveland, John 222
Clifford, Lady Anne 58, 78, 122n
Cosin, John 78, 123n, 129–30, 145
Counter-Reformation 80, 137, 140, 148, 150–1
country house poems 10, 29–30, 41n, 235–40, 246n
country life 29–31, 44, 160–70
Cowley, Abraham 118, 151–2, 222, 241, 244n, 245n

Crashaw, Richard 12, 124–53, 222; and martyrdom 137–9, 150; love of blood 135–9, 151; and the baroque 150–1, 153n; works: *Carmen Deo Nostro* 145–6; *Delights of the Muses* 126–7; *Epigrammata Sacra* 125–6, 152n; *Steps to the Temple* 126, 131–44; 'An Apologie . . .' 142–3; 'Hymn to the Name of Jesus' 137, 149–50; 'Hymn of the Nativity' 139–40, 192; Letter to the Countess of Denbigh 146–9; 'Musick's Duell' 126–7, 145; 'Ode on the Prayer Book' 143–4, 149; 'On our crucified Lord' 136; 'On the Assumption' 152; 'The Weeper' 131–5, 148, 153n
Crashaw, William 125
Cromwell, Oliver 13, 215, 221, 228–35, 242
Cupid and Psyche 209

Daniel, Book of 230, 238
Daniel, Samuel 34, 60
Danvers, John 75, 76
Davenant, Sir William, *Luminalia* 41n, 194
David, Psalms of 85, 190, 245
Dee, John 218n
Denbigh, Countess of 122n, 145–9, 153n
Denbigh, Earl of 145
Derby, Countess of 192, 202
Digby, Sir Kenelm 34, 38
Digby, Venetia 34
Diggers 234
Diodati, Charles 192, 198, 204, 212, 214, 219n
Donne, John 11, 28, 34, 42–74, 75, 86, 137, 215; attitudes to court life 44, 46–8, 52; attitudes to religion 48–50, 65–70; and Catholicism 42–3, 48–50, 61; death 45, 64–5, 67–70, 72n; family 42; marriage 54–5, 63; publication 52; relations with Countess of Bedford 60–4; relations with Magdalen Herbert 64; relations with Sir Robert Drury 56, 65–6; violence 52, 70n; works: *Anniversaries* 65–6, 69; *Biathanatos* 50; *Death's Duell* 69–71; Divine Poems 67–9; *Elegies* 50–3, 187n; *Paradoxes and Problems* 50; *Satires* 43–50, 52, 53, 60; *Songs and Sonnets* 53–64; 'Aire and Angels' 58; 'The Anniversarie' 54, 55, 56; 'The Apparition' 54, 56; 'The Autumnall' 53, 54, 64; 'The Baite' 54, 57; 'The Bracelet' 53; 'The Calme' 45–6; 'The Canonisation' 54, 55; 'The Comparison' 51; 'Elegie on Prince Henry' 66–7; 'The Expiration' 54, 57; 'The Extasie' 54, 58–9, 223; 'Hymn to God my God' 69; 'Love's Progress' 53; 'On his Mistress' 51; 'To his Mistress going to bed' 53; 'Nocturnall upon St. Lucies Day' 54, 63, 69; 'The Perfume' 51; 'The Relique' 54, 56; 'The Storm' 45; 'The Sunne rising' 55; 'The Triple Fool' 54, 57; 'Twicknam Garden' 54, 62; 'A Valediction forbidding Mourning' 54, 56, 223; 'A Valediction of the Booke' 54, 55, 56; 'A Valediction of weeping' 54, 56
Dorset, Earl of 68
Dowland, John 60
Drayton, Michael 24, 34, 60, 177
Droeshout, Martin 70, 71
Drummond, William 18, 24, 85; *Flowers of Sion* 94n
Drury, Elizabeth 65–6
Drury, Sir Robert 56, 65–6
Dürer, Albrecht 47, 201

Earthly Paradise 13, 66, 112, 118–22, 155, 194, 215–17, 232, 237, 239–43; source of idea 123n
Egerton, John Earl of Bridgewater 202, 204, 207
Egerton, Sir Thomas 45, 49, 55, 202
Elizabeth, Princess (daughter of Charles I) 98
Elizabeth, Queen 42
emblems 80, 101, 102, 134, 143, 146–8, 149
Essex, Earl of (Robert Devereux) 44, 60

Evelyn, John 118, 123n
Ezekiel 196

Fairfax, Maria 235, 239
Fairfax, Thomas Lord 13, 235–40
Falkland, Lord (Lucius Cary) 39
Felltham, Owen 115n
Ferrabosco, Antonio 57
Ferrar, Colet 129
Ferrar, Nicholas 77, 78, 79, 93n, 129
Ficino, Marsilio 197, 199, 219n
Fletcher, Giles 137
Fludd, Robert 218n
Foxe, John 24, 137
Fuller, Thomas 26
funeral verse 63–4, 65–7, 126, 171, 176, 211–14

gardens 13, 62, 155, 179, 216–17, 227, 236–43
Godolphin, Margaret 123n
Godolphin, Sidney 18–20
golden age 32, 193, 194, 201, 217
Goodyere, Sir Henry 57, 60, 74n

Habington, William 96
Henrietta Maria, Queen 37, 96, 126, 144–6, 165, 181, 194, 210, 227
Henry, Prince 66–7, 72n
Herbert, Edward (Lord Herbert of Cherbury) 58, 64, 75, 223
Herbert, George 9, 12, 64, 75–94, 101, 106, 108–10, 112, 114n, 115n, 124, 125, 129, 137; death 89–90; early career 75–8; motto 87; ordination 78; sense of order 90–2; works: *Musae Responsoriae* 79; *The Temple* 12, 79–93, 109, 114n, 124; principles of organization 81–2, 88–90; complexity 86; simplicity 85; 'Aaron' 94n; 'Affliction' 89; 'The Agonie' 82, 84, 91; 'The Altar' 80–1, 82, 101, 148; 'The British Church' 79, 91, 109; 'The Church Militant' 112; 'The Church Porch' 80; 'The Collar' 88; 'Easter Wings' 82–3; 'Employment' 90; 'The Flower' 90; 'The Forerunners' 85; 'The Holy Scriptures' 81–2; 'Jordan' 81, 85–8, 94n; 'Love' 81, 185; 'Man' 92; 'The Pearl' 76; 'The Pilgrimage' 101; 'The Posie' 87; 'The Sacrifice' 81, 82, 93n; 'Sunday' 93; 'The Temper' 84
Herbert, Sir Henry 74
Herbert, Magdalen 54, 58, 64, 72, 75, 122n, 132
Hermes Trismegisthus 199
hermetic philosophy 107, 218–19n
Herrick, Nicholas 171, 187n
Herrick, Robert 9, 11, 39, 96, 100, 154–87, 222, 224; aesthetics 164, 177–82; Cavalier qualities 178–83; fairy poetry 177–8, 196; and Horace 158–66; and ritual 168–77; Roman affinities 155–67, 169–75, 186–7n; works: *Hesperides* 154–87; *Noble Numbers* 100, 184–6; 'Corinna's going a-Maying' 172–3, 224; 'A Country Life' 162; 'The Country Life' 162–5; 'Delight in disorder' 178–9; 'Dirge of Dorcas' 184; 'Dirge of Jephtha's daughter' 184; 'Elizium' 183; 'His Age' 160–2, 183; 'To his father' 171; 'The Hock-cart' 162, 168–9; 'Julia' poems 177–80; 'The Lilly in a crystal' 181–3; 'To Live merrily and to trust to good verses' 158–60; 'Nuptiall Song to Sir Clipseby Crew' 174–6; 'Oberon' poems 177–8; 'The Parasceve' 184–5; 'Rex Tragicus' 184; 'To Sir Robert Pemberton' 30, 167; 'The Star Song' 184; 'The Vine' 187n
Heywood, John 42
Hilliard, Nicholas 72
Homer 159, 164, 192
Hopton, Susanna 116–17
Horace 10, 17, 21, 23, 28, 30, 31, 39, 40n, 156, 158–66, 187n, 224, 229
Howell, James, *Dendrologia* 114n

Isaiah 193, 196, 215, 238, 243
Israel 81; affinities with England 12, 83–4, 87–8, 102, 215, 230, 237–8, 243

James I 17, 27, 30, 32, 39, 42, 68, 69, 193, 218n; Court of 26–7, 39; *Works* 17
Jesuits 126, 129, 137, 148, 153n, 218n
Jones, Inigo 22, 39, 179, 210
Jonson, Ben 9, 10–11, 17–41, 45, 52, 57, 58, 60, 95–6, 100, 128, 154–6, 158, 162, 183, 187n, 193, 203–4, 218–19n, 224; and Horace 21, 23, 28, 30, 31, 39, 40n; Roman affinities 21–3, 28, 30–1, 37; relations with Sidney family 29–33; relations with women 33–4; works: *The Alchemist* 33; *Epicoene* 179; *Epigrams* 21, 22–8; *The Forest* 21, 28–35; *Hymenaei* 204; *Timber* 38; *Underwood* 37–8; *Volpone* 35; 'A Celebration of Charis' 36–7; 'Celia' 35, 224; On Chapman 26; On Donne 28; 'To Elizabeth, Countess of Rutland' 33; On Himself 38; 'To Penshurst' 29–30, 166, 167, 235; On Savile 25; On Selden 25–6; On Shakespeare 27–8; 'To Sir Robert Wroth' 29, 32, 162, 166; 'To Sir William Sidney' 32–3
Juvenal 30, 40n, 96–7

King, Edward 211–16

Last Judgement 12, 13, 45, 49, 67, 113–14, 195, 225, 230
latter days 67, 112–14, 225, 230, 232–4, 238–41
Laud, William 78, 129–31, 138, 145, 152n, 184, 186n, 202, 213
Lawes, Henry 184, 188, 202, 206
Levellers 112, 234, 238
Lincoln's Inn 42–3, 44, 45
Little Gidding 77, 78, 117, 129–30
Lovelace, Richard 35, 222

Marino, Giambattista 128–9, 132–3, 138
Marlowe, Christopher 46, 57, 218n
Marshall, William 188
Martial 10, 21, 23, 26, 30, 39, 40n, 41n, 155, 156, 158, 167
Marvell, Andrew 13, 30, 117, 215–46; and Charles I 227–31, 245n; and Cromwell 221, 228–35, 242; and Fairfax 235–40; literary influences on 222–4; millenarian strains in 230–1, 232–4, 237–43; works: 'Bermudas' 242–4; 'The Coronet' 87; 'To his Coy Mistress' 224–7; 'The Definition of Love' 223–4; 'The First Anniversary' 232–4; 'The Garden' 235, 240–2; 'An Horatian Ode' 228–32, 233; 'To Mr. Richard Lovelace' 222; 'Mower' poems 228, 235, 245n; 'The Nymph complaining' 227; 'The Unfortunate Lover' 227; 'Upon Appleton House' 30, 223, 227, 235–40
masques 39, 61, 98, 165, 193–5, 203–11; masquing elements in poetry 36–7, 61, 193–6, 227
Merrifield, John 177
millenarianism 12–14, 112, 118, 123n, 215–17, 230–1, 232–4, 237–43, 245n
Milton, John 9, 156, 188–220, 221, 234, 241; and chastity 192, 204–10, 220n; and fairies 196, 207; and music 194, 207–8; and neo-Platonism 196–211; as prophetic poet 191–217; and Virgil 190–1, 206, 212; works: *Paradise Lost* 14, 195, 215–17; *Paradise Regained* 217; *Poems*, 1645 14, 188–214; 'Arcades' 190, 192, 202; 'L'Allegro' 190, 198–9, 204; 'Comus' 190, 192, 196, 202–11, 217n; poem on the death of Bishop Andrewes 190, 218n; 'Epitaphium Damonis' 214; 'Lycidas' 190, 192, 211–15; 'Mansus' 217n; 'Nativity Ode' 190, 192–6, 207; 'The Passion' 190, 196; 'Il Penseroso' 190, 192, 198, 204, 216; Seventh 'Prolusion' 198, 200; 'At a Solemn Musick' 194, 196, 202; 'On Time' 192, 196, 202
Montaigne 48, 60
More, Ann 54–5
More, Sir George 55
More, Sir Thomas 42
Moses 81, 199
Muses 187, 190, 217n; migration of 40–1, 97

neo-Platonism 105, 194, 196–211, 218–19n
Nero 61
Newcastle, Earl of (William Cavendish) 39

Orpheus 192, 199–201, 206, 212–13, 219n, 233
Ovid 50, 100, 158, 159, 160; *Fasti* 170, 172, 186n

pastoral 58, 98, 100, 163, 165–6, 206, 211–12, 233; in Crashaw 139–40; in Herbert 85; in Herrick 163, 165–6; in Jonson 18; in Marvell 223, 240–2; in Milton 190, 193, 206, 211; in Vaughan 97–8, 111
Pembroke College, Cambridge 125, 129
Pembroke, Earl of (Philip Herbert) 78
Pembroke, Earl of (William Herbert) 21, 58, 75
Persius 96, 173
Peterhouse, Cambridge 129, 130
Petrarch 128, 227
Pico della Mirandola 197, 199, 204–5, 219n
Plato 114n, 199, 208
Platonic love 58–9, 96
Porter, Endymion 162–6
Promised Land 81, 87, 243, 246n
Propertius 159
Prospero 197, 217
Pythagoras 114n, 124, 199, 200

Quarles, Francis 148

Ralegh, Sir Walter 26, 44, 57
Randolph, Thomas 39, 96, 129, 222
Revelation, Book of 196, 214, 215, 225, 230, 234, 238, 242, 243
Rubens, Peter Paul 218n

St Buonaventura 116
St Paul 80, 94n, 207
St Teresa 130, 138, 140–3
Savile, Sir Henry 25
Second Coming, the 66–7, 105, 112, 215, 230, 232–4, 239
Selden, John 23, 25–6, 40n
Seneca 39, 40n
Shakespeare, William 27–8, 70, 177, 219n
Sidney, Sir Philip 29, 33, 46, 74, 124; *Arcadia* 53
Sidney, Sir Robert 29, 30
Sidney, Sir William 32–3
Smart, Christopher 122
Somerset, Earl of 52
Southwell, Robert 124, 132, 137
Spenser, Edmund 46, 128, 174, 197, 206, 209
Stanley, Thomas 129
Steward, Sir Simeon 162, 177
Strada, Famianus 126, 127
Strafford, Anthony 152
Stuart, Esmé 34
Suckling, Sir John 35, 39
Suetonius 46

Tacitus 23, 25, 40n
Tasso 128
Temple of Solomon 79, 233, 243
Theocritus 212
Tibullus 156, 158–60, 169
Tiresias 192

Townshend, Aurelian 98
Traherne, Philip 116, 119, 121
Traherne, Thomas 12, 116–23, 215, 241; and felicity 118–22; works: *Centuries of Meditation* 116–17, 119; *Roman Forgeries* 117; 'How like an Angel' 118; 'Innocence' 119–20; 'The Preparative' 120–1; 'Shadows in the water' 122; 'Solitude' 117; 'Wonder' 119–20
Trinity College, Cambridge 75, 222

Van Dyck, Anthony 179
Vaughan, Henry 12, 95–115, 116, 117, 118, 215, 241; works: *Life of Paulinus* 112; *The Mount of Olives* 114; *Olor Iscanus* 97–100, 111; *Poems*, 1646 95–6; *Silex Scintillans* 100–14; *Thalia Rediviva* 114; 'The Bird' 107, 111; 'The British Church' 109; 'The Charnel-House' 98, 100, 'Christ's Nativity' 109; 'Cock-crowing' 106–7; 'Corruption' 110, 'The Dawning' 112; 'The Evening-watch' 112; 'The Favour' 107; 'Isaac's Marriage' 110; 'The Jews' 112, 113; 'The Match' 110–11, 115; 'Midnight' 112; 'The Morning-watch' 108, 112; 'Regeneration' 101–4; 'Religion' 111; 'The Retreat' 104, 106, 110; 'To the River Isca' 97–8, 114n; 'Rules and Lessons' 111, 113; 'The Timber' 111; 'Upon the Priorie Grove' 96; 'White Sunday' 112; 'The World' 104–5
Vaughan, Thomas 107
Venus and Adonis 209
Virgil 10, 23, 30, 31, 39, 40n, 97, 139, 159, 162, 187n, 190–1, 206, 212; Fourth Eclogue 139, 193–4, 212
Virginia Company 75, 76, 93n

Waller, Sir William 35, 190, 222, 246n
Walton, Izaac 49, 56, 69–70, 72n, 79
Westmorland, Earl of (Mildmay Fane) 168
Wotton, Sir Henry 44, 57
Wren, Matthew 129
Wroth, Lady Mary 29, 32
Wroth, Sir Robert 29, 30–2

Xenophon 208